HOUSES
IN A
LANDSCAPE

MATERIAL WORLDS
A series edited by Lynn Meskell

HOUSES IN A LANDSCAPE

MEMORY AND
EVERYDAY LIFE IN
MESOAMERICA

Julia A. Hendon

DUKE
UNIVERSITY
PRESS
Durham & London 2010

© 2010
Duke University Press
All rights reserved
Printed in the
United States of America
on acid-free paper ∞

Designed by Jennifer Hill
Typeset in Quadraat by
Keystone Typesetting, Inc.

Library of Congress
Cataloging-in-Publication
Data appear on the last
printed page of this book.

FOR MY FAMILY—
*Rufus, Jane, and Alison Hendon,
and Viv Sutherland*

CONTENTS

ILLUSTRATIONS

TABLES

ACKNOWLEDGMENTS

The researching and writing of this book have bene-
fited greatly from a fellowship from the American
Association of University Women Educational Foundation American Postdoctoral Fellowship for the 2004–5
academic year. The project was further advanced by a
sabbatical from Gettysburg College in 2005–6. I am
especially grateful to the former Provost of the college,
Daniel DeNicola, for encouraging me to apply for the
AAUW fellowship and for making it possible to take
two years off from teaching. I am also grateful to Gettysburg College for its supplemental financial support
while I was an AAUW fellow as well as for its ongoing
support of my research at Cerro Palenque. Some of the
publication costs have been funded by a Mellon grant
to Gettysburg College.

This book draws in part on the results of my own

field research and in part on the work of others. The Instituto Hondureño de Antropología e Historia (IHAH) and its staff have been crucial to the success of my research in Honduras over the years. I am very grateful for permission to conduct research in Honduras and for the Instituto's ongoing support of my work. I thank the Director of IHAH, Dr. Dario Euraque, for his gracious permission to use data from Honduras in this study. The late Lic. Juan Alberto Durón, in his capacity as supervisor of sites and antiquities for the departments of Cortés and Yoro, was critical to my efforts to conduct research at Cerro Palenque and to those of myself and my codirector when we worked in the Cuyumapa valley.

The Corpus Archive Program of the Peabody Museum at Harvard University, Dumbarton Oaks, Kerr Associates, US Games Systems, Inc., and the National Museum of the American Indian (NMAI) gave permission to reproduce images from their collections or publications. I am grateful to Helen Najarian (Peabody Museum Press), Hilary Parkinson (Dumbarton Oaks), Bobbie Bensaid (US Games Systems), Barbara Kerr (Kerr Associates), and Lou Stancari (NMAI) for their prompt and helpful responses to my requests. Rosemary Joyce, Nancy Gonlin, Christopher Fung, and John Fox kindly gave permission to use drawings or photographs.

Parts of chapters 1, 3, and 4 were previously published as "Maya Home Life: Daily Practice, Politics, and Society in Copan, Honduras," in *Domestic Life in Prehispanic Capitals: A Study of Specialization, Hierarchy, and Ethnicity*, edited by L. R. Manzanilla and C. Chapdelaine. (Memoirs, no. 46, University of Michigan, Museum of Anthropology, © 2009, reproduced with permission). Part of chapter 4 previously appeared in "Textile Production as Craft in Mesoamerica," *Journal of Social Archaeology* 2, no. 2 (© 2009 by Sage Publications Ltd/Sage Publications, Inc., all rights reserved).

Financial support for the research I carried out has come from several sources over the years. The support of these organizations is gratefully acknowledged, and they are absolved of all responsibility for the ideas presented in this study. Funding for my work at Copan came from a National Science Dissertation Improvement Grant (BNS-8319347), the Proyecto Arqueológico Copan Fase II (directed by William T. Sanders), and the Owens fund of the Peabody Museum of Harvard University.

Claude F. Baudez, director of the first phase of the Proyecto Arqueológico Copán, and William T. Sanders, director of its second phase, graciously allowed me to work at Copan. Bill Sanders's willingness to allow me to base my dissertation on material from all excavations in the Sepulturas area represents a model of collegiality and intellectual generosity. The development of my understanding of Copan's archaeology and history began under the tutelage of William L. Fash, who was not only remarkably patient with me, an inexperienced fellow graduate student, but also had the good sense to let me sink or swim in the field. Meli Diamanti, Andrea Gerstle, and Ann-Corrinne Freter provided support of all kinds during the Copan field seasons. The late Gordon R. Willey set me on the path that led me to Honduras. Without his unfailing intellectual, emotional, and financial support, my experiences in Maya archaeology would never have happened and this book would not have been possible.

The work in the Cuyumapa valley was a joint effort with Rosemary A. Joyce. I thank Rosemary for inviting me to codirect the project, for sharing her stimulating ideas, and for offering supportive feedback, actions that have enriched my thinking about Cuyumapa, Cerro Palenque, and Copan and about Mesoamerica generally. Project funding for the Cuyumapa work was supplied by grants from the National Science Foundation to Joyce and to Joyce, me, and Christopher Fung in the form of a Dissertation Improvement Grant (BNS-9310671), by the Wenner-Gren Foundation for Anthropological Research to John G. Fox, and by the Peabody Museum Bowditch Exploration Fund. Russell Sheptak carried out the aerial photograph analysis at the beginning of the project. Rus, John, and Chris, along with Stella Kao, John Gerry, and Laura O'Rourke, contributed important field and analytical work to the project.

My fieldwork at Cerro Palenque has been supported by grants from the Gettysburg College Research and Professional Development fund and a Presidential Research Fellowship, the H. John Heinz III Fund (Heinz Family Foundation), the National Science Foundation (BCS-0207114), and the Stahl Endowment and Committee on Research of the University of California, Berkeley. Field, laboratory, and research assistance for the Cerro Palenque project has been provided by Kira Blaisdell-Sloan, Megan Case, Sarah Dunham, Brian Heinsman, Jeanne Lopiparo, Anne Norman, Mike Rhodes, Jenny Smith, Kirsten Triplett, and Amy Yarnell. Diane Ballinger carried out the analysis of the Cerro Palenque faunal and human remains. Shanti Morell-Hart carried out the analysis of the light fraction of the Cerro Palenque flotation samples. Rosemary Joyce's assistance with the classification of the Cerro Palenque pottery and artifacts from my excavations has been crucial to the comparative project discussed here. The hard work and creative energy of all these people is much appreciated.

I would like to thank Lynn Meskell for her interest in including this book in the series, Material Worlds. Her encouragement over the period it took to write the book is greatly appreciated. The two anonymous reviewers provided substantive comments that have improved the arguments presented here although they are not responsible for the direction in which I have taken those arguments. It has been a pleasure to work with Ken Wissoker, Editorial Director of Duke University Press, and the staff of the press. Thank you to Leigh Barnwell, Editorial Associate, and the design department for their work on the illustrations. Thank you also to Mark Mastromarino, Assistant Managing Editor, for his care in seeing the manuscript through to publication.

It is my parents, Rufus S. Hendon and the late Jane Bein Hendon, who are ultimately responsible for this book. They encouraged me in my chosen profession, supported me throughout the lengthy process of fieldwork, dissertation writing, and job searching, and always made me feel that my ideas had merit. Their experiences in Indonesia and Malaysia before I was born became a touchstone for me as I navigated my way through the culture shock, linguistic pitfalls, and excitement of living and working in Honduras.

Thinking About Memory

This is a book about memory and everyday life in three societies that flourished more than one thousand years ago in what is now Honduras, including the Maya kingdom in the Copan valley and its neighbors in the Cuyumapa valley and at the site of Cerro Palenque in the lower Ulua river valley. The people who lived in these places left behind monumental buildings, intricate works of art, fine examples of craftsmanship such as pottery, figurines, and stone tools, the remains of their dead, and the broken and discarded remnants of their daily life; but they left only a small body of written records. My project may seem quixotic because of this, but my contention is that an archaeological study of memory in past societies such as these based largely on material remains is both possible and worthwhile. It is possible because memory is not just a faculty of the individual mind operating in isolation but a social process of remembering and forgetting that is embedded in the materiality of human existence. It is a social practice intimately bound up in the relations people develop with one another and with the world around them through what they do, where and how they do it, and with whom or what—and results in physical traces that make up the archaeological record. It thus belongs with such processes as learning, knowing, and making sense of things, which have been productively studied by social anthropologists, philosophers, phenomenologists, semioticians, and psychologists and which, I argue, are susceptible to archaeological examination.

It is a worthwhile project because discussing memory in a specific historical and cultural context, moreover one so emphatically "non-Western" as pre-Hispanic Mesoamerica, sheds light on the how and why of social memory itself. The project also offers a new perspective on the complex societies of Mexico and Central America that developed outside of the influence of Europe for millennia before the shock of conquest and colonization beginning in the sixteenth century. These are societies that G. W. F. Hegel (1975:152–96) dismissed as being not just outside history but incapable of progress. This view is contradicted by the words of the people themselves and by the work of archaeologists, historians, anthropologists, epigraphers, linguists, and art historians, which reveal much about the historical consciousness of the Maya, Aztecs, and other groups native to the region. Yet the concept of history that permeates a great deal of this research is a restricted one. Approaches to Maya history during the Late to Terminal Classic periods, my focus here, have combined an intense engagement with art and hieroglyphic writing with a long-standing fascination with elite life to produce an overly narrow and fetishistic obsession with royalty. Shifting to a broader, theoretically more complex approach made possible by positing a more intimate and less disjunctive relationship between history and social memory, I am able to discuss how the "political economy of memory" (Melion and Küchler 1991:30) plays out at different levels of society and among three distinctive neighboring societies that were part of the greater Maya world.

Thinking about memory is also worthwhile precisely because I am working from the material remains to social context and questions of meaning, from physical residues to the actions and interactions that produced memory. I thus find myself challenged to reverse the analytical approach taken by much research on memory and related cognitive and social practices. These

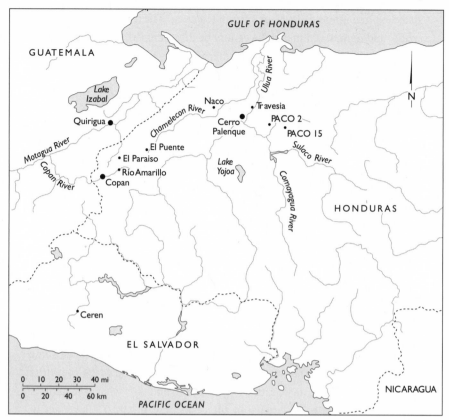

Map 1. Location of important sites in southeastern Mesoamerica. Drawn by Bill Nelson.

bodies of research, developed from various disciplinary perspectives, converge on their insistence that the ways through which people learn, remember, develop a sense of self, and understand are situated in social, spatial, temporal, and physical contexts. These contexts must be studied, not just set aside as complicating factors or background noise. Furthermore, these contexts are not only linguistic or discursive but also nonconceptual, based in action, and part of "the body's intelligent orientation to the world" (Carman 2005:71).

Taking seriously the proposition that making meaning, remembering, learning, and knowing are linked acts that people engage in through practice, I focus on how people interact with one another and with the world around them in contexts that are localized in time and space. The relationship between time and memory is obvious. Time's intimate connection to space is often ignored. As Nancy Munn (1992:94) asserts, "In a lived world, spatial and temporal dimensions cannot be disentangled, and the two commingle in various ways." I achieve this focus by subjecting the material culture itself to a concentrated scrutiny, resulting in an extended, creative, and fruitful engagement with the material remains of human endeavors. I draw on a panoply of analytical techniques and multiple lines of evidence, including what I can learn from the properties of the material remains themselves and what their spatial associations tell me about why and where people interacted. I also consider what kinds of comparisons I can draw with other groups from the information provided in documents produced from the sixteenth century to the eighteenth by Spanish and native writers as well as those produced by later explorers and ethnographers. Information conveyed through visual imagery and texts also adds to my understanding.

As an archaeologist, I approach the study of memory as lived out through everyday life from an intensely material perspective. Archaeologists find themselves enmeshed in the materiality of two worlds, that in which they live and that of the past which they study. I start with a body of materials recovered from excavations in and around ancient houses. These include the spatial proximity of certain buildings and artifacts—remains of at least some of the things people made, used, exchanged, and interacted with—as well as a knowledge of where those artifacts were found and thus what associations exist between objects and space in the residential group. I take a set of physical things—tangible and capable of being excavated, measured, analyzed to determine the characteristics of their material properties, compared, and represented—and use them to explore the significance of memory for people living at Cerro Palenque, Copan, and Cuyumapa from the seventh century through the eleventh CE, when their societies were at their largest and most diverse. The communities of memory (Burke 1989) that develop through actions and interactions bind individuals, places, and material culture together over time and in the process create a sense of relational personhood. Communities of memory are embedded in specific material domains that engrain memory, knowledge, and subjectivity in the human body through actions and interactions with people and things in particular spatial settings. I consider how the experience of living daily life, burying the dead and storing things, crafting objects and transmitting knowledge, and exchanging goods and feasting at home helped these people construct their particular histories and subjectivities.

My focus is on what people do at home as they live out their day-to-day life. I ask, How does everyday life become a locus of memory? Through the argument I present in this book I demonstrate how practices of everyday life in Copan, Cerro Palenque, and Cuyumapa turn domestic spaces into places of memory with important consequences for the production of social difference, the entrenchment of social hierarchies, and the ability of some to exert control over others. The multiple memory communities in these societies may be in competition or disagreement with one another or with the effort by some to produce a more encompassing and larger-scale totality through public acts of commemoration. The presence of multiple communities built around memory and practice opens a way to understanding how a historical consciousness is made manifest in material culture, practice, and landscape.

The ability of archaeology to discern associations among the built environment, the natural landscape, artifacts, and the remains of the dead speaks directly to how materiality, embodiment, and the spatiality and temporality of social life give meaning to people's actions and interactions at multiple social scales and in diverse settings. Archaeological materials and contexts recovered from excavation in living areas in Cerro Palenque, Copan, and Cuyumapa attest to the repetition of actions that involved more than one person, were carried out with and through things, and were productive of interaction. Archaeologists have typically divided these actions into those related to daily life, those with economic significance, those relating to ritual, and so on. The usefulness of these essentially functional distinctions is not great when one considers identity to be relational and intersubjective, although many archaeologists, like historians and cultural anthropologists, have given a greater role to ritual and commemoration than to the everyday in the production of memory. I find this emphasis debatable and explain why in the course of this book.

I cannot discern the actions and relations of any specific person. Archaeological data are too coarse grained to pretend to such ethnographic particularity. The hieroglyphic inscriptions created by the Maya living in the Copan valley might seem to offer hope of a more biographical insight. These carved and painted texts, mostly concentrated in one area of the settlement, have been used to produce lists of rulers and to identify a limited set of politically significant acts by royalty and a few favored relatives or noble supporters (see W. Fash 2001; Martin and Grube 2000; Stuart 2005). These documents serve the political purpose of reinforcing the authority of the king and his family, who deliberately limited which events and which people to record. They also determined when events should be memorialized, often preferring to create retrospective accounts on monuments erected long after the moment when the event took place (Grube 2006). From my perspective, therefore, they give insight into how one memory community attempts to perpetuate the memory of certain events and people through inscription in a permanent medium.

UNBUNDLING MEMORY

In Maya sculpture, women of high rank may hold large bundles tied up in cloth. Sometimes the bundle is shown with the wrapping folded back to reveal its contents: a clay bowl holding bark paper and sharp stone knives used to let blood as an offering to ancestors and deities (see Joyce 1993b, 1996). When I state that memory can be approached as embodied and situated intersubjective social practices of remembering and forgetting intimately bound up with the materiality of the world around us, I have presented readers of this book with the textual equivalent of that bundle.

If memory were indeed something that could be taken out of an offering bowl and turned around in one's hands, one would discover that memory takes on a different shape depending on the angle of view. One way scholars have tried to understand memory is by making a distinction between individual and social memory. From this angle, memory is seen as both a faculty possessed by individual people and a property of social groups or larger collectivities such as society. This also creates a seemingly neat division of labor between disciplines that study the individual and individual memory, such as psychology, the cognitive sciences, or biography, and those, including sociology, anthropology, and social history, that concentrate on the groups, structures, institutions, and beliefs that form society and culture. Whether one wishes to argue for the primacy of one of these forms of memory over the other or for their complementary coexistence, individual and social memory are taken to be a duality that separates memory into two disparate things. Research on the individual, however, has increasingly had to come to grips with the social, while research on the social has discovered it risks reifying abstractions if it ignores the individual.

THE SOCIABILITY OF INDIVIDUAL MEMORY

The study of memory as an individual faculty or a property of an individual mind may seem at first glance the obvious way to approach the subject. From this perspective, contemplative activity is inside of people, it is

D
1
2
3
4

E

A
1
2
3
4
5

B C
1
2
3

I. Royal Maya man (*left*) and woman (*right*) from a stone lintel. The woman holds a bundle of ritual paraphernalia. Drawing, YAX: Lnt. 5 from Corpus of Maya Hieroglyphic Inscriptions, Vol. 3, Part I, Yaxchilan, reproduced courtesy of the President and Fellows of Harvard College.

"intrapsychic," and thus "our only knowledge of reality comes through the representations we have formed within ourselves" (Taylor 2005:26), which must be stored and retrieved in some manner. A very old model of how this happens has been reconstructed by Frances Yates (1966) in her history of classical, medieval, and Renaissance arts of artificial memory. The anonymous author of *Ad Herennium* (ca. 86–82 BCE) instructs his rhetoric students that they can become better orators by learning the techniques of artificial memory, the invention of which is attributed to the poet Simonides of Ceos (ca. 556–468 BCE). Endorsed by Cicero and Quintilian, the art was said to help orators improve their ability to remember words, facts, images, and all the things necessary to deliver long, complicated speeches. The approach relies on a system of storage and retrieval that is entirely mental and intentional. A person creates a set of associations in his mind between what he wants to remember and a series of places (*loci*) and images that are vivid but not necessarily based on some real-world example already known to the person. This process is not only intrapsychic but resolutely unsocial: "It is better to form one's memory *loci* in a deserted and solitary place for crowds of passing people tend to weaken the impressions. Therefore the student intent on acquiring a sharp and well-defined set of *loci* will choose an unfrequented building in which to memorise places" (Yates 1966:7).

Revived in the thirteenth century by Albertus Magnus and Thomas Aquinas, the art of artificial memory, in its medieval practice influenced by the rediscovery of Aristotle, took on a moral tone as memory became an aspect of Prudence, one of the cardinal virtues, rather than a technique of rhetoric. Yates (1966:78–79) suggests that the Scholastics' recognition of the value of images to memory and more generally to the ability to apprehend spiritual matters may in part explain why visual imagery of religious subjects expands during this period. Images and places that the Roman students of rhetoric each held in their mind, in their individualized and imaginary memory palaces, have now become something that can be viewed and used by others in the form of paintings and frescos. During the Renaissance, the art of memory was taken up by the Neoplatonists, who continued the process of externalization, embodied most strikingly in Giulio Camillo's theater of memory. (Or at least it would have been if the wonderful project Yates describes had ever been finished and put into operation.)

More modern attempts to model how natural memory works turn out to mirror this shift from interior to exterior processes and from the individual in isolation to the individual as enmeshed in relations with other people and with things. Memory has been modeled as a set of mental operations based on the application of rules that are consciously applied by "a computer-brain isolated in the skull" (Fisette 2003:56). Such computational and representational models have become increasingly unsatisfactory, however, as the importance of dynamic interaction between individual cognitive processes and "content, context, environment and social setting" (Hirst and Manier 1995:108) has become more and more apparent (Gallagher and Varela 2003; Heath and Luff 2000; Küchler 2005). In other words, the notion of individual atoms of humanity sitting all alone doing something called remembering has become increasingly untenable as a way of approaching memory.

Social psychologists have emphasized how talking about events plays an important role in an individual's ability to remember experiences and feelings—and in their ability to forget (Pennebaker and Banasik 1997). At this point, we are moving from the intrapsychic to the interpersonal. The processes going on "inside people's heads" are thoroughly entrenched in and inseparable from the world in which people live and which they construct through their action (Lave 1993; Wenger 1998). Memories are created as much as they are retrieved through such practices as storytelling, conversation, participation in activities of daily life or ceremonies, visual cues, associations with objects or places external to ourselves, and the repetition of actions that perpetuate a sense of relationship (Boone 1994a; Connerton 1989; Fentress and Wickham 1992; Leibsohn 1994; Melion and Küchler 1991; Muriuki 2002; Petrov 1989; Rappaport 1990).

This phenomenon makes it possible for individuals to feel they remember events they did not experience or know people they have never met (Halbwachs 1994). Visiting London for the first time, Maurice Halbwachs has the sense that he knows the city, even parts that may no longer exist. His memories are based on the novels he read as a child and on conversations he had with friends who live there (Halbwachs 1997:52–53). Halbwachs is immersed in the palimpsest (Bender 1998) that is the complex urban landscape through which the past becomes part of a particular present enacted as the visitor experiences the city as social space (Lefebvre 1991b). Thus, the anxiety we seem to feel about whether memories are real or really our own stems in large part from a disjunction between a particular model, one might even say ideology, of memory and how remembering actually occurs. In *The Autobiography of Goethe. Truth and Poetry: From My Own Life* (*Aus meinem Leben: Dichtung und Wahrheit*), Johann Wolfgang von Goethe (1891:2–3) writes,

> When we desire to recall what befel [sic] us in the earliest period of youth, it often happens that we confound what we have heard from others with that which we really possess from our own direct experience. Without, therefore, instituting a very close investigation into the point, which after all could lead to nothing . . . our family liked to tell of all sorts of waggeries to which I was enticed by [the neighbors]. . . . One fine afternoon, . . . I . . . hurled [a pot] into the street. The [neighbors] . . . cried out, "Another." I was not long in flinging out a pot; and, . . . by degrees the whole collection, platters, pipkins, mugs and all, were dashed upon the pavement.

We remember through other people's statements about past events—in effect, we learn to remember. Like Halbwachs wandering the streets of London in the company of a long-dead author, Goethe in his memoir illustrates the degree to which remembering is a social act. He asks whether the pot-throwing incident was "a real memory," something he knows from "direct experience," but then decides it does not matter. Given how psychologists have shown that memories are not merely stored in the individual mind waiting to be retrieved but are instead developed through interaction and social relations, this question is not answerable and attempting to do so "could lead to nothing."

The distinction between poetry, fiction, or imagination (Dichtung) and truth, fact, or reality (Wahrheit) is ultimately irresolvable—if we assume that true or truthful memories can exist only through individual recall by Goethe as an autonomous, self-referential subject responsible for "his" memories. Goethe as a participant in intersubjective relations with others, however, contributes to the production of a sociable memory, the validity and value of which depend on more than just his contribution.

WHAT IS SOCIAL MEMORY?

The study of social memory reverses the analytical arrow. It takes some social group or society itself as its starting point and considers how memory can transcend the life span or mental capacity of the individual. Just as studies that begin with the individual had to find a way to move beyond the particularity of intrapsychic mental processes, so studies that start with society had to find a way to reincorporate people into social memory.

Halbwachs, profoundly influenced by Emile Durkheim, published his work on collective memory in 1925, thereby opening the way for the study of memory separate from the psychological focus on the individual (Coser 1992; Halbwachs 1992, 1994; Hutton 1993:77–90). By positing that "memory depends on the social environment," Halbwachs (1992:37) argued that the social groups with which a person interacts become the primary locus for recalling memories. Memory is more than an activity of an individual mind because it is the social context that determines how and why memories are recalled, recognized as important, and connected to places and events. Memories are not always there in a person's mind or immediately accessible but must be made to recur through social interaction.

The value of memory interlocutors is apparent in Vladimir Nabokov's description of how he revised his autobiography. The first edition had been written while he was isolated geographically and emotionally from his family and did not have access to materials that would confirm his remembrances. Years later, he traveled to Europe and renewed ties with his relatives: "At these family reunions, *Speak, Memory* was judged. Details of date and circumstance were checked, and it was found that in many cases I had erred, or had not examined deeply enough an obscure but fathomable recollection. Certain matters were dismissed by my advisers as legends or rumors or, if genuine, proved to be related to [other] events or periods. . . . Both my sisters angrily remonstrated against my description of the journey to Biarritz . . . and by pelting me with specific details convinced me I had been wrong in leaving them behind" (Nabokov 1966:14).

Remembering is thus a process of reconstruction or even construction, not merely preservation. Groups endorse a past that makes sense in light of present circumstances and attitudes. From this perspective, one should ask why Goethe's parents considered the dish smashing worthy of being remembered—of becoming part of their family's history—and how this memory shaped Goethe's relations with his parents, sister, and their neighbors.

The recognition by Goethe that our memories combine what we have been told with what we have experienced is certainly very close to the recent shift in emphasis among some psychologists toward a recognition of the social context of remembering. Halbwachs, however, emphasized the collective over the individual, taking such social formations as families, social classes, and religions as abstract entities that exist independently of any particular individual and can be said to possess an identity of their own. By identifying a variety of collectivities that serve as loci of collective memory, Halbwachs stressed that people are members of several groups, including more than one family through marriage or other social ties, but also community, social class, ethnicity, and they contribute to memory making in multiple contexts in which different memories are salient. This process leads to the creation of diverse bodies of memories that may be deployed by groups as they assert connections or differentiate themselves.

The anger of Nabokov's sisters at having been written out of the trip to Biarritz illustrates one of the criticisms leveled at Halbwachs: that he was indifferent to the possibility of conflict or disagreement in the process of reconstructing a past (Burke 1989; Cole 2001; Connerton 1989). A shared past is not derived solely from processes characterized by social solidarity and communication that are untainted by relations of power and differences in authority (Best and Kellner 1991). His lack of attention to this issue must be recognized but does not vitiate the value of his two main insights, which have proved productive for research on social and individual memory. One is that memories are made, not just retrieved, and that memory making is *work*, requiring not just remembering but also forgetting, debating, learning, reconciling or suppressing differences, and engaging across time and space with other people and ideas. The other is that groups of people that habitually interact furnish a prime opportunity for the work of memory making to go forward.

Since Halbwachs, the term *social memory* has become widely adopted as an alternative to as well as an expansion of his concept of collective memory. Social memory, it is argued, allows greater awareness of the individual (Crane 1997; Fentress and Wickham 1992) and expresses a sense of dissatisfaction with the Durkheimian notion of the collective (Cole 2001; Connerton 1989; Handler 1994). Nevertheless, it generally places greater emphasis on the social, that is to say, the group aspect of socially meaningful remembering, than on the individual.

Social memory has certainly become a widely evoked concept (see Canuto and Yaeger 2000; Van Dyke and Alcock 2003; Williams 2003; and Mills and Walker 2008 for recent archaeological applications). In a thoughtful attempt to characterize what they call "social memory studies," Jeffrey Olick and Joyce Robbins sum up this multiplicity of approaches and perspectives as a "nonparadigmatic, transdisciplinary, centerless enterprise" (1998:106). Maria Cattell and Jacob Climo (2002:4) go so far as to suggest that social memory is something "impossible to define" but that "we seem to recognize it when we see it." This rather startling alignment of social memory with pornography implies that at least some of the difficulty results from the reification of social memory as a static object (an "it") with commonly held properties regardless of context.

MEMORY AND IDENTITY

One's perspective on the memory bundle from this angle highlights the connection between memory and identity, which is widely held to be central both to the individual sense of self and to the group sense of coherence that makes people members of something larger (Burke 1989; Gillis 1994; Le Goff 1992). As an analytical concept, identity has been divided into the same two parts as memory: either it is something inherent in the individual person or it is a property of collectivities, groups that can be treated as a kind of individual writ large and clearly separable from other groups, just as individuals are distinct from one another physically and psychically. Writing on the relationship between memory and identity, Richard Handler suggests that one view social groups as situational and symbolic, "constituted and reconstituted through historical action" (1994:29). What we call social groups are neither merely agglomerations of individuals nor unchanging collectivities but practice-based sets of relationships and contexts for interaction and action, marked by varying degrees of participation and understanding that "inevitably subsume hostility and amity, rivalry and solidarity" (Jackson 1998:14). These relations are intersubjective but not always harmonious, as some approaches to intersubjectivity assume (Best and Kellner 1991; Smolka, de Goes, and Pino 1995). Any surface impression of integration and collectivity is the product of a great deal of work by the group's members.

Handler's analysis of identity has important implications for our understanding of memory. It argues that society is less a clearly bounded and integrated totality encompassing equally bounded and stable groups than a shifting congeries of relations and groupings. His suggestion does not lead back to an isolated atom of individualism. It recognizes that people do group themselves (or are grouped by others) into and consider themselves to be members of something longer lived and larger than any individual but asks one to be aware of the historical circumstances through which these groups come to be and which help explain why they matter. In this book I focus on how the Maya at Copan and their neighbors at Cerro Palenque and in the Cuyumapa valley formed themselves into social groups that endure over time through practice. One such group I am interested in is created through the sharing of domestic space and participation in the activities of daily life. As will become apparent, some of these domestic spaces were quite large and were home to larger numbers of people than we associate with domestic groups in contemporary society. This variation in size and scale reflects the fact that some households are longer lived than others, the greater time depth of their personal history resulting in a more substantial physical presence. It also may be related to differences in wealth (frequently the result of accumulation over time) and reflective of differences in social status. Despite this variation, certain fundamental kinds of actions and interactions emerge as integral to daily life in these societies.

Handler's ideas align with practice-centered approaches that argue that abstractions such as society, social groups, the individual or gender, power, economy do not have a prior existence that is reflected in and determining of relations and actions but are in fact constructed over and over again through these practices (Bell 1992; Bourdieu 1977, 1990, 1998; Farnell 1999; Keane

1995, 1997; Lovell 2000; D. Miller 1987, 2005; Moore 1994; Sawicki 1994; Weedon 1997; Wenger 1998). I see the significance for memory this way: accepting, as I do, the close connection between identity and memory, once the one (identity) becomes something recreated over time (historical and symbolic), then so does the other. In other words, memory is also something reconstituted over time in particular contexts. Social memory does not enshrine a collective narrative of events so much as it becomes a process through which people bring the past into the present.

MEMORY, HISTORY, AND MODERNITY

Shifting the memory bundle yet again reveals another set of issues, that of the relationship between memory and history. Any attempt to consider memory in diverse cultural and historical contexts must come to grips with an intellectual framework that has characterized the modern and the post-modern as different from preceding periods of European history (such as the medieval), rural society (peasants), and the non-Western. The modern and the postmodern (or the late modern) become stages in human world history and particular kinds of social formations that are also geographically and philosophically Western (Best and Kellner 1991; Harvey 1990; Lovibond 1993; Piot 1999; Poster 1997; Rabinow 1994). This condition corresponds to what Michel-Rolphe Trouillot (1991) calls the "savage slot," also known as the primitive, the traditional, the premodern, and the archaic, and apparently necessary to the self-definition of the Western philosophical subject as the sole possessor of history and culture capable of progress (Hegel 1975). Mesoamerican societies before European contact, like those of Africa and other parts of the non-Western world, are a large part of the conventionally defined premodern or traditional counterpart that provides the implicit comparison point against which modern life differentiates itself (Giddens 1981, 1990). The premodern is not so much a temporal division as a marker of difference based on assumptions about history, change, complexity, and evolution. The problem is not the recognition of the existence of cultural and historical difference fundamental to an anthropological project such as this one. It is how differences between groups labeled modern and premodern, Western and non-Western, have been framed and how they have been unreflectively absorbed into discussions of history and memory.

Premodern or traditional societies are supposed to lack historical consciousness, rely on myth for explanation, and be subject to the unconscious force of custom (Burke 2002; Rappaport 1990; Sweetman 2003; Trouillot 1991). Some have gone so far as to argue that there is a primitive or pre-modern kind of mind that differs in its cognitive abilities because of these disparate conditions. These assumptions permeate a range of literature in anthropology, psychology, sociology, economics, and history. They emerge in the attempt to oppose oral and literate cultures and the role and nature of memory in them (Connerton 1989; Goody 1986; Le Goff 1992; Hutton 1993; cf. Halverson 1992; Houston 2004; Parmentier 1987; Rappaport 1990; Rosaldo 1980; Schöttler 1995). Premodern or traditional people have memory, moderns have history. When Jacques Le Goff (1992:98) takes memory to be one of the objects of history, he assumes there is some coherent thing identifiable as memory that can not only be studied but also usefully contrasted to two things both called history—a critical, analytical mode of inquiry or the series of events and circumstances that make up the history of a people (see also Hutton 1993; Nora 1996). Other historians collapse the two, arguing that history is social memory (Archibald 2002; Burke 1989).

An example of the opposing of memory and history may be found in Pierre Nora's introduction to his collaborative work on French history and identity. The example is appropriate because some archaeologists have embraced Nora's organizing concept, *lieux de mémoire*, translated in an early version of his introduction as "sites of memory" (Nora 1989; see Alcock 2001; Holtorf 1997; Knapp and Ashmore 1999; Mills and Walker 2008; Moshenska 2007). The attractiveness of the English-language rendering of the phrase to an archaeologist is obvious. Not only does it incorporate a common term in the discipline but it seems to refer to something spatial and physical, the very essence of what archaeology studies. Monuments and other large-scale, enduring, visible constructions have been labeled sites of memory.

In his introduction to the later English-language edition of the work published under Nora's direct supervision, however, Nora notes that there is no "precise English equivalent" for the term and, as a result, asked the translator to "keep the French expression whenever possible, while substituting *place* or *site* only when these English words seem to capture the sense adequately" (Nora 1996: fn 1). Although the *lieux de mémoire* that loom large in the French national consciousness include monuments, they also encompass ideas, songs, books, fictional characters, and institutions.

More problematic for an archaeological study of social memory and historical consciousness in a particular cultural context is the degree to which the uncritical adoption of the concept carries with it acceptance of a specific perspective on the relationship between memory and history, so-called traditional and modern societies, that is part and parcel of the supposed disjunction between societies with and without history. For Nora, *lieux de mémoire* contrast with *mileux de mémoire*. In fact, *lieux de mémoire* exist in modern France only because "there are no longer any *mileux de mémoire*, settings in which memory is a real part of everyday experience" (Nora 1996:1). Peasants, that surviving remnant of premodern thinking in the West, were the last to inhabit *mileux de mémoire*. If these *mileux* still held sway, the French (or anyone living in modern or postmodern times) would not need *lieux de mémoire* because it would not be necessary to create external markers to force remembering. In fact, there would be no history. All acts "would be experienced . . . as a religious repetition of sempiternal practices" (1996:2). Memory, if one can even call it that, is undifferentiated wallowing in ritual; history is critical analysis of something outside of one's own experience. Our problem, according to Nora, is that modern society has acquired a historical consciousness but has not yet freed itself from memory. Therefore, we still need the crutch of something specific, whether concrete or imaginary, to serve as a memory marker. If we recognize historical consciousness as a universal yet culturally constructed category rather than a symptom or development of modernity, however, the distinction between *mileux* and *lieux* is meaningless, just as it makes no sense to argue that traditional societies have no history.

In fact, to say that moderns (and only moderns) have history implies at least three things: first, that moderns, which includes us, the contemporary analysts of ancient societies, are the only ones capable of recognizing that there is a difference between past and present which allows events to be defined by their temporal occurrence; second, that we have the right kinds of records, records that allow us to reconstruct past, or historical, events; and, third, that we construct narratives about the past with the goal of explaining causes or origins as well as preserving the knowledge of historical events (Parmentier 1987). Because we live in a society so wedded to a particular definition of history it is difficult for many of us to grasp the possibility that remembering over time can occur without a specific kind of historical record or evidence, the written text. This oversight allows us to label some societies as being without history and as lacking even the ability to think historically. From this perspective, social memory raises the specter of inaccuracy, at best, and fabrication, at worst. Thus Richard Bradley, commenting on the chapters in *Archaeologies of Memory*, worries about the "progressive distortion of history" (2003b:223) over time in societies without writing, even when material markers like monuments exist that function as temporal referents.

Similar worries may be discerned in the valorization of Maya documents dating from before the Spanish conquest. The texts that have survived (only a portion of what once existed) are most commonly carved on stone monuments, painted on pottery, or incised on portable objects made of jade, obsidian, bone, turtle shell, and other materials. Although their existence has been extensively documented since the nineteenth century, their translation proved difficult, and it is only in the past twenty to thirty years that large numbers of texts have been translated and published (see Coe 1999; Houston 2000; Wichmann 2006). Even now, large gaps remain, and some readings are disputed. The growing body of information made available through an understanding of these texts has led some Mayanists to claim they are now engaged in a historical enterprise rather than an anthropological one—Mayanists should be historians and the Maya emerge as possessors of a true historical consciousness, that is to say, one that looks like a modern or Western one (Coe 1999; Fash and Sharer 1991; Houston 2000; Pyburn 1998). These claims have been countered by those who feel that the sequences of events revealed in the texts, especially those on stone monuments, do not come up to the standard of history because they contain inconsistencies that make it impossible to construct a single coherent historical narrative for any one kingdom, such as Copan, or for the Maya area as a whole. The texts are deliberately inaccurate because they are the result not of a dedication to recalling the true sequence of events but of politically motivated decisions designed to hide the truth when inconvenient and bolster the fortunes of certain royal families—making them propaganda, not history (see Marcus 1992a, 1992b, 2002).

My approach is anthropological in that I argue that all societies have a sense of history but how they have defined the concept differs (Parmentier 1987; Rappoport 1990; Rüsen 2002). In other words, history is as susceptible to anthropological analysis as the family, the household, the economy, and other institutions: "In many other cultural realms . . . wide variations in form and content are acknowledged at the same time that family resemblances across cultures are recognized. Why should the sense of history be an exception to this general rule of anthropological analysis?" (Rosaldo 1980:91–92). History is a universal but culturally constructed category that provides a way for people to relate past, present, and future in a meaningful narrative that is expressed in various ways and takes various forms, not all of which mimic those we consider important or share the same concerns we do.

It is not a question of distinguishing true memories from false or accurate accounts from inaccurate ones but of trying to understand how and why people create connections in the present that are validated by a shared history. Who shares the history and what alternative histories coexist with one another, creating potential sources of conflict within or between societies? The Late Classic residents of Group 9N-8, one of the largest residential compounds in the Copan valley walked over the graves of at least eighty-eight people who had been buried over fifteen hundred years earlier (Davis-Salazar 2007).[1] By the time the later houses and associated buildings were built in the seventh century and the eighth CE, the collection of graves lay two meters below ground. Did the later residents of this compound know what was under their feet? What they knew and in what detail depends on what they considered worth remembering. Long-term retention of information is attested in Mesoamerican societies that lack written records, as is an interest in ancient objects, which may be found in burials and as offerings (Hamann 2002; Joyce 2003).[2] As I discuss in this book, the process of constructing social memory in Copan, Cerro Palenque, and the Cuyumapa valley involved, in part, an active engagement with buried remains of the dead and of valued objects. If, however, what mattered to the residents was their ability to claim in a more general sense that their forebears, whether directly related to the later inhabitants or not, were present because such a claim is sufficient to support a genealogy based on a sense of long-term being in one place, then that is the kind of memory likely to be cherished.

TIME'S ARROW, TIME'S CYCLE

Time—how it is measured and how it is understood—is taken to be a crucial difference between the modern and premodern or traditional mind that makes it impossible for traditional societies to be historical. Models of temporality underpin models of historical consciousness and everyday life (Munn 1992). A basic tenet of temporal models that seek to differentiate between modern and premodern concepts of temporality is that a dichotomy exists in how the movement of time is understood. Stephen Jay Gould called the two parts of this dichotomy, time's arrow and time's cycle. These metaphors represent two different ideas about the ways in which time moves, ways that Western thought conceives of as dichotomous.

Time's arrow is "history [as] an irreversible sequence of unrepeatable events. Each moment occupies its own distinct position in a temporal series, and all moments, considered in proper sequence, tell a story of linked events moving in a direction" (Gould 1987:10–11). The ability to apprehend time's arrow is central to arguments for how the West became different from the rest and began its historical development toward modernity. Time's arrow freed the West from the prison of a cyclical view of time and history. A distinctly Western historical consciousness, it is argued, develops from the radically different sense of time and history created by Christianity's recognition that human history is moving toward salvation, a recognizable end-point. This view, however, has been called into question: "It is often said that history comes to be seen as meaningful and goal-directed under the impact of Christianity. This is true, but not in the sense in which it is usually meant. History comes to be seen as meaningful as a result of . . . apologetical disputes with the non-Christian Greeks and Romans; the idea of history as goal-directed is not so much theological as rhetorical" (Press 1982:22). The rhetorical force of telos or a goal-directed movement of history does not diminish when the religious model is replaced by secular developmental sequences, such as social evolutionary frameworks, with different proposed or implied endpoints (Burke 2002).

The privileging of time's arrow and the assumption of a telos become the basis for an idea of history, both as an object of study and as a definition of how the history of something should be presented. This idea of history can be a powerful tool for the elucidation of events and relationships, but it has also made it possible to argue that non-Western societies have no sense of history because they do not share this particular idea of it or because they do not produce appropriately structured narrative accounts of the past (Parmentier 1987; Van de Mieroop 1999). Such an argument applies not only to societies that do not write things down but also to those with a long literary tradition. Orientalists, European specialists in the study of South Asia in the eighteenth century and nineteenth, dismissed "Indian civilization as being ahistorical" (Thapar 2002:181) because they claimed that only one of the many written sources of information produced in India over centuries could qualify as an example of a historical way of thinking. This deficit meant that it was up to the Orientalists to provide that history.

Time's cycle encapsulates the idea that "events have no meaning as distinct episodes with causal impact upon a contingent history. . . . Apparent motions are parts of repeating cycles, and differences of the past will be realities of the future. Time has no direction" (Gould 1987:11). Premodern (or non-Western) peoples are caught in this eternal repetitiveness that precludes an understanding of time's forward movement, Nora's sempiternal practices. Always returned to point zero by their entanglement with the natural rhythms of the body, the seasons, or the movement of celestial bodies, they find themselves in a situation in which "neither history as a whole nor any individual historical event can have any particular meaning or value" (Press 1982:7). Instead of events, they experience nothing more than the reoccurrence of seemingly eternal forms. The present recapitulates the past rather than the past informing an understanding of the present. This assumes that repetition means stasis and results in a kind of amnesia caused by the lack of anything distinctive to remember.

Reserving the sequential as the superior framework for history impedes understanding of what different models of history and what different kinds of historical consciousness might be possible (Herzfeld 1991; Press 1982; Rappaport 1990; Rüsen 2002). An insistence on sequences and cycles as two opposing modes of understanding time also downplays the coexistence of sequential and cyclical temporal models in many cultural contexts, including Western ones. Scholars attempting to write the history of the Aztec empire (ca. 1430–1521 CE) or of how one group of Nahuatl speakers, the Mexica, came to dominate much of what is now Mexico and Central America have been confronted with variant accounts of this history preserved both in indigenous forms of recording information and in the roman alphabet introduced by Spanish colonizers.[3] These accounts, written by societies conquered by the Mexica, allied with them, or successfully resistant to them, have proved difficult to reconcile into a single narrative and to attach to a firmly dated chronological framework. Several reasons have been put forward to explain the difficulty (Gillespie 1989). It has been argued that Mesoamerican peoples are subject to time's cycle rather than to time's arrow, in effect reflecting a premodern sense of the relationship between time and event. It has also been suggested that the accounts reflect a merging of mythical and historical elements and causes in a way that a modern understanding of history rejects; this tendency also afflicted many Spanish writings, especially those of members of religious orders, who were eager to fit Mesoamerica into their own mythic (religious) universe and millenarian traditions (Phelan 1970).

Rather than assume that time's arrow and cycle are mutually exclusive, that sequential chronologies are inherently superior, or that the inclusion of myth renders narrative unhistorical, I consider how these elements help make sense of lived experience and memory as part of a process of the cultural construction of past, present, and future (Munn 1992). The value of the written documents that have survived lies in their ability to offer one insight into a Mesoamerican idea of what history should be, an idea that may not match a modern Western idea. Maya hieroglyphic inscriptions and later, colonial-era writings by Aztecs and Spaniards share an interest in presenting the significant people, relationships, places, nonhuman forces or entities, and events of their own memory communities (Boone 1994a; Gillespie 1989; Leibsohn 1994; Marcus 1992b). The variation they exhibit suggests that the ability to crystallize memory in more permanent form becomes part of the attempt to privilege one body of memory over another (Hassig 2001).

PHILOSOPHIES OF TIME

Understandings of time in Mesoamerican societies have been most commonly approached by looking at the methods these societies developed to measure and structure it. The most widespread of these calendars are cyclical in that the elements they record repeat themselves over some period of time. Mesoamerican peoples were aware of and interested in many astronomical cycles, including that of the sun, moon, and the planet Venus. The Late Postclassic Mayan book the Dresden Codex contains tables charting eclipses and the passage of Venus (Lounsbury 1983; D. Tedlock 1992). One of the most important cycles is based on the solar year and has a repeat of 365 days. The 365 days are divided into 18 months, each with its own name and each lasting 20 days, plus a final period of 5 days' duration. One purpose of this calendar is to structure agricultural activities such as sowing, but it was used primarily to organize a series of small-scale and large-scale, often community-wide or statewide religious events (Bricker and Bricker 1988; B. Tedlock 1992a). According to the elaborate descriptions in the Florentine Codex, compiled in the sixteenth century by the Spanish Franciscan missionary Bernardino de Sahagún with the help of Nahuatl-speaking students and elders, these ceremonies were celebrated in a specific sequence—in specified months and at specified times in the month—over the course of the year (Sahagún 1953–82; see also Durán 1971; Tozzer 1978).

A second way of structuring time, one which survived Spanish conquest and continues in use today among some Maya in Mexico and Guatemala, is a 260-day cycle created by combining 20 day names and 13 numbers; this cycle is referred to by some scholars as the sacred almanac (Sharer 1994:560–62).

Like the 365-day cycle, this one is both sequential and cyclical in that the day names follow one another in order, as do the numbers. This means that having entered the cycle at any point one knows what the next combination will be.[4] Achieving a competent understanding of the 260-day calendar is not just a matter of grasping the mathematical relationships or of being able to move backward and forward as needed from any point in the cycle. Each day and each number and their combinations have associated meanings (Quiñones Keber 1995; B. Tedlock 1992b; D. Tedlock 1992). The 260-day cycle provides a way to keep track of ritual observances that often must take place in specific locations and as a way to carry out divination. These seem to be rituals and actions of concern to small-scale social groups such as individuals, families, and households. People who have been specially called and trained divine in response to problems and questions brought to them by people. The questions are often quite specific and involve marriage, illness, and other concerns, but somehow they always work back to people's relations to a larger world made up of humans and nonhumans, animals, plants, corporeal and noncorporeal entities, ancestors, deities, and natural forces, the living and the dead. Divination is thus a social act carried out in the context of the people involved, the question asked, the day on which the question is asked, and other factors (B. Tedlock 1992a, 1992b).

Peter Furst (1986) has discovered that some contemporary users of the 260-day system note a similarity between its duration and that of a woman's pregnancy. His sources did not claim that the cycle was invented as a way to keep track of pregnancy, only that the two could be seen as similar. This correspondence is interesting because of the light it sheds on the meaning of cycles in the context of everyday life. Over the course of gestation, the passage of time is signaled quite obviously by changes in a woman's body, changes that are most apparent to her but are also increasingly evident to those around her. These are sequential changes. At the conclusion of the pregnancy, with the birth of the child, one could claim that the cycle has returned to its starting point and things are exactly as they were before. But this is not the case. The social group has been increased by the addition of a new individual, whose presence changes what people do and how they relate to one another. New relationships have come into existence and old ones have been redefined. The infant has begun its passage through the life course, an experience that is again a sequential series of changes. The mother may seem to have returned to a pre-pregnancy state, but her body is no longer the same as it was before. Even if this is not her first pregnancy, the physical effects are not identical each time; if anything, they are cumulative. Neither is her social identity the same. Cycles are thus as likely to be about transformation as about repetition.

The one form of time measurement that matches our understanding of a linear chronological system has been named the Long Count, known to us through inscription on permanent media from several areas. Although the earliest surviving texts come from the coast of the Gulf of Mexico, it was the Maya who used it for the longest period of time. Even they stopped using it in the early part of the tenth century CE, and it was not in evidence when the Spanish arrived, although the 260-day cycle, the 365-day cycle, and others not described here continued to be important. We know most about the Long Count from its use by Maya rulers on their monuments. It is the existence of these dates that has allowed epigraphers to construct king lists for different Maya cities and, by extension, to create a chronological sequence for some royal activities (see Grube 2006; Martin and Grube 2000). Although the Long Count seems eminently linear to us and appears to reflect an understanding of time's arrow, it may also be understood as an extremely large-scale example of time's cycle. The Maya saw the Long Count as measuring the passage of time within a very long cycle of years that began in their distant past (equivalent to 3114 BCE) and would come to an end in the distant future (2012 CE), then to start over again if all went well (Sharer 1994:567–68). Mesoamerican philosophies of time, in fact, continually stress the working out of sequential actions that are also subject to repetition that makes them part of smaller- and larger-scale cycles.

Histories of the creation of the world further illustrate how sequence and cycle form part of the same understanding of event. In the Popol vuh, for example, a history of the Quiché Maya that has come down to us in a colonial-era transcription, the gods attempt to create beings that will worship them. This process requires several attempts. First, the gods create beings who are unable to interact properly with the deities because, although they make noise, they cannot speak. The gods therefore demote them to being the ancestors of the animals who will serve the people to come. The deities next make a person out of clay, who proves incapable of moving or speaking or reproducing. This inherently static, unsocial creature is done in by the instability of the very material itself. Then the deities try wood, but these people, although able to speak and reproduce in a more humanlike way, turn out to be too stiff necked to submit to the gods' authority and must be destroyed. Finally, the gods decide to use corn and make people out of *masa*, the dough made from grinding corn with water (D. Tedlock 1996). The individuals formed from corn are the ancestors of the Quiché. They are "beings who will walk, work, and talk in an articulate and measured way, visiting shrines, giving offerings, and calling upon their makers by name, all according to the rhythms of [the 260-day] calendar" (D. Tedlock 1996:32). Events and actions, whether, by our standards, mythological or historical, religious or political, are in one sense repeated—the gods consult, choose a material, fabricate people, observe them, find them deficient, and destroy them. Yet no recurrence is identical to its predecessor, being rather a logical extension of the earlier state of affairs. The gods consider what has happened before trying again. They choose different raw materials they hope will correct the problems evident in their previous choices.

It is tempting to see the Long Count as evidence of a temporary shift from time's cycle to time's arrow, from premodern cyclicity to something approaching modern linearity, that for several centuries allowed the Maya to somehow surpass their contemporaries and successors in the development of a modern understanding of time and history (Pyburn 1998). The cycles, however, never disappear during the period in which the Long Count marked royal events. The Maya did not abandon cyclical modes of time reckoning, including the notation of the corresponding position in the sacred almanac, solar year, and lunar month. And the Long Count itself was never free from its connection to the very large cycle in which it was embedded. Not all Maya cities put up dated monuments, which suggests that alternative ways of keeping track of important genealogies and events existed. This is certainly the case for the later Aztec, who did not tie their history to fixed dates but nevertheless recorded genealogies and historical narratives that are sequences of events and relationships that separate conceptually past action from present.

The Long Count as a mode of defining temporal relationships is closely bound to the support of the political actions of certain royal houses. It becomes a medium for the construction and dissemination of the royal memory community's process of remembering and forgetting, a process made possible by the discourse structure of the text and the associated imagery (Maxwell 1997). By attempting to limit the use of permanent records of these events and their occurrence to certain memory communities, these royal houses present their idea of which (and whose) memories should be given prominence. For the histories of other memory communities and for the rest of the history of these royal communities of memory, one must turn to the ways in which the lived actuality of the everyday becomes a source of social memory.

Everyday life at home creates an appearance of patterned repetition of actions and interactions. While not necessarily planned or deliberate, the production of repetition is the result not of automata but of people making decisions, sometimes consciously, sometimes unconsciously, about how to use their time, how to expend their energy, how to structure their daily interactions with others, and how to interpret what is done. These practices are temporal as well as spatial in nature, enacted through the movement of the body as it performs its tasks. These actions create a sense of continuity. Continuity is often represented as timeless—as the same thing over and over—and therefore not productive of memory. This view ignores the dynamism inherent in the actions and interactions of daily life. There seem to be two assumptions informing this notion. First, that what is repeated must be perceived as the same by the person performing the action and by those observing it. And second, that memory must be precise and tied to a codified temporal sequence.

The distinction between time keeping and time telling in imperial China affords another way of approaching this issue. Time keeping "allowed the government to regulate seasons, months, days, and hours" through horology and astronomy, knowledge that was the province of the few, while time telling "conveyed a standardized official time to a large population" (Wu 2003:108). Time telling emphasized patterned rhythms of action. The drum tower was the primary means of time telling for many centuries in Chinese towns and cities, but it was not a clock. It transmitted information about time by making sound at certain points during the day, conveying an "official schedule of projected operations and recurring events" (Wu 2003:108).

Time keeping in Mesoamerica is made possible through the use of multiple calendars that marked the passage of time in 260-day, 365-day, and longer intervals. Segmenting time allows the scheduling of practical action and religious ceremonies at home and in the plaza (Bricker and Bricker 1988; Durán 1971; B. Tedlock 1992a). Time keeping played a central part in the assertion of royal control at Copan by providing a framework for public commemorative, religious, and political events. Neither Cerro Palenque nor Cuyumapa society were as highly centralized politically or as socially differentiated as the kingdom of Copan. Both societies, like Copan, did build ballcourts (see chapters 1 and 7). These monumental arenas suggest a means of time telling and its importance since ballgames were played on a schedule that was tied in to calendars and astronomical events (Gillespie 1991; Joyce, Hendon, and Lopiparo 2009). Calendars were not employed only by the state. The 365-day calendar was also of concern to people because of the relationship between date of birth, one's destiny, and personhood (see chapter 5). Perhaps even more central to individuals and their immediate circle was the 260-day cycle. Curing illness, deciding whom to marry, and mourning the dead are examples of concerns that would loom large in the life of people at all levels of society. Divination is integral to these concerns and would have taken place either in a domestic setting or at sacred places in the larger social and geographic landscape (Boone 1983; Brown 2000; Brown, Simmons, and Sheets 2002; Durán 1971; Tozzer 1978; Sahagún 1953–82; B. Tedlock 1992a; D. Tedlock 1993; Viesca Treviño 2001). The ability to deploy the 260-day calendar in this way comes from specialized training and the mastery of a specific body of knowledge integrated with the study of ceremonial and medical knowledge. Such expertise was not restricted to the elite or to those holding high political or religious office, although it does seem that status distinctions separated the specialists.

No evidence has been found in the societies I study here of any official means of time telling comparable to the Chinese drum tower's ongoing intervention in daily life, an intervention made possible by the nature of Chinese cities. However, the perceptual aspects of the periodic, often daily actions that take place in the domestic space of the residential compounds—particularly the combination of sights, sounds, and smells attendant on these actions—provide a form of time telling that, while not controlled by a centralized authority, nevertheless produced a rhythm by which residents scheduled their lives and provided a framework around which memory grows.

THE POLITICAL ECONOMY OF REMEMBERING AND FORGETTING

I have exhausted the usefulness of the two angles of vision discussed so far. Memory is not just an individual faculty or social property. Neither is it the poor relation of history, emblematic of a premodern mindset incapable of thinking historically. It is time to turn this thing we removed from the offering bowl so as to achieve a more productive perspective on memory. The new angle I propose to explore in the chapters that follow argues that "memory is best conceived of in verb form" (Hirst and Manier 1995:109).

Memory is remembering and forgetting and thus changes from a static object to an interactive and intersubjective process that forms part of Handler's historical action, "stretched across individuals and the wider social and cultural environment that they inhabit" (Cole 2001:29). Memory is not something people *have* but something they *do*. People interact with one another and are bound together in webs of social relations. These relations and interactions may be transitory or enduring, connected to situations that are unlikely to ever be repeated or which recur over and over, even beyond the life span of any individual participant.

Recognizing that memory does not reside only in the mind, waiting to be retrieved from some neurological equivalent of the Roman orator's memory palace or the computational model's hard drive, frees one to consider how the inescapable sociality of human beings undermines any simplistic equation of the individual and remembering. At the same time, dismantling the reification of social groups as bounded and unchanging entities allows one to reconfigure them as collections of people connected through practice and meaningful interaction. Identity and memory are practices that are constituted and reconstituted over time, practices that involve forgetting of certain aspects of history as much as celebrating others. This makes them potent political forces. The promulgation of memory may become an attempt to impose someone's preferred narrative or to elevate some group's social memory to the level of the official (Bodnar 1992; Cole 2001; Forty 1999; Koshar 2000; Levinson 1998; Nora 1996; Prost 1997; Tai 2001). This is in fact part of what elites do, not just through written texts but also through performances and how they live their lives. They wish to elevate particular genealogies and sequences of events over others (see, e.g., Kan 1989). Such exercises in legitimation are often associated with attempts to maintain social hierarchy (Cressy 1994; Gillis 1994) or with colonialism (Rappaport 1990; Thapar 2002), where they have been analyzed as attempts to impose a cultural hegemony (Comaroff and Comaroff 1992).

No matter how insistent the voice of elite or official memory, however, the "multiplicity of social identities" guarantees "the co-existence of rival memories, alternative memories" which reflect "different views about what is significant or 'worthy of memory' " (Burke 1989:107). I adopt Peter Burke's term *memory communities* to refer to groups that coalesce around bodies of memory. Thus memory communities are also communities of practice in which learning takes place and knowledge is constructed (Lave and Wenger 1991; Wenger 1998). From this vantage point, the fact that the residents of some domestic places claim to endure over generations results from the social, political, or economic consequences of these shared practices rather than from the group's achieving some kind of transcendent life independent of the people who reproduce it through practice. Furthermore, the multiplicity of narratives present in Mesoamerican societies offers a glimpse of the accommodations with and resistance to such attempts to sustain a cultural hegemony, whether through religion, conquest, exchange, and all the other forms of coercion and co-optation practiced by those attempting to acquire and hold on to power. At the same time, these narratives allow an anthropological analysis of memory, history, and historical consciousness as cultural categories.

I have been most concerned here with demonstrating how different approaches to memory converge on remembering and forgetting as interpersonal and intersubjective, embedded in the web of human sociality. I have argued that memory and identity are intersubjective, situated in spatial, temporal, and social contexts and created through practice—constituted and reconstituted through historical action. I have suggested that we think in terms of multiple memory communities interacting with one another, an approach that provides a way to consider the political economy of memory, an economy based on remembering and forgetting that is strategic and also a potential source of conflict as well as of productive connection. Remembering and forgetting are embodied and contextualized social practices that are intimately bound up with materiality. It is through an intensive and ongoing engagement with materiality that people do the work of memory across time and space.

It is precisely the inextricability of this connection that makes it possible to approach the study of memory communities by way of their material remains. As practices, they are externalized onto objects that have an existence separate from ourselves, engrained in the body, and dependent on context (Hirst and Manier 1995). My reason for considering the activities, material world, and interactions of people living together in such depth is that by attending to these elements as components of a constituting process of social practice, I can rethink ritual, daily life, artifacts, art, and burials (to name some of the most heavily studied archaeological domains) as integral components of social practice.

I have mentioned what could be considered to be different kinds of memory, first individual and social, then intersubjective. In the following chapters I expand intersubjectivity to include embodied remembering and relations with personlike objects. That different ways of remembering and different kinds of memory may be possible is explored as part of my discussion throughout the rest of the book. I have deliberately avoided presenting a typology of memory because such an approach tends to produce categories that must be treated as dichotomous and discrete in order to justify their differentiation. As my review of the individual–social memory distinction and the linear–cyclical time opposition makes clear, typologies obscure connections. I am interested in determining how diverse modes or ways of remembering interact. Rather than state a priori that memory can or should be divided into categories, with the concomitant developmental or sociological implications such a statement would carry, I prefer to use the detailed exploration of domestic life in the valleys of Copan and Cuyumapa and at the site of Cerro Palenque in the Ulua river valley as an opportunity to consider when and how particular modes become salient. The ways in which meaning is constructed through action, semiotics, materiality, perception, and sensation are applied to the material world in which the people in Copan, Cerro Palenque, and Cuyumapa embedded themselves.

My discussion now moves to the relationship between materiality, identity, and memory in order to grapple seriously with the interaction between practices, object domains, and how memory develops in multiple social venues. I point to the importance of understanding how memory communities assert connections between memories and identity in ways that bring the past into the present. Several processes are central to this endeavor. One is that action and interaction create society, which does not have an abstracted or reified existence separate from the practices that constitute it. A second is the active and formative role of material objects in how people make meaning and understand their subjectivity. Chapter 1 introduces the three societies in detail and discusses the material traces of life in three river valleys and their larger historical context. I also consider residential space as meaningful places inhabited by communities of practice, drawing on anthropological studies of place and phenomenological studies of perception.

In chapter 2 I examine research on the relationship between people and objects to consider how memory and identity intersect with multiple object domains to create contexts for remembering and forgetting at different social and spatial scales. Objects can be like persons. They can act as social agents, participants in relationships, and subjects in their own right. In chapter 2 I draw on Alfred Gell's discussion of the enchantment of some kinds of objects and Daniel Miller's on the humility of others to underscore that objects, such as monuments, are not fossilized memories or static repositories. Work on ephemeral monuments argues instead that objects play a central role in remembering and forgetting because of their ability to facilitate and shape the recall of something absent.

In chapter 3 I bring together the discussion of places and communities of practice in the first chapter with the treatment of materiality in chapter 2 to expand understanding of how people living together become a memory community, always mindful that other memory communities exist as well. This discussion requires the crossing of conventional analytic boundaries to bring together practices that are integral to everyday life and those considered to be ritual in nature: the burying of people or caches of objects, the building of houses, and the storing of food. The reopening of burials, the rearrangement of caches, the frequent rebuilding of houses, and the constant putting in and taking out of goods from storage containers are dynamic processes that make the past part of the daily lives of the living through selective remembering and forgetting.

In chapter 4 I look at the relationship between memory, knowledge, and learning. I focus on doing and making, confounding the traditional archaeological separation between domestic or subsistence activities, such as food preparation, and craft production, such as weaving cloth, in order to reorient the discussion toward the importance of productive action to an intersubjective, embodied identity. I address questions of identity in greater depth in chapter 5 through a discussion of relational personhood. I present individual identity as the result of social relations and situations involving people and objects to support further my argument that memory in these societies cannot be assumed to enshrine a single narrative of events or take a constant point of view.

In chapters 6 and 7 I discuss periodic ceremonies that provide another context for the construction of social memory. In chapter 6 the text stays rooted in domestic space as it explores the implications of the celebration of important events that make up the history of the coresident community of practice. The emphasis is on feasting as a "total social phenomenon" (Mauss 1990:3) that presents opportunities for interaction among groups of people belonging to different communities of memory and, in the process, for the reinforcement of a local sense of identity. The next chapter introduces another setting, that of the ballcourt. Ballcourts, although a specialized kind of architectural construction with the specific purpose of providing a venue for the playing of the ballgame, have close connections with

domestic space in pre-Hispanic Honduras. They are also a form of monumental construction common to all three societies studied here. Like feasting, the ballgame is best viewed as a kind of umbrella term subsuming a
series of activities, events, and interactions, including dancing, sacrificing,
eating and drinking, processions, and dramatic or comedic performances as
well as the games themselves, that together create a riveting spectacle. I sum
up my discussion in the conclusion, in which I return to some of the larger
issues raised here.

ONE

Communities of Practice in Honduras in the Seventh Century through the Eleventh

The seventh century through the eleventh are conventionally referred to as the Late Classic and Terminal Classic (or Early Postclassic) periods by archaeologists working in the region (Chase and Chase 2004; Joyce 2004; Rice et al. 2004). When first coined, these terms conveyed assumptions about cultural evolutionary development that have since been discarded by Mesoamerican scholars. For my purposes, the terms serve as convenient referents for the centuries under discussion when Copan, Cuyumapa, and Cerro Palenque attain their greatest size. They do not follow the same growth trajectory, however. Copan reaches its peak population in the eighth century, during the Late Classic, under the rule of a series of kings who see their centralized political control disintegrate between 800 and 850 CE, although people continue living there for several centuries afterward. The Cuyumapa area maintains a more stable population and organization until a much later decline, after 1000 CE. Cerro Palenque is first settled during the seventh century and remains a small community until the middle of the ninth century. Then it grows quickly to become the largest Terminal Classic settlement in the lower Ulua valley.

GEOGRAPHY AND SETTLEMENT

The three societies are located in different areas of modern Honduras. Here I summarize the important features of the geography of the Copan, Ulua, and Cuyumapa valleys and their pre-Hispanic history of occupation as well as introduce the sites that provide the archaeological data used in my study (see table 1).

TABLE 1. Important Residential and Monumental Areas in the Three Regions

RESIDENTIAL	MONUMENTAL
CUYUMAPA VALLEY	
PACO 2 Groups 5-2 and 6-2	PACO 2 ballcourt and associated platform
PACO 15 residential area	PACO 5 ballcourt
	PACO 14 ballcourt
CERRO PALENQUE	
CR-44, including Group 2[a]	CR-44
CR-157 Groups 1, 3A and 3B, 5A and 5B, Groups 6A and 6B, Ballcourt residential group	Great Plaza and ballcourt
CR-171 Group 4	
COPAN VALLEY	
Inner zone: Groups 9N-8, 9M-22, 9M-24	Main Group, including the main plaza, ballcourt, Hieroglyphic Staircase, and
Foothills: 7D-3-1, 7D-6-2, 11D-11-2, 32B-16-1, 34A-12-2, 34C-4-2, 99A-18-2	Acropolis, with Temples 11, 16, and 22

[a] CR-44 is the earlier occupation and dates to the Late Classic period. All the other areas listed are part of the later occupation during the Terminal Classic.

THE COPAN VALLEY

The Copan river has created a series of small alluvial valleys or pockets as it flows through the mountains of western Honduras near the border with Guatemala. Archaeologists have discovered the remains of settlement in Copan dating back to at least 1400 BCE (W. Fash 2001:63; Hall and Viel 2004). The most densely settled of these pockets is also where the main center is located. The residents of this pocket and the adjoining ones were, by the Late Classic period, organized into a single political entity that included people living along the river and in the surrounding foothills. Settlement in the neighboring valleys was closely linked to Copan culturally and economically and may have been politically subordinate (Nakamura, Aoyama, and Uratsuji 1991). Copan's political influence extended as far west as the smaller polity of Quirigua in Guatemala. The early ninth century saw the kingdom fall apart, in part because of local circumstances such as environmental degradation, population growth, and possibly political factionalism among the ruling elite. Economic and political realignments affecting Mesoamerica as a whole also played a role (Fash, Fash, and Davis-Salazar 2004; Viel 1999; Webster, Freter, and Storey 2004). Although dynastic political control did not survive, the valley was not immediately abandoned and not all forms of social difference disappeared.

The relatively narrow width of the valley floor and the way the walls rise quite steeply, especially at its eastern end, create a feeling of enclosure. The contrast between the flat floodplain and the slope of the hills is noticeable. The river is a constant presence as it winds through the valley. The Main Group, the collection of monuments and massive religious, governmental, and residential buildings built for and used mainly by the rulers of the Copan polity, sits on the valley floor. A large open plaza takes up the northern part of the area, where most of the free-standing monuments are located. The plaza is enclosed by buildings and, on the south, bounded by the rise of the Acropolis. The top of the Acropolis is divided into two enclosed courtyards, the East and West Courts. In the area at the foot of the Acropolis is the main ballcourt and the Hieroglyphic Staircase (see W. Fash 2001; Longyear 1952).

The massive and elaborate nature of the architecture throughout the Main Group tempts one to perceive it as something permanent and immutable. Especially so when we think about the limited technological means at its builders' disposal and the correspondingly large investment of human labor and strength its construction required. What we see now, however, is only a

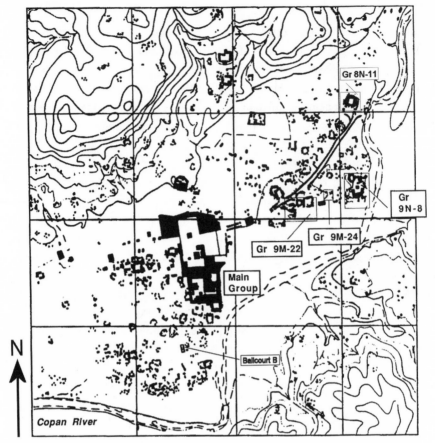

Map 2. Copan valley settlement around the Main Group. Courtesy of the Instituto Hondureño de Antropología e Historia.

moment in what was a long-term, ongoing process of rebuilding individual structures, relocating monuments, and redesigning whole areas of the complex. We see the moment when this process of movement and change came to a halt as political authority broke down in the eighth century CE. The ballcourt, the Hieroglyphic Staircase, the Acropolis, and the buildings on top of it contain within their walls and underneath their floors superseded structures that go back to a period between 100 and 400 CE, based on radiocarbon dates and the kinds of pottery recovered by archaeological excavations (Sharer, Sedat, Traxler, Miller, and Bell 2005). This period is prior to the founding of royal rule in the fifth century CE (Martin and Grube 2000). Such durable histories and long periods of occupation exist in domestic settings as well, especially in the urban area. The implications of

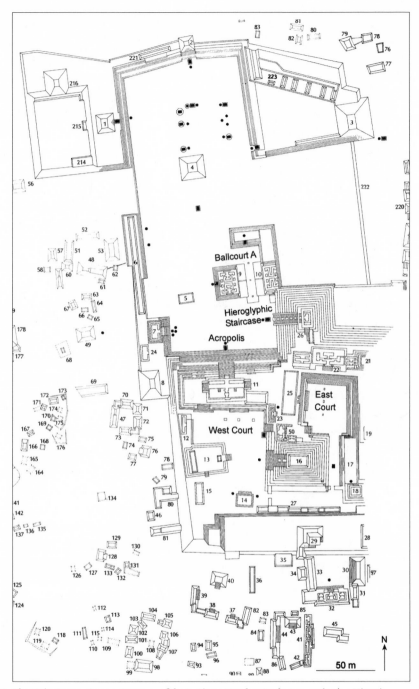

Map 3. The Main Group, Copan. Courtesy of the Instituto Hondureño de Antropología e Historia, redrawn from Fash and Long 1983:Map 12.

duration for the development and perseverance of memory communities are explored in chapter 3.

Spaces like the Main Group are closely connected to the effort on the part of some members of society to centralize and concentrate political authority in the hands of the few. Such authority cannot be separated from the person of the ruler or the royal house, making these spaces a kind of domestic setting writ large. The royal family inhabits the entire complex even though their living quarters occupy only a small portion of the area. The location of early residences lies underneath the Acropolis. By the time of the last ruler (Ruler 16) in the eighth century, the royal family was living behind the Acropolis, in an area much lower in elevation, separated from the large plaza and ballcourt by the bulk of the Acropolis itself (Andrews and Bill 2005; Andrews and Fash 1992; Bill 1997a; Doonan 1996).

The Copan valley floor and sides are dotted with groups of low stone platforms supporting residential structures, many rebuilt more than once. In many cases, Copanecos arranged their houses and other buildings to enclose a rectangular courtyard. Sylvanus Morley, one of the earliest archaeologists to work in the valley, remarked that "every available spot in the valley was intensively occupied [by the Late Classic period]. Wherever one strays from the beaten tracks, one encounters the vestiges of former occupation: fallen buildings, fragments of elaborate sculptural mosaics, pyramids, platforms, terraces, and mounds" (1920:14). Systematic survey of the valley, including all the alluvial pockets, the foothills, and the tributary drainages, has confirmed this impression, with over 4,000 structures mapped (Canuto 2002; W. Fash 1983b; Fash and Long 1983; Freter 1988; Leventhal 1979). While many of the residences consist of a single courtyard and its surrounding buildings, others are aggregates of several such courtyards.

The density of buildings reaches a maximum in an area extending approximately 2 kilometers (1.24 miles) around the Main Group. The remains of about 2,000 buildings have been located and mapped in this area. The largest number of aggregated groupings of courtyards is found here, the tallest supporting platforms, and the most labor-intensive forms of construction, using cut stone blocks, rubble fill, and stucco plaster. Many of these aggregated groups are the result of growth over time. Group 9N-8, one of the largest such compounds, was made up of at least fourteen patios at its largest extent and, as mentioned in the introduction, was built over earlier houses and burials. It is this dense area around the Main Group that is considered by Copan researchers to be occupied by the most elite members of society after the royal family and to represent a more urban settlement (e.g., W. Fash 2001; Sanders 1989; Webster 1999). Significant variation exists within this area in terms of material culture, however, suggesting that social difference was not just a simple division between elites and commoners because not all inner zone residents are alike in terms of wealth or prestige (Gonlin 1985; Hendon 1989, 1991, 1992, 2000b, 2003b). It is not possible either to make a simple urban/rural distinction between large, dense settlement around the Main Group and small, dispersed settlement elsewhere. Large residential compounds with multiple patios may be found in the foothills (W. Fash 1983a; Whittington and Zeleznik 1991). Smaller centers with monumental architecture that developed in some of the eastern pockets and along tributary streams were incorporated into the expanding Copan polity as well (Canuto 2004; Morley 1920; Pahl 1977; Saturno 2000).

The most complete body of information on daily life in the Copan valley comes from horizontally extensive excavations in two different parts of the settlement. One is the eastern part of the urban core, known as the Sepulturas zone. My discussion is based primarily on three residential compounds from this zone. Their excavation in the 1980s provides one of the most complete recoveries of information about the Late Classic occupation. Group 9N-8, as noted, has at least fourteen patios, which have been designated A–M. Patios A and B share a raised artificial platform that puts them at a slightly higher elevation than the adjoining patios. Of these, Patios A–F, H–K, and M have been excavated. Group 9M-22 is a three-patio compound, two of which (Patios A and B) were excavated. Group 9M-24 is a single-patio group (see Diamanti 2000; Gerstle 1988; Gerstle and Webster 1990; Hendon 1987, 1991; Hendon, Agurcia, Fash, and Aguilar P. 1990; Hendon, Fash, and Aguilar P. 1990; Gonlin 1985; Mallory 1981, 1984; Sheehy 1991; Webster, Fash, and Abrams 1986). All three were slated for restoration to expand the tourist park; this made it possible for us to clear off all of the final phase of the buildings and excavate the full depth of the deposits of trash behind them. The restorers needed to dismantle the surviving walls in order to reset them to vertical, giving the excavators a chance to explore the earlier phases of construction and to locate burials and caches. Nancy Gonlin's analysis of the excavation results of eight smaller residential groups in the less densely settled portion of the valley farther away from the Main Group provides a look at daily life among the more rural sector of the population. The foothill sites are all small, no larger than Group 9M-24 (Gonlin 1993, 1994; Webster and Gonlin 1988). They vary in the number of buildings and consequently in

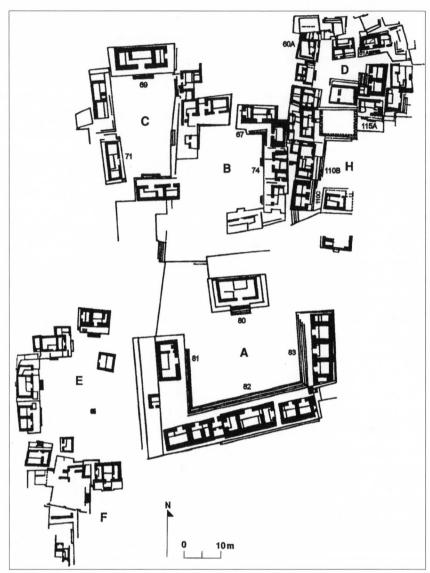

2. Plan of Group 9N-8, one of the largest residential compounds at Copan, made up of contiguous but separate patios, indicated by a letter on the plan. Courtesy of the Instituto Hondureño de Antropología e Historia.

how closely they approach the quadrilateral arrangement of structures, but they do share with their larger examples an orientation toward a common patio. These diverse groups are a comparable sample based on similar excavation strategies and methods which exposed the final phase of the buildings, recovering materials inside rooms and in the trash deposits behind the buildings. Excavators also dug trenches for burials.

CERRO PALENQUE AND THE LOWER ULUA VALLEY

The lower Ulua valley (sometimes called the Sula valley) is both broad and long, formed by the Ulua and Chamelecon rivers as they flow north into the Caribbean Sea. One of the major rivers in the country, the Ulua has a large, fertile floodplain with high agricultural productivity. As in the Copan valley, occupation of the lower Ulua valley has a long history, dating to at least 1600 BCE (Joyce and Henderson 2001). The area was heavily occupied during the Late and Terminal Classic periods. Several major centers, including Travesia, La Guacamaya, and Cerro Palenque, developed here but none exercised the kind of centralized political control over the residents of the valley that existed in the Copan valley. In fact, lower Ulua occupation is better understood not as a single, politically unified society with a well-defined social hierarchy, but as a set of more and less bounded settlements held together by multiple coordinate economic, social, and political networks that created heterarchical relations based on shared practices (see Henderson and Joyce 2005).

Many people lived on the relatively flat, fertile (but also often flooded) valley bottom, but the residents of Cerro Palenque chose to live in the foothills at the southern end of the valley. They built first on the highest peak. This sector consists of five architectural groups which include domestic and religious buildings as well as a reservoir. The architecture here exhibits the same sort of features used to argue for elevated social status at Copan and other parts of southeastern Mesoamerica, including an overall massiveness of construction, the use of worked stone and lime plaster, and the presence of architectural sculpture. The relatively small group of people living here (compared to the later occupation) had access to such imported materials as jade and the spectacular marine shell *Spondylus* (spiny oyster). They used these materials in socially meaningful rituals, including the creation of caches in domestic and ritual contexts (Joyce 1985, 1991).

After 850 CE, settlement moved to the ridge tops of the lower hills, leaving the earlier buildings still visible. Over 500 structures have been mapped

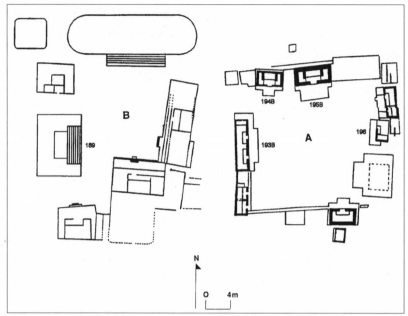

3. Plan of Group 9M-22 at Copan, a residential compound with several patios, two of which are shown here. Courtesy of the Instituto Hondureño de Antropología e Historia.

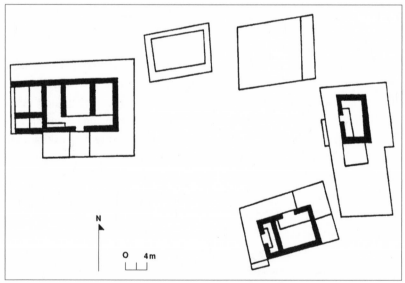

4. Plan of Group 9M-24 at Copan, an example of a single-patio residential compound. Although small, this group has well-built stone structures. Courtesy of the Instituto Hondureño de Antropología e Historia.

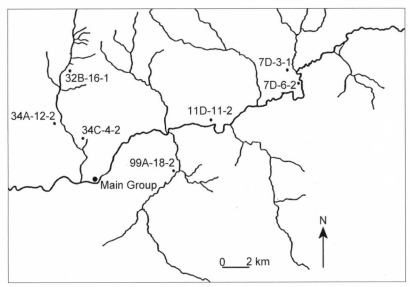

Map 4. Rural sites in the Copan valley. Courtesy of the Instituto Hondureño de Antropología e Historia, redrawn from Gonlin 1993:3.1, used with permission.

at Cerro Palenque, making it the largest settlement in its valley during the Terminal Classic but considerably smaller than Copan at its peak (Joyce 1982, 1985). Even if comparison is limited to the dense area around the Main Group, Cerro Palenque is only about one-fourth the size of Copan.

Three concentrations of Terminal Classic construction have been identified (Joyce 1991). The largest, CR-157, includes domestic spaces with houses, shrines, and kitchens to the east and west of a new concentration of monumental architecture. This Great Plaza was the architectural and spatial focus of the ancient community during its Terminal Classic occupation. Although functionally similar to Copan's Main Group and conventionally monumental in scale, the Great Plaza does not contain carved stone monuments or inscriptions. In the Main Group, buildings subdivide the open area into separate plazas of unequal size and different elevation. The placement of stelae and other sculpture further breaks up the space. At Cerro Palenque, aside from a low platform used for religious offerings, nothing intruded into the open space of the plaza. Two raised walkways that lead from the northern end of the plaza to a tall building further enhance the expansive sense of space. A ballcourt is located at the southern end along with an adjoining group of residential structures.

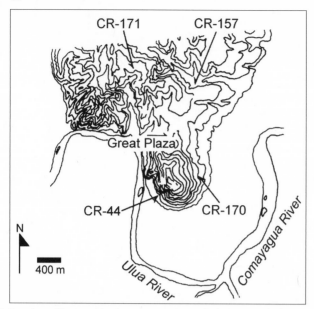

Map 5. Location of the Late Classic (CR-44) and Terminal Classic (CR-157, -170, -171) settlement clusters at Cerro Palenque. Courtesy of the Instituto Hondureño de Antropología e Historia, redrawn from the original map by Rosemary A. Joyce, used with permission.

A second locus of residences, CR-171, is located northeast, and the third, CR-170, to the east of the earlier occupation. Each of these areas is built on top of a ridge that slopes down from the Late Classic hilltop. Each has a single plaza with monumental architecture that is a smaller version of the Great Plaza. Occupation on the same ridge is thus separated by differences in elevation, while the ridges themselves constitute discrete segments of the ancient settlement pattern. Residential groups in CR-157, CR-170, and CR-171 are made up of small, low cobble mounds arranged in formally oriented, rectilinear groups or in less formal, looser groups around small courtyards. The important spatial pattern is that the orientation of the buildings is toward the courtyard.

The ridges create a strongly marked north–south orientation for the Terminal Classic settlement, enhanced by the layout of the Great Plaza. Interaction with people living on the same ridge would have been easy, although movement across ridges must also have taken place given the integration of the site in terms of material culture and the presence of the ballcourt in the Great Plaza. The decoration of jars suitable for carrying liquids such as water or *chicha* (fermented corn beer), for example, is distinctive of

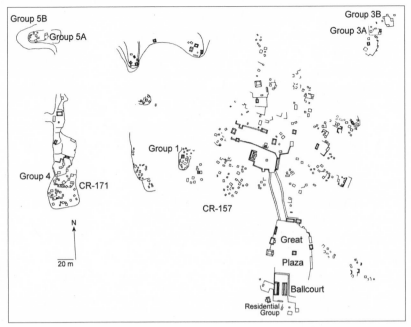

Map 6. Houses and monumental architecture in CR-157 and CR-171 at Cerro Palenque.
Courtesy of the Instituto Hondureño de Antropología e Historia, redrawn from the original
map by Rosemary A. Joyce, used with permission.

Terminal Classic Cerro Palenque as a whole when compared to other sites in
the lower Ulua valley (Joyce 1987a), reinforcing a sense of community identification spanning the three clusters of settlement.

Horizontally extensive excavations in six Terminal Classic residential
groups located in different parts of the site provide information on domestic
life (see Hendon 1998, 2000a, 2002a; Hendon and Lopiparo 2004; Joyce
1985, 1991). The residential group southeast of the ballcourt stands out by
virtue of its proximity to the Great Plaza and its size. It shares the raised
terrace supporting the ballcourt, putting it on the same level as the monumental architecture. Only 20 meters (65 feet) separate the ballcourt and the
northern end of the living area. The area in between was paved to create a
walkway that made for easy access between the two areas (Hendon 2005;
Hendon and Lopiparo 2004). This residential area is larger than the others,
which are Groups 1, 3A and B, 5A and B, 6A and B in CR-157 and Group 4
in CR-171. These features make it sufficiently distinct from the residential
groups already excavated to suggest that its residents may have differed from
their neighbors in social status, political role, or economic activities.

THE CUYUMAPA VALLEY

The Cuyumapa river flows westward through a mountainous section of central Honduras to merge with the Comayagua river, which in turn flows into the Ulua river where it enters the lower Ulua valley. The earliest occupation in the Cuyumapa valley has been dated to about 900–800 BCE (Hendon and Joyce 1993). Settlement in the Cuyumapa valley is located in clusters along the river and its two main tributaries, the Cataguana and Oloman. Some 511 structures have been identified through survey and excavation (Hendon and Joyce 1993; Joyce, Sheptak, Hendon, Fung, and Gerry 1989). The number of structures suggests a population scale approximately equal to that of Cerro Palenque at its peak but distributed across a much larger area, resulting in a lower density of population (Joyce and Hendon 2000).

Most of the Cuyumapa settlement consists of small-scale structures (below 1.25 meters or about 4 feet in height) arranged in clusters on the landscape that are unevenly but not randomly distributed. In some areas of the valley, especially along major drainages, clusters are close enough to form larger conglomerations of structures. Excavation has shown these structures to be residences and associated types of buildings usually arranged around a shared courtyard, similar to the plan of residences at Copan and Cerro Palenque. Clusters may contain many such residential groups. In this sense, they are comparable to the ridge-top groupings at Cerro Palenque. Something similar may also be seen at Copan in the way the massive residential courtyards cluster along the river around the Main Group and in the way residential groups farther away and in the foothills were sometimes built in proximity to others. What the Cuyumapa settlement system lacks is a single architectural concentration of monumental buildings and plazas like that found in the Main Group and the Great Plaza. The region does have large-scale structures, but they are found in many clusters. These large-scale structures vary in shape, some being tall and pyramidal, others long and low. They also differ in function. Some were residences, others ritual buildings or ballcourts. Although some clusters of small-scale structures are near ballcourts, in the sense that they are distributed along the river, they are not nucleated around the cluster of monumental architecture (Fung 1995; Hendon and Joyce 1993; Joyce and Hendon 2000).

A program of test excavations at six sites, three in the Oloman valley and three in the Cataguana (PACO 1, PACO 2, PACO 5, PACO 11, PACO 14, and PACO 15), established the presence of a Late to Terminal Classic occupation that continues after 800 BCE, contemporaneous with Cerro Palenque. More

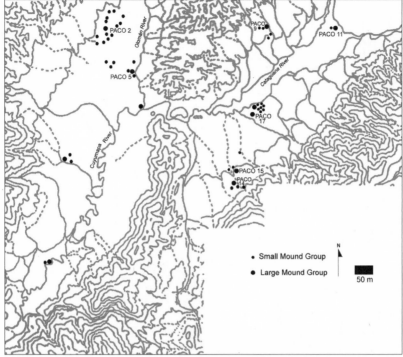

Map 7. The Cuyumapa river valley. Its two arms are formed by the Oloman and Cataguana rivers. The location of sites with ballcourts is shown. Courtesy of the Instituto Hondureño de Antropología e Historia, redrawn from the original map by Rosemary A. Joyce, used with permission.

intensive excavations have been carried out at residential areas and ballcourts at the sites of PACO 2, 14, and 15 (Fox 1994, 1996; Fung 1995, 1996; Joyce, Hendon, Fung, and Fox 2001).

COMPLICATED SOCIETIES IN SOUTHEASTERN MESOAMERICA

The people living at Copan, Cerro Palenque, and in the Cuyumapa valley, like their neighbors in southeastern Mesoamerica, were neither modern nor Western as conventionally defined. They did not live in the same social, cultural, economic, political, technological, or territorial world people do today. Their history was built around events unfamiliar to us but was based nevertheless on a consciousness of the passage of time and the need to relate past and present. These histories contribute to the construction and

5. Plan of part of the site of PACO 2 in the Cuyumapa valley, showing the relationship between the ballcourt and the nearby cluster of houses. Courtesy of the Instituto Hondureño de Antropología e Historia, redrawn from the original plan by Rosemary A. Joyce, used with permission.

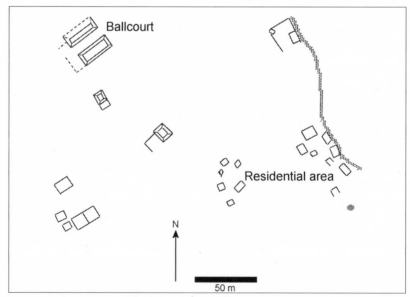

6. The Late to Terminal Classic period ballcourt and associated houses at the site of PACO 14 in the Cuyumapa valley. Courtesy of the Instituto Hondureño de Antropología e Historia, redrawn from the original plan by Rosemary A. Joyce, used with permission.

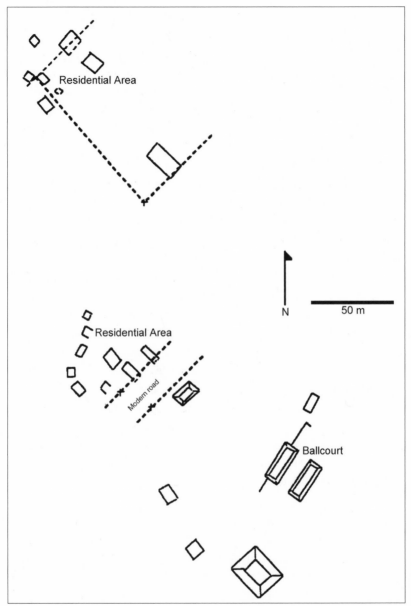

Residential Area

Residential Area

N   50 m

Modern road

Ballcourt

7. Location of the Late Formative ballcourt at the site of PACO 15 in the Cuyumapa valley. Courtesy of the Instituto Hondureño de Antropología e Historia, redrawn from the original plan by Rosemary A. Joyce, used with permission.

reconstruction of identities over time and place significant happenings in temporal relationship to the present. I am not interested in claiming they were modern, although such an argument has been made (Pyburn 1998), because to do so leaves intact, or at the least does not address, the validity of the distinction itself. What I am suggesting is that the lack of the particular things we see as creating an unstable, fractured, distanced world does not mean these so-called premodern people lived in unchanging, stable situations or in bounded, delimited societies. These were complicated societies, what Piot (1999:23) has called cosmopolitan, with "a social life characterized by flux, uncertainty, encounters with difference, and the experience of the processes of transculturation."

Many aspects of such societies were productive of uncertainty, instability, and ambiguity (Cobb 2005; Muriuki 2002; Piot 1999). Archaeological and historical sources of information offer insight into at least some of these aspects. An impressive array of languages were spoken in Mesoamerica before European colonization (Campbell, Kaufman, and Smith-Stark 1986). People of varying ages, genders, occupations, classes, ethnicities, and languages lived in close quarters, so much so that in 1519 the Chontal Maya of Mexico's Gulf Coast were able to provide Hernán Cortes with a translator fluent in their tongue in addition to her native language of Nahuatl; she rapidly learned Spanish as well, making it possible for Spanish conquistador and Aztec emperor to speak to one another (Karttunen 1994). The presence of hieroglyphic inscriptions in the Copan valley argues that one of the large family of Mayan languages was spoken there. Fine-grained research on primary sixteenth- and seventeenth-century Spanish documents from the area around Cerro Palenque by Russell Sheptak (2005) suggests that the lower Ulua valley was occupied by speakers of several languages at the time of Spanish contact, including a Mayan language and Lenca (see also Chapman 1985, 1986; Joyce 1988). The Cuyumapa region was occupied by Tol (Jicaque) speakers after the Spanish conquest (Ardón Mejía 1986; Chapman 1978). This information postdates the time period I consider here but is suggestive of linguistic diversity that did not stand in the way of frequent and ongoing interaction.

Exchange with societies living far away was central to the economies of these societies. Not only goods but also technologies, ideas, and people moved over long distances regularly—perhaps not as far as we are used to or as rapidly but quickly enough, from far enough away, and over long enough periods of time to create enduring networks of exchange and to necessitate ongoing interaction with foreigners. Shifts in exchange networks are also evident, which would require the establishment of new social ties and economic arrangements. Prior to the Late Classic period, pottery and sculpture demonstrate the movement of materials and ideas between the Copan valley and the southwestern highland area of Guatemala (Fash and Stuart 1991; Viel 1998). By the eighth century, these networks had shifted. Late Classic Copanecos imported substantial numbers of the striking painted polychrome vessels known as Ulua polychromes that were produced in the Comayagua valley and Lake Yojoa area to the southeast as well as in the lower Ulua valley. Similarities between Copan valley and central Honduran storage vessels also show that the Copan people maintained important connections with their eastern neighbors (Hendon 2003b; Joyce 1993a; Longyear 1952; Schortman and Urban 2004; Viel 1993a, 1993b). Jade, marine shells such as *Spondylus*, and marble vessels are among the materials and objects that were exchanged. The residents of Cerro Palenque received obsidian from outcrops in Guatemala some 300 kilometers (180 miles) away and pottery from Belize, transported by people maneuvering canoes through the Caribbean sea and up the Ulua river (Hendon 2004a; Sheptak 1987; Yarnell 2005). People in the Cuyumapa valley acquired pottery from near and distant neighbors in several parts of Honduras, including Cerro Palenque (Fung 1995; Joyce et al. 2001).

All three societies experienced and contributed to ongoing processes of political and economic realignment among groups and regions in Mesoamerica as the Late Classic gave way to the Terminal Classic. Mesoamerican societies were never stable or unchanging. Realignments occurred throughout the history of the region, and sometimes they are visible to archaeologists because of the nature of the associated material cultural changes. The Late to Terminal Classic transition was a time of changing ties, population distribution, and forms of political integration. It has received a great deal of attention from archaeologists because it is marked by the gradual cessation, over a period of about 150 years, of the practice at many Maya sites, including Copan, of installing commemorative stone monuments recording the significant events of royal dynasties tied to dates in the Long Count (Chase and Chase 2004). Although these changes were once taken as symptomatic of the breakdown of an entire civilization on a regional scale (a so-called Maya collapse), more recent work has argued that they represent the dissolution of a particular mode of political organization in the Maya area centered on the royal person and dynasty (Rice, Demarest, and Rice 2004). During the eighth century through the eleventh, we see the decline of some settlements, the continued occupation of others, and the development of new cities and towns as well as the development of new kinds of material culture and aesthetic traditions, shifts in exchange relationships, and changes in political organization (Demarest, Rice, and Rice 2004; Hendon 2004c).

People at Copan had to cope with the changes caused by an expanding population during the seventh century and the eighth and its decline in the ninth and tenth. They lived in a society with a long history of social differentiation signaled by variation in wealth and markers of status, even longer than the establishment of dynastic royal rule. It has been suggested that the last confirmed ruler, the sixteenth, found it necessary to share power and privilege more widely among members of high-status families in order to secure their continued support in the face of declining resources and a lower standard of living and resources (W. Fash 2005; Fash and Stuart 1991). Competition for authority and privilege predated this particular ruler's tenure, however. René Viel (1999) has argued that more than one royal lineage existed and that, over time, rulership shifted, perhaps to some extent in a patterned fashion, among at least two and possible more noble houses who had legitimate but contested claims on the kingship and other political offices.

Cerro Palencanos experienced an expansion of settlement and population size that happened even more quickly than that in the Copan valley. Concomitant with this change was the decline of the other large settlements in the lower Ulua valley, leaving Cerro Palenque with the biggest population and most consequential conglomeration of monumental architecture. Other indicators, such as the distribution of imported obsidian and pottery as well as of locally produced marble vessels and pottery, suggest that the Cerro Palenque community was developing a greater degree of internal social differentiation during the 800s than had been the case earlier, with the residential group next to the ballcourt emerging as the locus of greatest variation and quantity of such materials (Hendon 2004a, 2005).

Excavations in the ballcourt residential group have found foreign pottery of diverse origin. These include the kinds labeled by archaeologists Blanco Gray from the Cuyumapa valley, Las Vegas Polychrome and Tenampua Polychrome from southern Honduras, Belize Red from Belize, and some that may be from El Salvador. The presence of this pottery attests to the fact that residents of Cerro Palenque maintained social contacts with diverse groups of people in the Terminal Classic Mesoamerican world and were thus able to adjust their networks in the face of regional upheaval. These contacts involved them with new modes of material culture. This is most vividly demonstrated by the changes in the locally produced pottery used for food serving and eating, often in sociable or ritual contexts. After 850 CE, the residents of Cerro Palenque sharply reduce their use of Ulua polychrome pottery. I excavated a cache, or ritual deposit, in the ballcourt residential group containing a bowl of Santana Polychrome, a very late Ulua type (Hendon and Lopiparo 2004). Some sherds have been found in other excavations, but the overall frequency is very low and reduces to nothing over time.

A new kind of pottery becomes the preferred fancy tableware even as pottery used for cooking and storage continues in the same vein as before. The new pottery, known as fine paste, is generally unpainted and often quite plain (Joyce 1985, 1986, 1991; see also Rice and Forsyth 2004). When decorated, the surface is incised, molded, or modeled into shapes and patterns. The appearance of fine paste pottery is quite distinctive from that of the Ulua polychromes, although certain stylistic elements do connect them. Moreover, fine paste pottery resembles similar kinds of pottery that appear in the Maya area of Guatemala and Belize around the same time (known as Fine Orange pottery) and which also represent a shift from a former polychrome tradition (Joyce 1987b). Analysis of the clay from which the Cerro Palenque pots were made demonstrates that they, like those found at other sites in the valley, were produced locally at several production centers (Lopiparo 2003; Lopiparo, Joyce, and Hendon 2005). Local manufacture is further supported by the occurrence of the molds used to make the vessels and pottery kilns at the site (Hendon 2005; Hendon and Lopiparo 2004). Cerro Palencanos capitalized on the regional political and economic changes to become more important locally and used material culture to construct an identity that reiterated its connections with groups in the Yucatan peninsula and lowland Guatemala and Belize during an unstable period. These connections are further indicated by the presence of elaborately carved vessels made from marble in Belizean and Guatemalan sites (Joyce 1986). These marble vessels were manufactured in the lower Ulua valley (Luke 2004; Luke and Tykot 2002).

Cuyumapans also valued exchange relationships with multiple groups, including the Aguan valley to the east, the Sulaco river drainage and the Lake Yojoa area, and Comayagua valley to the south. In the mid-800s, imported Ulua polychromes are replaced by fine paste wares from the lower Ulua valley, confirming the presence of ties between the two areas, ties already suggested by the occurrence of Blanco Gray pottery from Cuyumapa at Cerro

Palenque (Hendon 2005; Joyce, Hendon, Fung, and Fox 2001). Settlement remains quite constant in Cuyumapa, in contrast to Copan and Cerro Palenque. Moreover, the inhabitants of Cuyumapa continue to build and use multiple ballcourts. The fact that settlement and social relations in Cuyumapa do not show the marked changes found in the other two valleys during the centuries under discussion might be taken as evidence of a stable, unchanging situation. Maintaining heterarchical relations with relatively little social difference, however, in the face of the larger-scale shifts going on around them, suggests that stability was something to be achieved, not merely continued.

CONTEXTS OF IDENTITY

Many years ago, when I first began wrestling with the question of the meaningfulness of domestic life (Hendon 1999b), I discovered a description in Evon Vogt's magisterial ethnography of Zinacantan, Mexico, that I found quite illuminating. Although Vogt himself was preoccupied with defining Tzotzil Maya social groups through the classic anthropological paradigm of kinship and descent, his description included what the Tzotzil themselves considered important: men and women, adults and children bound together through a shared residence (either a house or a set of houses in a compound), a common corn supply, and a wooden cross placed outside the main dwelling (Vogt 1969:127–29). Through their productive and ritual actions as well as through their relations to one another, the coresident members exemplify consciously and implicitly the beings desired by the gods in the *Popol vuh* capable of walking, working, and talking "in an articulate and measured way, visiting shrines, giving offerings, and calling upon their makers by name, all according to the rhythms of [the 260-day] calendar" (D. Tedlock 1996:32). From this perspective, the Tzotzil coresident group emerges as a social group of men and women who see themselves bound together through economic and religious activities that connect them to a particular place over time. There are several ways to think about these kinds of historically constituted identities that are tied in some way to places. Archaeological and biological anthropological research indicates the possibility of several contexts of identity which defined how people became part of long-lived social groups with economic, social, and political significance. The important ones discussed here are biological lineages, households, sociological houses, and communities of practice.

BIOLOGICAL LINEAGES

One way of thinking about forms of affiliation may be discerned at Copan on the basis of the sizeable sample of human remains from the Main Group, the urban zone, and the more distant areas of settlement recovered over decades of excavation.[1] Recent work by Megan Rhoads on the distribution of genetically inherited dental traits, used "as a proxy to determine biological distance between or among groups," reveals that the Late Classic Copan population was remarkably homogeneous in terms of biological related- ness. Only one clear distinction emerged from a range of analyses: that two biological lineages could be differentiated (Rhoads 2002:44, 215–21). Rhoads notes that these two lineages, called here for convenience A and B, crosscut the spatial distinction of rural versus urban residence, the status distinction of higher and lower status, the economic distinction of greater or lesser wealth, and the social distinction of gender. In other words, members of both biological lineages were found in burials in the Main Group, in the dense and conventionally elite residential area around it, and out in the more dispersed foothill settlement. In those cases where it is possible to consider the burials from one particular residential patio or from agglomerations of such patios as found in the urban zone, it turns out that men and women from the same domestic setting most often belong to the same biological lineage. Furthermore, no genetically foreign (from outside the valley) en- claves could be identified. Take the three groups from the Sepulturas area that I study here. Group 9M-24, the smallest, was occupied by people be- longing to Lineage A. The two excavated patios of Group 9M-22 contained burials belonging entirely or mostly to Lineage B. Both lineages were found in the largest group, 9N-8. Patios A, B, C, D, E, F, and H have more burials belonging to Lineage B than A, while those from Patio J are members of Lineage A. Even the residents of Patio D, suggested to be immigrants from outside the valley (Gerstle 1988), are biologically indistinguishable from their close neighbors in the adjacent patios. The distribution of lineages does not correspond to sex in any regular way, suggesting that people fre- quently married members of their own biological lineage. Other excavated groups in this area are occupied by Lineage A (Rhoads 2002:Table 7.8).

These biological data do not mean that people in the Copan valley neces- sarily had no sense of different degrees of relationship. Kinship may be defined in ways that emphasize smaller-scale or shorter-term connections and is not directly dependent on shared descent. But the data do suggest that over time the residents of the alluvial pocket around the Main Group had built up a wide-ranging, long-lasting set of relations and connections that were both biological and social. These may have complicated the construction of clearly defined social difference based on location, wealth, or descent (see chapter 3).

HOUSEHOLDS

The concept of the household captures certain aspects of the relations and practices that bound people together in these societies. Archaeological interest in the household developed in response to a desire to place the actions of coresidential groups in some kind of analytical framework that avoided defining social groups on the basis of kinship—as a "family" (Hendon 1996, 2004b, 2006a; Wilk and Rathje 1982). The study of households emphasizes small-scale economic relations that are often the responsibility of such coresidential groups. The Tzotzil sharing their residences, corn stores, and wooden cross are in one sense a household, an economically cooperative group that may be defined on the basis of task and activities as "the most common social component of subsistence, the smallest and most abundant activity group" (Wilk and Rathje 1982:618) with four main functions: transmission, reproduction, distribution, and production.

The economic interdependence of people living together in Late to Terminal Classic Honduras comes through in the consistent association between domestic space and evidence for a range of productive action over time. Given the size of some of the residential groupings discussed here, some households were large indeed, yet they display a similar pattern of activities conventionally defined as economic. In all cases, analysis of the architecture of these residences, the artifacts recovered, and their contextual associations, including where they are found and what they are found with, allows one to see the kinds of activities of daily living that took place there, activities I discuss in detail in chapters 4 and 5. Pottery jars, plates, bowls, and basins for mixing, cooking, and serving; basalt or rhyolite *manos* and *metates* for grinding corn; sharp cutting tools made out of obsidian; bones from deer and other animals—all of these objects demonstrate that food preparation, food consumption, and food storage took up people's time. But daily life during this time period included more than just making sure everyone was fed and housed. People made things while at home. Thread, cloth, jewelry, pots, clay figurines and whistles, cutting tools, and bark paper were the kinds of objects that might be manufactured. They celebrated important family events and carried out rituals crucial to their religious lives.

SOCIOLOGICAL HOUSES

The sociological house represents another locus of identity and memory in Mesoamerican societies (see Chance 2000; Gillespie 2000b, 2000c; Hendon 2007; Joyce 2000a; Lopiparo 2007; Monaghan 1995:244–46; Sandstrom 2000).[2] More so than the household, the sociological house provides a richer social context for the work of memory. Based on the *sociétés à maison* (house societies) model developed by Claude Lévi-Strauss (1982, 1987:151–94), subsequent work has emphasized the ways in which sociological houses are created and sustained through practice (Carsten and Hugh-Jones 1995; Gillespie 2000a; Joyce 2000c; Kan 1989; Waterson 1995). Sociological houses are an example of how the work of memory and the work of identity converge to support relations that endure over time and space. Although not limited to people who live together or are of equivalent social status, sociological houses in Mesoamerica, like those elsewhere, rely heavily on connections between people, physical houses, and material objects for their perpetuation (Gillespie and Joyce 1997; Hendon 2002c, 2007; Joyce 2001; Lopiparo 2007; Weiss-Krejci 2004).

People become members of a sociological house through various means. In contrast to a lineage model, descent from other members is only one of several possible ways to use relatedness as the basis for a claim of membership. Other ways include marriage to someone already part of the sociological house, adoption, capture, or living in the same area. People are brought together through genealogy and alliance, kinship and locality, to create a flexible but enduring social group of variable size. Although sociological house members often use kinship as a way of referring to one another, this is as much a rhetorical strategy as a reflection of what we would call actual blood relationships (Waterson 1995). Membership is really oriented around common investment in the house estate, an investment embodied in shared participation in ritual and day-to-day interactions, and combines material possessions with intangible property or wealth (Lévi-Strauss 1982; Weiner 1992). Intangibles might include what we would think of as rights, such as the right to perform certain ceremonies or produce particular items (often regalia used in such ceremonies) or the right to employ specific names and titles (Gillespie and Joyce 1997; Kan 1989).

Living house members must be concerned with contributing to continuity over time through their actions and interactions for the whole enterprise to keep going and for a sociological house to stay in existence over multigenerational time spans. In many house societies, members of sociological houses contend for position within their house and strive to make their house more prominent than neighboring houses or distant allied rivals (McKinnon 1991). As a memory community, the sociological house is both a vehicle for the perpetuation of memory and something that exists in the collective memory of its members, allies, and rivals. Accumulation of honors, continuity of identity, and perpetuation of the house estate may be more feasible for noble houses or may merely be more visible because of their greater ability to invest in material markers of their identity. Economic constraints and changes may undermine house stability, especially for groups that are not wealthy or firmly entrenched (Sandstrom 2000).

As noted earlier, royalty at Copan may have been divided into several competing and cooperating sociological houses that included members of the urban area. Altar Q, a monument carved for the sixteenth ruler and placed in the East Court of the Acropolis, shows Ruler 16 facing the first ruler. This ruler, who is credited with founding the royal line of succession in the fifth century CE, hands him a scepter. Fourteen other figures line up between the first and last kings. These figures, which can be identified as the second through the fifteenth rulers, cover all four sides of the low rectangular monument. All sit on objects that are large hieroglyphic signs corresponding to their names or other identifiers (Baudez 1994:95–97; W. Fash 2001). Viel (1999) has noted that the pectorals worn by the Altar Q figures fall into six types. Study of other monuments adds another two styles. That of Ruler 1 is unique. Viel argues that the other pectorals denote different social groups, which I would suggest are in fact different sociological houses. Based on similarities in the components of the pectorals, Viel further groups these styles into two larger sets, one of which predominates in the latter half of the kingdom's history. This larger grouping, made up of several sociological houses, may be associated with the northern and eastern areas of the urban zone, through the occurrence of appropriate jewelry on sculptures of young men attached to large houses in Sepulturas and on royal monuments (see chapter 5).

Altar Q has been cited as an egregious example of the propagandistic nature of Maya monumental art and texts (Marcus 2002). The idea that two individuals, Rulers 1 and 16, could have actually done what they are depicted as doing is absurd given the centuries that separate them. Therefore, the image lies. There are two difficulties with this argument, however. One is that it assumes monumental imagery and texts are intended to depict actual events as they happened. Allegory and metaphor play a role in many

8. Copan rulers wearing their pectorals as carved on Altar Q in the West Court of the Acropolis. Ruler 1, with his unique pectoral, is the second figure from the left. Ruler 16 faces him. Photograph by Julia A. Hendon.

traditions of public art, including our own. Monuments, even if realist in style, are not like newspaper photographs. The other problem is that labeling Altar Q as propaganda ignores the likelihood that it reflects a variant approach to history (as opposed to an inability to perceive history), one that valorizes connections across time and admits of the possibility that such connections were believed to be possible in actuality as well as metaphorically to the people who lived at Copan. In other words, here is a glimpse of a historical consciousness different from our own but no less valid within its cultural context.

COMMUNITIES OF PRACTICE

What the concepts of household and sociological house do not fully address is the meaningfulness of coresidence, of living together, or of the places themselves. Sociological houses represent one important locus of memory making that supports multiple memory communities. Not all members live together, however. Since I see the groups of people living together as an important source of identity and social memory, I have found it more productive to think about the occupants of houses in Cuyumapa, Copan, and

Cerro Palenque as communities of practice, created through mutual engagement in a joint enterprise defined and sustained through practice (Wenger 1998). Communities of practice develop out of the ways in which people engage "in actions whose meanings they negotiate with one another" (Wenger 1998:73) as they do what they need to do to further their collective enterprise. It thus "shifts the ground of definition from either language or social structure per se to the engagement of actors in some project" (Hanks 1996:221). The actors' shared occupancy of a particular kind of space involves them in a series of interactions, relations, actions, and practices through which memory and identity are constituted and reconstituted over time. "Through their capacity both to signify appropriate behaviors and to accommodate them, house forms and their resident social groups are mutually constituting" (Birdwell-Pheasant and Lawrence-Zúñiga 1999:4), a relationship that makes agents out of houses as well as out of their occupants (Preucel 2006). Communities of practice may also develop from constituting interrelationship between place, material culture, and social relations in different settings, most notably, for my purposes, ballcourts and monumental precincts. In all cases, the important relations and interactions are not just between people but also between people and the places they inhabit and the material culture they deploy (Gell 1998; D. Miller 1987, 1998b, 2005).

Such a perspective allows me to argue that practices occurring in the spatial setting of the home (or residential places) and thus against the background of these places take on a meaning that is shaped as much by location as by who is involved and what is being done. Phenomenological studies of perception draw attention to the relationship between figure and ground. Making sense of the figure (what you are explicitly focusing on), knowing what you are seeing, can be achieved only by taking into account the (back)ground against which the figure appears and of which it is a part (Kelly 2005). Changing the background changes the perception and meaning of the figure and in the process changes our understanding of the world we inhabit as a "locus of shared understanding organized by social practice" (Taylor 2005:31). By considering figure and ground together—in this case action and interaction (figure) at home (ground)—I am suggesting that we cannot assume actions or events carried out in distinct spatial and social locations differ only in terms of scale and otherwise are essentially the same and have the same meaning. The household economy, for example, is not merely the economy writ small (Graeber 2001; D. Miller 1987; Moore 1992, 1994; Schöttler 1995). And rituals carried out within the confines of a residential compound are not merely scaled-down versions of those performed in the Main Group, the Great Plaza, or in association with ballcourts in Cuyumapa. Even if such observances involve the same kinds of materials or actions, they do not have the same meaning or consequences.

People residing together in Late-Terminal Classic Honduras participate in multiple communities of practice centered on joint enterprises, some situated in residential places, others not. The maintenance of place and identity over time makes the coresidential group a case of mutual engagement. By concentrating on communities of practice defined by the shared project of living together, I can bring forward the central role of practice, not as part of some duality with structure or as a reflection of some abstract set of norms, but as the means through which day-to-day reality is produced and changed over time. Memory communities are communities of practice in which learning takes place and knowledge is constructed (Lave and Wenger 1991; Wenger 1998). From this vantage point, the fact that some sociological houses claim to endure over generations results from the social, political, and economic consequences of these shared practices rather than from the group's achieving some kind of transcendent life of its own independent of the people who reproduce it through practice.

In this sense, the idea of communities of practice is a more flexible and useful way to approach the significance of daily life at home to memory and identity than *habitus*. "As an acquired system of generative schemes, the *habitus* makes possible the free production of all the thoughts, perceptions and actions inherent in the particular conditions of its production—and only those" (Bourdieu 1990:55). Bourdieu's insistence on *habitus* as structuring, its sedimentation in the body (bodily *hexis*) and on practical, embodied, or second-nature forms of knowing has been taken by many to mean that *habitus* is determinative and that practical knowing is irrelevant to agency or meaning. The problem is that *habitus* can be turned into a fixed background to social interaction, one that becomes an unyielding structure that exists prior to human action and interaction (Farnell 1999, 2000). Thus things that should be approached as performative, relational, and situational, such as gender relations, can be explained away by facile assumptions about the embedding of social agents in particular social structures. One can see how *habitus* provides a powerful explanation for how children become differentiated into socially recognized and, for Bourdieu, class-based categories of male and female. Yet, as Terry Lovell (2000:33) points out, "It is clear that this by no means always happens, requiring as it does that female and male children *position themselves* as girls and boys. . . . Those which posit a glove-like 'fit' between *habitus* and social position are in danger of binding subjectivity too tightly to the social conditions in which it is forged." Communities of practice, like any form of social action, are embedded in and influenced by history that justifies how things are done the way they are and what kinds of relations and meanings result. Conceptually, however, the emphasis is much more on the dynamic consequences of practice through which both day-to-day and long-term realities are produced. Communities of practice are characterized by "shared histories of learning" (Wenger 1998:86) that are both intersubjective and based on some material domain. They are also contexts for remembering and forgetting, open to reinterpretation over time.

TWO

The Enchantment and Humility of Objects

In 738 CE, a ruler of Quirigua, in southeastern Guatemala, claimed the honor of having captured and sacrificed the reigning ruler of the Copan kingdom, Ruler
13.[1] The event became a touchstone for the Quirigua
ruler, who referred to it on four of his free-standing
sculpted monuments, Stelae E, F, and J and Zoomorph
G. This ruler, who had previously acknowledged the
Copan king as his political superior, now styled himself as the fourteenth king, as if he had succeeded his
victim. Royal monuments at Copan, in contrast, record
nothing about this event or its consequences until some
twenty years later, when the date of Ruler 13's death in
battle is noted in a text commissioned by the fifteenth
ruler as part of his renovation of a massive monument
known as the Hieroglyphic Staircase (Fash, Williamson, Larios, and Palka 1992). Among the statues of

9. The south side of Stela E at Quirigua as photographed in the nineteenth century by A. P.
Maudslay. This monument, put in place in 771 CE, is one of three stelae recording the capture
of a Copan king by the ruler of Quirigua thirty-three years before. Image reproduced from the
facsimile edition of *Biologia Centrali-Americana* by Alfred Percival Maudslay. Published by
Milpatron Publishing Corp., Stamford, Conn., 06902. Further reproduction prohibited.

10. The Hieroglyphic Staircase (Structure 10L-26) in the Main Group at Copan. Photograph by Julia A. Hendon.

Ruler 15's predecessor kings seated on the staircase is one of the thirteenth ruler dressed as a warrior. Ruler 15's monuments also construct an apparently smooth and seamless line of succession from Ruler 13 to Ruler 14 to himself, working just as hard to forget the fiasco as the Quirigua did to keep the memory of their triumph green (Looper 1999, 2003; Riese 1984; Martin and Grube 2000; Sharer 1990; Stuart 2005).

HOW DO OBJECTS HELP US REMEMBER?

Here I begin my exploration of how memory communities assert connections between a body of memory and a desired identity. I focus on the ways in which memory is externalized through objects. The erecting of monuments to create a permanent and public commemoration of particular events or people is something that has been widely studied because we assume that monuments "are intended to outlive the period which originated them, and constitute a heritage for future generations" (Giedion, Léger, and Sert 1984:62; see also Serageldin, Shluger, and Martin-Brown 2001). They are intended to record some event, person, or concept considered to be so significant that it merits a permanent memorial with names, dates, and appropriate visual imagery. This notion of heritage has been extended to things that are monumental, such as buildings, statues, monoliths, and tombs. Monuments and the monumental are interpreted as being tangible, enduring reminders that enshrine some kind of shared identity and history. Even vernacular architecture and city streets, elements of the built environment not originally designed with commemoration in mind, can become monuments to something and thus deemed worthy of preservation (Norkunas 2002; Williams 2001).

The sad truth about monuments is that, left to their own devices, they fail to provide the kind of permanent instantiation of memory we think they should (see Elsner 2003; Herzfeld 1991; Nora 1996). And yet I agree that they are important to social practices of remembering and forgetting because they can be drawn into the work of memory. The question is how. In this chapter, I consider how things external to ourselves that we somehow use, perceive, or interact with become integral to remembering and forgetting even as they shape our sense of self. Such things go by many names, whether artifact, material culture, or art (Gell 1998; Küchler 2002). Quite often the emphasis is on things that people make, use, and exchange (Graeber 2001; D. Miller 1987), but it is debatable whether this is a necessary distinction for my purposes. The line between the natural and the human-made world is not nearly as obvious as we may think—naturalized rather than natural, historical rather than eternal, symbolic as much as practical (Frémont 1997; Knapp and Ashmore 1999; Schama 1995; Stilgoe 2005).

I primarily consider what I refer to as material objects, keeping in mind that a material object may be a tool, a piece of jewelry, a small three-dimensional figure of a woman made out of clay and designed to serve as a whistle, a house, a monument, or an entire landscape. I call these things material objects (or material culture) in order to try to maintain some differentiation between such things and emotional, psychological, cognitive, philosophical—that is to say, mental—objects that are part of the process of objectification or the process of differentiating between subjects and (philosophical) objects (D. Miller 1987; Tilley 2006). Material objects are physically separate or separable from us, have a period of existence different from our own, and possess properties that we experience and that somehow contribute to people's ability to remember and forget. They are sometimes objects, sometimes subjects as they become part of the process of creating persons and a sense of self.

I begin with two widely invoked explanations that I feel are inadequate: objects as archives and as memory fossils. After explaining why these approaches fail to fully capture the memory potential of people's relations with objects, I consider how objects become dynamically involved in the generation of remembering and forgetting. This leads me to a discussion of the importance of the experiential and semiotic nature of objects, followed by a consideration of how the enchantment and humility of objects make them effective participants in the construction of social memory.

ARCHIVES AND FOSSILS

The archival explanation argues that objects may serve as memory aides because they function as external storage devices. Nowadays such devices surround us—things we read, things we watch, things we listen to, things we touch. Such devices are a subset of the object world in which we live and certainly store information, but it is debatable how they actually help us remember. "Memory has begun to keep records: delegating the responsibility for remembering to the archive, it deposits its signs as the snake deposits its shed skin" (Nora 1996:8). Archives, however vast and complete, are of value only if someone wants to use them and is allowed to do so and if anyone else wants to hear the results of the work (Ketelaar 2002). Once again, it comes back to how and why the past is brought forward into the present. Having records (which implies having a means to make records and social institutions designed to preserve them) does not ensure memory. History does not write itself. Neither is it always written down. If we were to limit ourselves to the answer that objects externalize memory only when they are its record, then we must admit that our perspective is equally limited by the idea that memory crystallizes into something we would recognize as history only under a narrow range of circumstances having more to do with certain technologies of remembering than anything else. This puts us at risk of assuming that only some things are worthy or capable of being remembered and everything else must be allowed to fall by the wayside into an undifferentiated morass of experience and the endlessly repeated lived moment. An alternative point of view, the one I take here, is that social, political, and historical circumstances result in some things being remembered differently and through different means than others.

An alternative approach, equally problematic, views objects as memory fossils. Objects like monuments may serve as memory repositories but without necessarily containing a literal transcription of what they are intended to commemorate. They may become memory surrogates as a result of the human propensity to ascribe meaning to things with a physical presence. Historians and archaeologists have tended to foreground monuments as some kind of special case of this kind of representation through symbolism because of their presumed public or collective nature and because so often they seem to us to have been intended as permanent memory markers. They obtrude on our notice so forcefully through their sheer scale and mass, which make them seem permanent, enduring, immobile, and indestructible and thus ideally suited to the perpetuation of social memory. Adrian Forty (1999:2) admirably summarizes this view even as he offers insight into its limitations: "It has been generally taken for granted that memories, formed in the mind, can be transferred to solid material objects, which can come to stand for memories and, by virtue of their durability, either prolong or preserve them indefinitely beyond their purely mental existence." This perspective extends a remembering function beyond what to us are conventional ways of archiving, but it suffers from the same fundamental limitation because it assumes that the point is to offload the responsibility for remembering onto the object. If we treat objects as memory stand-ins, as some kind of body double for memory that takes care of the tedious or distasteful aspects of remembering while memory waits off camera, primped, coiffed, and buffed, for its close-up, we find ourselves circling back to memory as something "purely mental" and as an object itself rather than a process—either memories are in the mind or they have been extruded in the form of some physical object which becomes the equivalent of a memory fossil.

OBJECTS AS GENERATIVE RESOURCES FOR
REMEMBERING AND FORGETTING

Ephemeral monuments furnish an instructive alternative perspective on the role of material objects that suggests that forgetting or removing something from view can be a generative resource rather than a defect of human mental capacities. Susanne Küchler has considered remembering and forgetting in the context of malanggan,[2] which refers both to a part of the extended series of events, often extending over many years, that make up the funerary ritual practiced by some societies of New Ireland Island in Papua New Guinea and to the effigy that is an important part of the ceremony

(Küchler 1987, 1988, 1992, 1999, 2002; Melion and Küchler 1991). The effigy takes many months to make and is revealed during the malanggan ceremony, housed in a special structure. It is treated as a living person, but it is visible for only a short period of time, perhaps no more than an hour or so before it is taken away and destroyed. Its sacrifice helps release the dead from the social relations they were part of while alive and make them an ancestor. Those attending the ceremony scrutinize the effigy while it is on display. The effigy itself and the comments of those who see it trigger a process of remembering of the motifs used in malanggan carvings. The effigy also facilitates the forgetting of the deceased person as a living social being. Because they are not preserved, knowledge of how to create and decorate a new malanggan comes only through the memory, memory which is valid only if it comes from people who stand in a particular kinship relationship to the dead.

One way to destroy wooden malanggan is to sell them to outsiders, who then remove them by taking them away from Papua New Guinea. That these outsiders have carefully preserved the carvings as art objects in museums and private collections is an ironic consequence of the shifting meaning of the objects as they move across cultural borders. The ability to keep producing effigies that are like previous ones in the absence of any physical prototype is one aspect of malanggan production that I take up later on, with its implications for memory as a generative resource. Knowledge of malanggan imagery, how it should be applied in specific effigies, and the right to carve another one is a kind of intellectual and intangible resource that is not alienated when the effigy is sacrificed, even if the method of sacrifice involves a cash sale and subsequent installation in a vitrine in the Metropolitan Museum of Art in New York or the Museum für Völkerkunde in Basel.

Here I want to concentrate on another aspect of Küchler's discussion of memory resulting from her extended meditation on these figures. She is especially interested in how objects such as malanggan, both as physical presences and as sets of images that people think about, make possible a kind of remembering that may be defined as the recall of something that is absent rather than the recovery of something forgotten. Speaking more generally of the use of effigies in funeral ceremonies, she suggests that such figures "are not a representation, referential in nature, which adds a public definition to that which it replaces . . . but represent what is not present by fashioning an image that recalls what is absent into memory" (Küchler 2002:112). This suggests that monuments do not preserve a memory or stand in for that memory but instead serve as a point of focus around which and through which recollection is made possible, a generative and dynamic process. Remembering is as inseparable from thinking as it is from other cognitive processes often treated as distinct, such as knowing and learning. Küchler considers remembering an example of analogical thinking that binds together people, things, events, sensations, images, and other elements. Recollection may thus be active rather than passive, "the coming to life of the past as a performatory experience with its own distinct temporal dimensions; momentary and point-like in nature in which past, present, and future collapse together" (Küchler 1999:60).

Monuments seem to provide a way to commemorate some memorable person or event that, like a written text, can endure beyond individual (that is, intrapsychic) memory and communicate a message to a wide audience through a combination of text and image. Once the monument has been put into place, no doubt as part of some commemorative ceremony, its communicative capacity evanesces unless renewed over time. The ways in which Stelae E, F, and J at Quirigua communicated the triumph of its king cannot be fully grasped if we assume that the monuments were meant only to be observed and their hieroglyphic texts read by solitary spectators.

In the eighth century CE, Quirigua and Copan were living societies, not national parks, as they are now. People could not wander the royal precinct at will merely by paying a modest entrance fee. They had their lives to lead and social conventions to respect. Of the people who might have gazed at Stela E, the number who could have read the hieroglyphic text's statement of the capture of Copan's king was small, for two reasons. First, this kind of literacy was not widespread and may not have included even all members of the royal family. If the production of texts were the only mechanism available to the royal family, the assertion of memory and identity would not be very effective, given that even in societies in which literacy is widespread people remember, learn, and make meaning through other means.

Second, the stela's physical form discourages ready viewing of most of its text. The total length of the monument is 10.6 meters, of which about 3 meters were buried below ground, making it the "largest stone ever quarried by the ancient Maya" (Looper 2003:147).[3] Standing almost 25 feet high, Stela E is clearly a monument conceived on a larger-than-life scale. The reference to the sacrifice of Copan's Ruler 13 appears on its west side, about halfway down from the top of the monument (Maudslay 1974 Vol. II:Plate 30; see also Looper 2003:Figure 4.41).

A photograph of Stela E taken in the nineteenth century by A. P. Maudslay (see fig. 9 on page 64) shows the monument canted sharply to the right. The photographer placed two men in the shot to give a sense of the size of the stela. One stands on the ground just behind the base of the monument, and the other has climbed about two-thirds of the way up its inclined side to stand next to the ruler's head. I don't know how tall these men are, but undoubtedly they are no shorter than the people who lived at Quirigua in the eighth century, when Stela E was erected. Archaeologists who have excavated at Quirigua found very few burials with human skeletons that could be studied, but a large number have been found at Copan, and they provide a reasonable point of reference. Rebecca Storey (1999) has reconstructed the height of the people who lived during the same time period on the basis of these remains. Rounding her results off to whole numbers gives an average height for women of 155 centimeters (5 feet, 2 inches) and for men of 163 centimeters (5 feet, 5 inches) (see also Storey 2005).[4] It is true that Stela E at Quirigua is an unusually tall example of this kind of monument. So also are the other two stelae that record Quirigua's triumph. Stela F stands 7.3 meters high and Stela J is around 5 meters tall, or about 24 and 16 feet (Looper 2003:100, 123; Maudslay 1974 Vol. V:12–15). Other stelae at this site and those found at Copan are generally shorter, but they are still not particularly human-scaled so as to facilitate reading of their texts.

Stephen Houston (1994) thinks that monumental inscriptions were periodically recited or their content incorporated in some other way into commemorative and dedicatory events that were part of royal public life during this period and provided opportunities for expanded social contact and interaction (Baudez 1991, 1994; Houston and Taube 2000; M. Miller 1986; Stuart 1998). Such events brought a wider range of people than usual into royal precincts, including those of lower social status and from outside the polity. Rosemary Joyce (2003) argues that the short inscriptions found on some body ornaments, for example, earspools, were also recited in the more intimate confines of life cycle rituals. These are both plausible suggestions given the importance Mesoamerican people placed on such modes of expression as recitation, oratory, poetry, music, and dance (Boone 1994a; León-Portilla 1969; Looper 2003; Monaghan 1994; D. Tedlock 1983). These modes of expression move away from text to a more sociable and interactive kind of remembering involving people and of objects. Such remembering takes place through the medium of the expressive performance itself and its appeal to the senses (Farnell 1999; Küchler 2002; Mitchell 2006). Stela E was not meant to be gazed at as a work of art or read like a book. It was incorporated into events that heightened the sensory impact through the interplay of sights, sounds, odors, movement, color, and feeling. This experience invoked memories of other ceremonies and recalled significant events (Gell 1977). In the absence of periodic affirmation through performance, Stela E loses its ability to reiterate the political claim made by Quirigua's rulers.

Remembering as a participatory act or process makes it as much a spatial phenomenon as a temporal one. This kind of remembering was emphasized by the royal memory community's ongoing process of monumentalizing at Quirigua and its more powerful neighbor, Copan. Copan, too, has its collection of stelae with images of human figures and hieroglyphic texts. Most were placed in a large plaza in the royal precinct, where they are surrounded by monumental architecture. Their placement spans several reigns, although later rulers also relocated monuments pertaining to their predecessors. Copan stelae, like those at Quirigua, create images of action, both in the content of their texts and in the carved images of elaborately dressed people. One sign of the ceremonies associated with these monuments is the stelae caches. Objects like pottery vessels were deposited in stone-lined chambers beneath the monument (Strömsvik 1941) when it was first put in place.

The texts themselves provide further notice of these events. Although these inscriptions often refer to prior actions by the ruler or other personages, such as the capturing of prisoners, they also put in written form the actions surrounding the monument's dedication. Recording of actions in and around the monument itself may indeed have been one of the main purposes of these texts (Stuart 1998). Furthermore, the images themselves signal activity and performance (Grube 1992; Houston and Taube 2000; Looper 2009; Meskell and Joyce 2003). The placement of a hand, foot, head, and torso implies a body caught in mid-movement. The acts of holding, displaying, carrying, wearing, seeing, and hearing are suggested by the figure's posture, accoutrements, costume, and associated elements. Monuments, both as a spot on the landscape and as a bearer of information about events and people, were incorporated into the periodic ceremonies that took place in these royal precincts in ways that brought the content of the image and text out into the open through recitation and performance. The conjunction of ceremony and monument becomes an opportunity for remembering through which royalty's achievements and importance are not reviewed as a historical sequence but collapsed into a single moment of recollection that recreates the past and the present every time the ceremonial events are carried out. These monuments are not like malanggan in that they are not destroyed once the ceremony is over (although there are instances in which stelae are removed, relocated, defaced, or buried). They remain in place, but most people did not see them or interact with them except in the context of the periodic events that brought monuments and people together. These events provide intermittent moments of recollection organized by the royal house for its own purposes. As I elaborate in subsequent chapters, there are other opportunities for recollection in these societies that are not offered by royalty and are not encompassed in royal rites.

The recurring commemoration of the capture of Copan Ruler 13 by the Quirigua ruler is also an example of how cycles and sequences fit together and reinforce one another in the political remembering of royal houses. The three stelae that remember the event are linked to one another through the use of Long Count dates to establish a temporal sequence that marks the progress of the Quirigua ruler's reign. In this sense, the texts on these monuments become part of a historical account that accords well with our modern understanding of history because each monument inscribes a different moment in the ruler's progression through time. The accounts also help reproduce structures of authority, assertions of power, and the privileging of certain ideological claims over others (Bodnar 1992; Maleuvre 1999). These monuments do so by circling back to the same past event, the capture of Ruler 13. Furthermore, that event is marked in the same way each time, by the carving and raising of a stone monument and by how it is referred to in the inscription. This congruity in form, in conjunction with the practices of commemoration carried out as part of the ceremonies, allows memory to appear to recreate a past event that many participants had not directly experienced.

INTERPRETING OBJECTS: ICONOGRAPHY, PRACTICE, AND SEMIOTICS

To really think about how remembering and forgetting intersect with material objects, I need to broaden the scope to consider how objects connect to processes and practices of making meaning. Interpretation of Mesoamerican visual imagery, art, and ritual occupies a venerable place in research on this subject, and I therefore start with this category of object, a category that includes monuments. Maya art is generous in its presentation to the inter-ested interpreter of images evidently intended as representations of objects and entities; the images are often arranged in scenes that seem to tell a story (represent action) and frequently are accompanied by hieroglyphic texts (a highly visual and artistic form of writing in its own right).[5] A well-dressed woman weaving at her loom modeled in clay, a royal personage reviewing subordinates carved in stone, four men playing ball painted on a ceramic vessel epitomize the mimetic quality of Mesoamerican art.

DECODING SYMBOLS: READING TEMPLE 22

Much scholarly effort has been expended on decoding the meaning of individual elements and their co-occurrence and on delimiting what artistic conventions and the way symbols are deployed reveal about society (see, e.g., M. Miller 1999; Schele and Miller 1986). Two assumptions underlie this effort. One, that much of this art is indeed mimetic—holding a mirror up to nature—even if the concept of nature it reflects differs from our own, con-taining beings, creatures, places, and concepts not allowed for in our philos-ophy. Two, that analysis should conform to "the intellectualist conception that . . . conceive[s] the perception of a work of art as an act of decipherment, a *reading*" (Bourdieu 1993:266, see also Gell 1998; Küchler 2002). Decipher-ment requires a knowledge of the underlying system. One cannot read with-out knowing the language the "text" is written in. Work on Mesoamerican art draws on several rich veins of information to read these visual texts without the help of any actual informants. The contents of contemporane-ous hieroglyphic texts, information available from colonial-era sources, and the results of ethnographic work among present-day descendents have been intensively mined for keys to this system of signification.

Many buildings at Copan, particularly those in the Main Group, are deco-rated with sculpture inside and out. One such building is Temple 22, located in the East Court on top of the Acropolis. Based on their decoding of some of the sculpture of Temple 22, epigraphers and art historians argue that the building is an imitation mountain (W. Fash 2001; Stuart 1997). Two repeated images are taken as diagnostic of this act of architectural mimesis. Faces of a fantastical reptilian creature with large fangs and long, protruding lips are placed one on top of the other at the corners of the building. More faces are set into the outside walls. The entrance to Temple 22 is carved to make it into the open mouth of this creature: "The two upper steps of the stairway form the lower part of the jaw. The riser of the top step is carved to represent

11. Temple 22 in the East Court of the Acropolis at Copan. The entrance to the building is carved to represent the open mouth of a fantastical reptilian creature. The curving fangs of its lower jaw rise from the top of the narrow staircase, the uppermost riser of which was carved with the rest of the creature's teeth. Photograph by Julia A. Hendon.

teeth. . . . At either end, resting on the top step, is a huge curling fang fashioned from a single stone and fitted into a specially cut socket in the step" (Trik 1939:100). The creature has clusters of beads arranged in an inverted triangle on its forehead and lip, the "motif that is used in Maya iconography to mark items of stone" (Stuart 1997:14; see W. Fash 2001:Figure 78). This crocodilian or ophidian creature, especially when decorated with the triangular clusters of beads, has been read as a conventionalized sign representing a personified and deified mountain, whose mouth symbolizes a cave, and is the embodiment of the generative forces attributed to these natural features of the landscape (Stone 1995).[6] The triangular clusters of beads, whose reference to "stone" reiterates the message inherent in the fact that the building is made of stone, have been interpreted even more specifically as denoting "a specific kind of sacred stone [that] represents cave formations dripping sacred virgin water" (B. Fash 2005:117).

The sculptural decoration of Temple 22 also includes carvings of the heads and upper bodies of young men conforming to Maya standards of male beauty (Bachand, Joyce, and Hendon 2003; Joyce 2002) that have been identified as anthropomorphic corn plants (Baudez 1994; B. Fash 2005; see also Gordon 1970; Maudslay 1974). These statues encode the generative power of mountains in human creation even further. When the gods in the *Popol vuh* finally decide on corn as the proper raw material from which to make human beings, it must be extracted from a specific mountain, the source of all wonderful foods (Brotherston 1992; D. Tedlock 1996). The labeling of Temple 22 as a mountain was an enduring one, continuing to be marked as the building was rebuilt several times (W. Fash 1998).

As the *Popol vuh* and similar creation stories from the Aztecs and other groups attest, mountains are important places to people in Mesoamerica. They are not merely inanimate elements of a natural landscape. They have names, gender, relationships with one another that mirror those of human society, and they own animals, just like people. Ancestors, deities, and spirits live on or in them. Mountains are supernatural entities in their own right. They want to be fed, may take an active role in human affairs, and are themselves deified. They contain caves which afford entrance into their bodies and provide a place for offerings (Bassie-Sweet 1991; Laughlin and Karasik 1988; Stone 1995; Stuart 1997; B. Tedlock 1986, 1992b; D. Tedlock 1993; Vogt 1969).

Treating visual imagery, works of art, and, more broadly, material objects as part of a conventionalized and therefore culturally specific set of symbols confronts us once again with material objects (or some feature of them, such as their design or decoration) as reflecting some idea that is behind the object. Signs become "the garb of meaning . . . that must be stripped bare" (Keane 2005:184). Whether listening to what people say, observing what they do, or studying works of art or other products of human endeavor, researchers strive to see through to the meaning behind the material world in the hopes of approaching those mental processes of which the material world is a representation (Myers 2001; Preucel and Bauer 2001; Sperber 1975; Taylor 1993).

Knowing that mountains matter to people in Mesoamerica assists the reading of the sculpture of Temple 22 as a set of symbols. Its sculpture makes the building a mimetic image of a specific mountain that recalls important formative events and relations without which life as the Maya knew it would not exist. Furthermore, this knowledge can be integrated into an understanding of how the temple's significance develops through other kinds of relations and other forms of signification, in ways that lead to a further understanding not only of Temple 22 itself but also of the Acropolis on which it rests.

UNDERSTANDING THE PRACTICAL AND SEMIOTIC COMPLEX

Webb Keane (1997:10) has argued that "if we treat words, things, and performances together as media of action, the mimetic function is only part of the story. Mimesis does not disappear, but is resituated as one component of a practical and semiotic complex." This complex allows meaning to be made in multiple ways that expand beyond, but do not exclude, the conventionalized or mimetic. It also embraces practice and materiality, allowing one to think about how and where material objects are deployed as part of a process of meaning making. The inclusion of practice and materiality is important because I am interested not only in replacing the limited study of signs as symbols with a larger suite of signs, but also in considering how the properties of things offer ways to think about the relationship between material objects and meaning making.

Recognition of broader forms of signification and of the importance of action augments my ability to carry out an archaeological study of memory. I acknowledge the insights that the more traditional approach to Mesoamerican symbolism has generated, but its orientation restricts its usefulness. Its reliance on mimesis, on ideas given concrete form, does not help me figure out how to engage with objects that don't seem very "symbolic," such as those found in domestic contexts. The identification of the long-lipped creature and the male figures as personifications of natural phenomena that evoke particular associations and beliefs relies on linking together bits of information on Mesoamerican religion. This reliance on culturally specific exegesis is fruitful but incomplete because it does not account for other ways of arriving at meaning and thus other forms of meaning making.

To do this, I turn to the semiotic complex referred to by Keane, which derives from the work of Charles Sanders Peirce (Hanks 1996; Keane 2006; Lele 2006; Parmentier 1987; Preucel 2006). It includes three major categories of signs: indexes, icons, and symbols. Although it is easy to assume that these terms refer to things ("an icon"), the terms refer to relationships: "To say that a sign is an index is to say that it functions by virtue of an indexical relation between the perceivable form of the sign and whatever it stands for" (Hanks 1996:39). Icons, indexes, and symbols are the kinds of relationships

I employ here. A fuller explanation of other kinds of relations in the Peircean typology may be found in Preucel (2006). The term *symbol* refers to conventionalized or nonnatural signs that must be decoded. Much of the interpretation of Mesoamerican art, including that of Temple 22, exemplifies this kind of relationship. Icons and indexes furnish a way to expand the focus on the object itself. Material objects may enter into each and all of these relations because the complexity of their physical properties makes multiple meanings possible (Gell 1998; Hanks 1996; Keane 2005; Preucel 2006).

Indexes allow us (you, me, someone at Cerro Palenque) to make meaning through causal inferences based on some specific character of the index that we can connect to something else. Common examples include the movement of a weathervane indicating the direction of the wind or seeing smoke and inferring that there is a fire (Gell 1998; Knappett 2005). Rosemary Joyce (2007) presents a Mesoamerican example through her study of a distinctive type of clay figurine from Honduras in the Playa de los Muertos style (ca. 900–200 BCE) and made by earlier inhabitants of the same river valley as those who lived in Cerro Palenque. Figurines of this sort were constructed by first making an armature of clay for the body, to which was joined a separately modeled head. The joined body and head were then coated with a layer of clay to make a smooth surface. The figurine makers worked on this surface, incising, impressing, modeling, and otherwise taking advantage of the clay's plasticity to create details of the physical appearance, such as muscle markings, facial features, hair style, and folds of flesh. This technique of manufacture, in terms of both the component parts and the sequential process employed, recreates through practice the relationship between the skin and interior substances that make up the body of living beings. It thus indexes the composition and process of production of the living body, which was also something to be shaped and modeled in the womb and after birth (see Joyce 1998; Monaghan 1995)

Icons suggest relations through a resemblance based on some set of shared properties. At its simplest, this is a mimetic relationship but more complicated kinds of iconicity exist (Preucel 2006). Joyce notes the anthropomorphism or zoomorphism of her figurines as an example of the iconicity of the clay figures. Her figurines look like people or animals because they have humanlike or animal-like heads, limbs, torsos, and so on. At the same time, she argues that figurines and clay vessels from the same time period also resemble one another in other ways. Some vessels are decorated with a stylized depiction of a fantastical zoomorphic creature, one that, like the creatures on Temple 22, cannot be identified as an actual species of animal but is nevertheless like the human and animal figurines in being animate, corporeal, and capable of being rendered in an image. Thus vessels and figurines resemble one another in that both may be a vehicle for the depiction of animate beings. Joyce notes another relationship. Figurines and vessels share the property of being containers, the one for bodily substances, the other for food and drink. This is made most obvious by those vessels that in fact look like Playa-style figurines, but relations of iconicity do not depend on such complete likeness.

COPAN'S ACROPOLIS AS ICON, INDEX, AND SYMBOL

The Copan Acropolis is also a complex congeries of icons and indexes shaped by the materiality of the built environment. Consider the physical sensations you feel when you are climbing a mountain—the strain on the thighs and knees as your body hauls itself up the slope, how the unevenness of the path makes it impossible to fall into an even stride, the feeling of release at the top when you can straighten your back and feel the breeze you were cut off from below, and the shift in perspective achieved by being so far above ground level. All of these experiences are replicated when I ascend the Acropolis at Copan, an astoundingly tall, steep artificial construction that rises some 22 meters (72 feet) high (Hohmann and Vogrin 1982:Plan II).

When I first came to Copan in the early 1980s, a time when almost no tourists visited the site because of the political violence in neighboring Guatemala, the current prohibition against climbing the stairs on the front, or north, side of the Acropolis had not gone into effect, and I went up them often. The steps of this north staircase are made from beautifully shaped blocks of stone that are very large. Standing 61 inches (or approximately 152.5 centimeters) tall, I am close to the average height of ancient Copan women. As I move from one step to the next, the knee of my climbing leg bends at a sharp angle, drawn up nearly to my chest, as my standing leg extends until it is almost straight. I strain the thigh muscles of my bent leg to pull my weight upward, sometimes pushing with my hands on the next tread up. The steps vary in height, forcing me to pause to readjust my weight as my body accommodates itself to the unevenness of the stairs, which are so steep that all I can see in front of me is the next one. Leaning back to see how much higher I must climb, I discover the mass of the Acropolis looming over me. I feel like I am clambering up a steep and rocky mountain, not climbing stairs.

When I remember the ascent today, some twenty-five years later, I realize how much it mirrors what I experienced when I spent two months checking the accuracy of site maps by revisiting previously recorded sites in the foothills. Like the Main Group, the present-day highway is on the valley floor. Getting to these rural sites required that I climb from where the truck dropped us off along the road up a steep footpath to reach the places where ancient farmers had built their houses. Moving up and down the face of the Acropolis and climbing those tracks evoked comparable sensations. The resemblance between tall, pyramidal structures such as the Acropolis and mountains has been noted by modern scholars and the original builders alike but deserves to be explored further (e.g., Ashmore 2004; Stuart 1997; Vogt 1969). Experientially as well as visually, the Acropolis indexes "mountain-ness," leading to the conclusion that it is a mountain in its own right.

The experiential perception of the Acropolis as mountain is further reinforced in two ways: by the presence of buildings on its summit through which the living could interact with ancestors, deities, and noncorporeal sacred forces, and by containing within its mass the remains of the houses, tombs, and temples built by people, including royalty, now dead and apotheosized. Archaeologists who have excavated inside the body of the Acropolis have argued that among these tombs are those of the founder of the Copan royal dynasty (or Ruler 1), his successor, and a close female relative, perhaps the wife of Ruler 1 and the mother of the second ruler (Bell, Sharer, Traxler, Sedat, Carrelli, and Grant 2004; Stuart 2005). They have found precursors of the Acropolis itself in the form of platforms supporting increasingly large-scale, elaborate architecture (Sedat and López 2004; Sharer, Sedat, Traxler, Miller, and Bell 2005) and the remains of residences identified as those of early royalty and other high-status members of society (Traxler 2001, 2004). The mountain-ness of the Acropolis may not have been something that seventh- or eighth-century Copanecos spent much time discussing with one another. The materiality of the Acropolis, made up of its presence, its history, and its ability to invoke particular sensations, experiences, and associations, makes it a form of signification that "gives rise to and transforms modalities of action and subjectivity *regardless* of whether they are interpreted" (Keane 2005:186). The Acropolis as mountain becomes salient through what people do or what kinds of intersubjective relations they emphasize through these actions. The properties of the Acropolis, such as its scale, material, history, and experiential effect, demonstrate how meaning develops through multiple attributes, the co-occurrence of which seems natural and inevitable but which in fact is not (Keane 2005).

The buildings on top of the Acropolis become part of the process of signification. What the twenty-first-century tourist sees as she climbs to the East and West Courts by the now-approved side stairway (less steep and more human-scaled but still indicative of a mountain ascent) is the product of several centuries of urban renewal. Temple 22 is on the north side of the East Court and was built during the reign of Ruler 13 before he met his end at Quirigua. Temple 18, opposite on the south side, is the construction of the sixteenth ruler, finished some years before he died in the early 800s (Andrews and Bill 2005:253; Looper 1998; Stuart 2002). The complex of Acropolis and massive buildings on its summit confronts one with a reiteration of mountain-ness, of mountains on top of mountains.

Other buildings make this association as well. Temple 16, the tallest building on the Acropolis, sits between the two courts, facing onto the western one. During its final phase of construction, its exterior decoration was not explicitly referential of mountains, but a lower jaw with large tusks, like the one at the entrance to Temple 22, was placed in the interior wall of one of the rooms (Baudez 1994:184–89, Figure 93). An earlier version, buried within the final structure, had the long-lipped reptilian creature and corn plants built into the exterior walls (W. Fash 2001). Another example of a room entrance decorated as the creature's mouth may be found in Temple 11, built at the north end of the West Court and thus in a line with Temple 22 (Baudez 1994:170, Figure 84). This places the status of Temple 22 as a mimetic mountain into a broader context in which meaning comes from multiple sources repeated over time.

Temple 22 and the Acropolis are icons of one another because they are both containers that hold within them moments and materials of origin and the passage of time. Inside or underneath the Acropolis is the origin of the Copan dynasty in the form of honored dead bodies and superseded structures. Temple 22 holds its earlier versions within its foundations and the living people within its rooms who enter into the mouth of the corn mountain of creation as they walk through the main doorway. The materiality of mountain-ness thus derives not only from symbols, or even from the confluence of icons, indexes, and symbols, or even from these different signs brought together by action and experience, but also from the implicit history resulting from the way in which all these architectural constructions encompass earlier instantiations of origins and creation, in the process conflating the history of one set of people, the royal dynasty, with all human beings. The prior presence of material objects may continue to be important even when absent or hidden. Their materiality continues to inveigle meaning even when no longer in plain view.

THE ENCHANTMENT OF OBJECTS

Objects may become part of the construction of social memory and identity because they participate in this semiotic complex. Our understanding of the complex can be further expanded by bringing in Alfred Gell's discussion of the enchantment of objects. Gell explores the particular domain of objects that Western society designates as art (Gell 1992, 1998). Gell wishes to call into question the assumption that it is possible to characterize certain things as art through recourse to a notion of pure aesthetics (see Halliwell 2002). To this end, he works to connect things not conventionally designated as art with those that are in order to determine why certain objects are treated and thought of as being like persons. He argues that objects are semiotic indexes that make manifest social relations through their involvement in social action with people and other objects.

Gell points to the capacity of certain material objects to enchant us and to draw our attention through their appearance and other qualities that bespeak a set of skills and knowledge responsible for their impact that we acknowledge but can only partially comprehend. Enchantment emanates from things that are not traditionally considered to be art by Western society. He insists on the "cognitive stickiness" of such objects, which, through such physical attributes as form and decoration, present us with a kind of perceptual puzzle. The sensory complexity makes it difficult to differentiate the whole into its constituent parts while also allowing people to perceive new connections and elements in the overall design through repeated interactions with the object (see also Küchler 2002). The object's effect on us causes us to relate to it in certain ways that Gell characterizes as similar to the way we relate to persons in that they can be "sources of, and targets for, social agency" (Gell 1998:96).

Objects are more than an intermediary between human beings who are in a relationship to one another. Objects are another possible participant in "interpersonal" and intersubjective relations, a participant that is not merely a tool, a device, or a means to an end, but an agent that helps shape the relationship through its properties, its purpose, and its connections to larger social projects. In arguing for the agential nature of objects—not as some absolute or essential characteristic but as a product of social relations and action—Gell rejects intentionality or some state of being (being alive, being human) as the criteria for determining agency. Objects do not have intentions, but they do have properties that cause things to happen and induce people to relate to them in particular ways. Objects are not alive in the biological sense, but they can be considered to be animate. People have intentions and may even be aware of them at times, but it is the outcome of what they do, in some context and in relation to some other (human or not), that makes them agential. The meaning or significance of objects develops through these relations between object properties and human action. Social agency is defined not by something's biological status (alive or dead) but by its relational status (subject or object, cause or acted upon). Such objects have physical properties that engage us and the capacity to index complex intentionalities (Gell 1999b).

Material objects (indexes) allow agency to be distributed beyond any individual and assist in the development of relational personhood. Distributed agency and relational personhood are important to processes of bringing the past into the present and to the ways in which memory communities develop their collective memory. Gell wants to restrict primary agency to humans. This strikes me as more reassuring (to those made uneasy by the prospect of ceding agency to things that are not human or not biologically alive) than necessary since "in practice, people do attribute intentions and awareness to objects like cars and images of the gods" (Gell 1998:17). It is the "in practice" that most interests me because it moves us away from a fixation on memory fossils to how material objects like monuments can play active roles in the social relations and processes through which remembering and forgetting occur.

Quirigua Stela E is a cognitively sticky and enchanting object that causes things to happen and that permits the making of causal inferences. Its height alone draws the eye, as does its placement among earlier monuments in Quirigua's monumental precinct, the design of which mimics that of Copan (Sharer 1990). The ruler, larger than life, appears on two sides of the monument. These relief carvings create a visual complexity that draws in the viewer through the elaboration of the ruler's costume and his regalia which, along with his person, fill the space with an exuberance of carving. Elements of the design may be extracted from the whole after some study, and these elements —what he wears, what he holds, what surrounds him—can be treated as symbols. The object he holds in his hand, for example, has been labeled the "manikin scepter" and identified as a specific deity, "God K" or "God GII," that is also a symbol of rulership when held in this way (Looper 2003; Miller and Taube 1993:110; Schele and Mathews 1998:412). The elements are also, however, indexes that naturalize his claims to power and authority.

The presence of Stela E is a focal point for ceremonies and for the recall of one of the highlights of his reign, his capture and sacrifice of his Copan counterpart. The reiteration of this event on this monument suggests a number of inferences about the relationship of the Quirigua ruler to the participants in those ceremonies and those hearing about the capture. For some, this would be a repetition of earlier moments of recall, but for others it would be the first time they had had the events of 738 CE brought to their attention. Stela E was erected in 771 CE, thirty-three years after the event, and it was the latest of the three stelae to refer to it, Stela J having been erected in 756 CE and Stela F in 761 CE (Looper 2003). The Quirigua ruler himself was older than he was when he captured Ruler 13 and would soon be dead (Martin and Grube 2000:221). Estimates by paleodemographers suggest that people living in Classic period Maya settlements tended to die young. Maya kings, who sometimes beat these odds and lived into their seventies or eighties, nevertheless ruled over a population mostly under the age of fifty (Márquez, Hernández, and Serrano 2006; Storey 1999; Tiesler Blos 1999). This suggests that by the time Stela E was dedicated only a few of the participants in the ceremony had been alive when Ruler 13 was captured. Most of the Quirigua king's subjects would have been born after that year and would have no direct experience of whatever sequence of events led up to his moment of glory. By having the stelae carved and placed in his plaza, the ruler realized a way of bringing these events into the present over and over again through interaction with the monuments themselves and with people by way of the monuments.

THE HUMILITY OF EVERYDAY OBJECTS

The objects that acquire a capacity for agency through their enchanting qualities require one to recognize that people engage as much with the material world as with some abstracted body of knowledge or set of ideas (or, to put this more strongly, to recognize that even such ideas are ultimately material [Küchler 2005]). Gell's claims for object agency have been subject to scrutiny and criticism from a number of directions, usefully summarized in Meskell (2004). His ideas about agency must be understood as part of a larger discussion of objectification that "is not about persons, but also about material entities that motivate inferences, responses, or interpretations" (Küchler 2002:10). Material objects are not just signs or a medium for making relations among people possible but are integral to how people develop a sense of themselves as subjects and of the reality of such abstractions as society: "It is not just that objects can be agents; it is that practices and their relationships create the appearance of both subject and objects through the dialectics of objectification" (D. Miller 2005:38). Miller argues that material objects play a fundamental role in how the relationship between people and the material world is constituted and given meaning. Important relations are not just interpersonal, that is, between people, but also between object and person and even object and object.

Material objects, as a result of their properties, context, the relations they are part of, and the actions they contribute to, embody a range of possibilities for how they will be used and how they can enter into relations with people. The possibilities remain as a potential only until taken up by agents in the course of action (Keane 2005). At the same time, the fact that these objects are part of the physical world means that their meaning is never entirely arbitrary because they cannot be completely detached from their material properties (Keane 2001). Cloth tears, pots break, stone weathers, bone splinters, wood rots. Take, for example, that mundane object of everyday life in Mesoamerica, the *metate*, a tool made from a large piece of rock. Its shape, material, and weight make it a stable and durable platform on which to grind corn, seeds, spices, and other foods with a second, smaller stone implement called a *mano*.

The metates found in the Cuyumapa valley, like those at Cerro Palenque and Copan, are mostly made of volcanic stone such as rhyolite or basalt (Fung 1995; Joyce 1991; Spink 1983; see also Doonan 1996; Willey, Leventhal, Demarest, and Fash 1994). There are some differences in shape and size. Basalt metates at Cerro Palenque, like many at Copan, have legs, for example, while others at Copan and those from Cuyumapa are rectangular or basin shaped and have no legs. Metates decorated with geometric designs or animal heads, often of birds or jaguars, have been found in Honduras (Stone 1941, 1957). A few examples of these are known from Copan (e.g., Gerstle and Webster 1990; Longyear 1952:105, Figure 89a). The ones I discuss here are undecorated and seem to have been exclusively the product of practical needs. They are neither commemorative nor symbolic, neither a fossilized

12. *Mano* and *metate* behind Structure 9N-68 (Group 9N-8, Patio B). The metate, which is upside down, is typical of the grinding stones without legs used by many people at Copan. Photograph by Julia A. Hendon.

memory nor a work of art. Compared to the rich visual text provided by Temple 22, these tools are a blank page.

Studies of modern-day material culture have had to engage this issue as well since they primarily deal with ordinary or everyday objects. Yet much of this research relies heavily on the ability to talk to people about their stuff or observe them in the process of shopping, giving gifts, decorating, and inhabiting their object world (D. Miller 1987, 1998a, 1998b, 2001). This avenue is closed to me. I do not have the ability to project myself back in time to a summer morning in 850 CE to watch the women of Cerro Palenque grinding corn in the early hours for the family's first meal of the day. Exciting as the prospect would be to meet the people behind the artifacts, to ask these women what they think their labor means or what symbolism they associate with the corn they grind, I am arguing that being in a position to pose these questions would not exhaust either the ways available to me to discern meaning or the ways it is likely to manifest itself (see Bourdieu 1977; Keane 1995; Sperber 1975). Like the students of Mesoamerican iconography, I can and do turn to colonial-era documents and ethnographic information. These sources palliate somewhat my inability to travel back in time,

13. A woman using a *mano* and *metate*, this one with legs. Detail of a scene painted on a Maya poly-chrome vessel. Photograph © Justin Kerr, K631.

augmenting but not replacing the study of the material remains. Even though I cannot be like those ethnographers who have participated as well as observed (Greenfield 2004; Keller and Keller 1996), joining these women at their labor, taking a turn pulverizing the soft kernels on the rough surface of the metate, no doubt to the amusement of all as they observe my clumsiness with the mano and my lack of stamina, I can consider the objects themselves and what they can tell me about the practices that they, as a particular kind of object, engaged in with other objects and people.

Archaeological discussions of tools like these focus on function above all else. The function of metates, to grind corn and pulverize other edibles, is almost self-evident to Mesoamerican archaeologists by now, and for this reason the heavy stone artifacts are not considered to be especially interesting. They tell us that food preparation took place, a useful piece of information, but how much more can they convey? The answer from a functionalist perspective is, not much. Of course households have to subsist. Metates result from this need to adapt to local resources and process corn into food. A semiotic and practice-oriented perspective suggests there is more to be learned.

Metates are heavy rocks shaped as much by the gradual wearing away of their upper surface by the patient movement of the mano, day after day, by women and girls intent on transforming corn kernels into tortillas, porridge, or other foods to sustain their household and support their members as it celebrates important events. Metates lack any obvious means of enchanting anyone along the lines of Gell's argument. They do not display, in any noticeable way, an intent to communicate some kind of social message through decoration or symbolism. Yet they do have physical properties, embody complex intentionalities, and intersect with several material domains. They exemplify "the humility of the common object" (D. Miller 1987:101) that becomes part of the background, necessary but unnoticed. Yet "artifacts [are] often most effective in social reproduction when they [are] assumed to be merely trivial and not to matter" (D. Miller 1998b:12).

Metates unassumingly index social practices integral to an everyday arena of action. They index someone's repeated, ongoing daily labor that resulted in the wearing down and polishing of the hard volcanic rock they are made from. Bringing in other sources of information, I can argue that they index the labor of women and girls. Depictions of food preparation in art are rare during this time period in southeastern Mesoamerica, but some scenes show women grinding corn. In a complicated and heavily populated scene painted on a cylindrical serving vessel, a kneeling woman works at a metate, one end of which has been propped up to make a slanting grinding surface. A three-legged plate holding food sits in front of her, representing the finished product of her labor. Two richly dressed nobles sit on a bench or stairs behind and above her (Kahn 1990:380; Kerr 1989:29). Another vessel depicts, in a style that exaggerates the size and scale of the figures, a standing woman bent almost double to reach the metate at her feet (Coe 1982:94–95). A third example is a figurine of a woman with a small child on her back kneeling over her metate (Meskell and Joyce 2003:Figure 3.6).

Information gathered at the time of the Spanish conquest reports a consistent association between women (people gendered socially as female) and the preparing and cooking of food. Female deities ground corn or bone with blood and water to create humans; girls were taught by their mothers what to do, and women were linked through poetry and metaphor to the hearth-stones, the metate, and the storage bin (see Hendon 1999a, 2000b). Corn was a central element of daily diet, but crucial as well to religious ceremonies and events that were also vehicles for social striving (Hendon 2003b). In many Maya texts, the term for unleavened cakes of corn becomes a shorthand for all kinds of food. The same term stands in for the more general notion of making an offering, regardless of whether the offering is edible

(Bill 1997b; Bricker 1991; Love 1989; Taube 1989). The context of corn grinding is domestic, and the places where grinding took place index the communal nature of economic production created by this sort of repeated cooperative production. Integral to a repeated activity that drew several people together, some more senior than others and from different households and sociological houses, metates create the circumstances through which people create and recreate their social relations.

The materials from which metates are made point to other sets of relations and interactions. Rhyolite and other less commonly used materials such as tuff and sandstone are softer than basalt, a difference that would be evident to the person pecking away at a chunk of raw material. Yet it is the harder material which received more careful work. The basalt metates with legs have evenly shaped bodies and tapering supports whereas the rhyolite ones are often only minimally finished after being sized and shaped. In fact, their shape is mostly the result of wear induced by use over time. At Copan, basalt metates are more common in domestic contexts associated with residential groups in the urban area closer to the Main Group than in more rural homesteads in the foothills (Gonlin 1993; Hendon 1987, 1991; Spink 1983). At Cerro Palenque, they are the only kind of metate found (Joyce 1985, 1991). In Cuyumapa, the distribution of basalt and rhyolite metates between living areas does not overlap, although the households using these different materials lived right next to each other (Fung 1995, 1996).

Both Mary Spink, for Copan, and Christopher Fung, for Cuyumapa, suggest that the differential occurrence of the two raw materials connects to processes of social differentiation. Spink sees the use of basalt metates as a reflection of social status; Fung takes a more practice-oriented approach to argue that the deployment of metates made of different materials distinguished the residents of the neighboring households every time the tools were used.

Grinding stones, no matter how pleasingly shaped, have not been the usual stuff of archaeological attempts to determine social status in southeastern Mesoamerica. Taking them in context and considering the relative variation they display, one can see that metates do provide a way to construct a social space in which differentiation takes place. Bourdieu has described this space as one "of differences, in which classes exist in some sense in a state of virtuality, not as something given but as *something to be done*," something that is relational and that people "construct, individually and especially *collectively*, in cooperation and conflict" (Bourdieu 1998:12). The important process is the continual creation or reaffirmation of difference and distance among individuals and groups. The particular markers of distinction through which groups differentiate themselves do not and cannot remain stable. In Cuyumapa these markers are less overt than at Copan and Cerro Palenque. Architectural variation between PACO 2 residences is almost imperceptible, and the variety of material culture even less so. Nevertheless, the presence of basalt metates indicates an enhanced ability on the part of some households to acquire things through exchange or, more accurately, to acquire things that come from farther away. Here is another way metates index social relations, in this case ones we might want to further specify as economic, that in turn may contribute to these relational processes of differentiation or similitude. This is not to insist that basalt metates are always more desirable, but just that in some cases they were more desired.

Gell's focus is on art objects (or objects that Western society has designated as art). He is thus examining one object domain in which objects contribute to objectification in particular ways (D. Miller 2005). The ability of objects to serve as indexes or icons or both, to invite causal inferences, and to enter into relations that involve objectification and agency extends beyond this particular domain (Gell 1999b; D. Miller 1987). They thus also become "mechanisms for social reproduction and ideological dominance" (D. Miller 1998b:3) in ways that often go unnoticed and unchallenged because they are embodied in things, not stated through language. Objects have their own properties and "prior presence," which may extend beyond the physical limits of the object itself through its ability to generate sound, odor, or other appeals to the senses (Tacchi 1998).

Studies of social memory want their object of study to be the result of acts intended to be commemorative. The tacit remembering that takes place as one grinds corn and that is both enabled by and embodied in objects such as metates seems too vague and undifferentiated. It usually does not come with names and dates attached and thus does not make remembering approximate history (or a particular idea of history). It seems to be a "timeless" repetition of unthinking and routine domestic tasks which are held to be outside the arenas of social action in which memorable things occur (de Certeau 1984; Giard 1998). I argue against this assumption of irrelevancy and reconsider the putative atemporality and lack of meaning attributed to nonconceptual forms of knowing and the repetitive actions of everyday life, keeping in mind that "repetition does not exclude differences, it also gives birth to them" (Lefebvre 2004:7).

THREE

The Semiotic House
Everyday Life and Domestic Space

Thinking about daily life turns our attention to a range of actions beyond the heroic, the large scale, the overtly commemorative, the unique (Featherstone 1995). Studying what people did when they weren't gathered for commemorative ceremonies in public places further brings out the ways in which objects, some humble, others enchanting, become part of the semiotic complex through which meaning is produced and contested. Considering quotidian actions in particular types of places demonstrates how closely the everyday connects with the kinds of ritual and special events that have been more commonly highlighted in research on social memory. A focus on life at home also allows me to bring into the discussion people who did not have the social position, political clout, or economic means to erect hieroglyphic monuments or live in the monumental center but who nevertheless make up the multiple communities of practice and of memory present in these societies. The actions and relationships captured by the terms *daily life* or *the everyday* and the places labeled residential or domestic together create a context for memory that coexists with and interpenetrates that created by acts of monumentalizing and commemoration taking place in the large-scale plazas and their associated monumental buildings. The relationship between everyday life and events in Copan's Main Group, Cerro Palenque's Great Plaza, and the Cuyumapa ballcourts is reciprocal and recurrent because residential compound and plaza are dynamically interconnected spatial and social places.

RITUAL OR RITUALIZATION?

Commemoration and its monumental traces have received so much emphasis in discussions of social memory, especially for societies with little to no use of writing, because commemoration is a form of ritual. It has been argued that rituals are much more likely to preserve memory in the absence of the ability to archive through writing. Research on memory and history has often taken for granted that the whole point is to remember in a particular way, to inscribe in as permanent and unvarying a form as possible (writing if available, if not, rescued perhaps through ritual, epic poetry, or oral memory) some body of knowledge in order to overcome the frailty of human memory. Remembering, it is argued, requires special actions and events that take place under the spotlight of ritual. Forgetting, for the most part, is what happens outside the bright glare of that circle of light.

Certain features attributed to ritual are held to make it especially well suited to serving a preservative function. These are formality, repetitiveness, and the attempt to maintain an unvarying form and content (Connerton 1989; Halbwachs 1992, 1994; Le Goff 1992). As Catherine Bell (1992) has demonstrated with great effectiveness, however, these features are not invariant aspects of ritual. Bell switches focus from rituals to *ritualization*, defined as a culturally specific "way of acting that sets itself off from other ways of acting by virtue of the way in which it does what it does" (1992:140). In other words, attention shifts from an object of study (ritual) to practices (ritualization) through which people act and interact. Formality, repetition, and fixity become one way to engage in the practice of ritualization rather than defining characteristics of ritual. Bell remains mainly interested in

finding a way to recast ritual as ritualization in order to invigorate the anthropological discussion of ritual itself. She demonstrates that it is analyti-
cally useful to study the social meaning of ways of acting that can be distinguished from one another by paying attention to the practices required to
carry out these ways of acting.

I have found ritualization helpful in studying the significance of domestic
places in ancient Honduras for two reasons. First, "it is not at all clear that a
discrete category of ritual action ever existed" in Mesoamerican philosophy
(Monaghan 1998a:48). As a result, domestic space was also religious space. It
is true that people in all three regions were involved to some extent in formally
organized special events in monumental spaces that match the conventional
idea of ritual. Those in Cuyumapa attended ballgames. Residents of Cerro
Palenque and Copan congregated in the centers for certain occasions, including ballgames. But these events do not exhaust the ways in which people
participated in rituals. Excavation of living areas demonstrates that much of
religious life was inextricable from daily life spatially and conceptually.

Second, incorporating this concept into the study of social memory at
home has the potential to give insight into actions not usually identified
as ritual or religious by archaeologists. Bradley (2003a:20–21) argues for
the ritualization of daily life "in which everyday acts could take on special
qualities until they assumed the character of a theatrical performance."
According to Bradley, the occurrence of everyday objects and basic foodstuffs
in carefully placed and arranged deposits indicates that ritual action and
religious beliefs were not separate spheres of activity but were integrated into
and dependent upon daily life. Bradley's ritualization of daily life offers a way
to overcome assumptions about ritual as being somehow apart from everyday life. He shows that material objects that seem inherently mundane and
practical may move between domains of signification one might assume are
distinct. Even as Bradley's application of the concept expands understanding
of the meaning of daily life, however, it risks leaving intact the division
between ordinary and ritualized domains. We still need to consider the
significance of daily life even when it did not assume features of a theatrical
performance in order to "reveal the extraordinary in the ordinary" (Lefebvre
1987:9). By doing so, we can overcome the "static conception . . . of everyday
life [that] presupposes a clear-cut separation between the spheres of everyday
life and the noneveryday [in which] everyday life is the preschool, as it were,
for the sphere of noneveryday eventfulness" (Lüdtke 1995:6).

THE PROBLEM OF THE EVERYDAY

I discussed in chapter 1 why people in Mesoamerica before European contact did not live in bounded, stable, homogeneous, and static societies ruled by custom and unlikely to have changed if not "roused from their ethnological slumbers by the rape of colonization" (Nora 1996:1–2), a violation that, for Nora, nevertheless forced these people into history. The people whose lives I am trying to address, separated from us by so much time, have an everyday life both in the sense of a "lived actuality" (Highmore 2002:1) that can be described and in the sense of a significant set of practices that creates meaning through repetition and ritualization. In this sense, "everyday life has always existed, even if in ways vastly different from our own" (Lefebvre 1987:10). The things people do, day in and day out, over and over again, and the spaces in which they occur are fundamental to the constitution and reproduction of society yet are often the least remarked upon.

Everyday life is a complicated object of study, however, because it has many contexts and encompasses many activities and relations (Featherstone 1995; Gardiner 2000; Highmore 2002; Lefebvre 1987, 1991a). My interest is in the places where people lived. Studies of modern everyday life, however, have demonstrated a curious ambivalence toward the home and home life (Schor 1992). It is as if the home is too everyday, too routine, too natural to serve as a site in which the meaningful features of the everyday emerge: "Only the domestic sphere is deemed to exist outside the dynamic of history and change" (Felski 2000:82). As a result, the contributions of everyday life to social identity are more widely appreciated than those to remembering and forgetting. Halbwachs (1992) certainly argued that the family was one crucial social environment in which these processes took place. Yet others have assumed that the very features of everyday life that give it such an important role in forming identity preclude it from becoming a locus of memory making through which a historical consciousness is expressed. The repetitiveness, the sameness, the supposed presentist orientation, and the routine nature of domestic life impede a sense of the passage of time and prohibit an awareness of moments in time to which unique or notable events could be anchored (Assmann 1995; Bloch 1977).

Processes and actions that are repeated, which must be repeated by their very nature and purpose—cooking, cleaning, repairing, and making anew— are not meaningful because they are seen as the reiteration of eternal forms endemic to time's cycle. These are tasks "deprived . . . of visible completion,

[that] never seem likely to get done" (Giard 1998:156). They are also actions with ephemeral outcomes. Even the most elaborate meal is consumed, the remnants disposed of, and the sensory effects dissipated, to be replaced by others. Clothing is woven, worn, mended, and washed but eventually wears out or is outgrown. Dwellings must be built and preserved, constructed and maintained. Iris Young (1997:136) points out that even Martin Heidegger's emphasis on dwelling as "habitual human activity [that] reveals things as meaningful" nevertheless gives far greater weight to building, as an active and creative act, than it does to preserving and maintaining what has been built.

In other words, as lived actuality the everyday is often studied as exemplary of small-scale processes, relations, and institutions that emphasize the experiential and the personal. In this sense, it aligns with many studies of the household. As a result, it has seemed more obvious how to model the ways that the larger scale (however constituted) impinges on and encompasses the small scale than to develop a model of how the smaller and the larger are mutually constituting (Graeber 2001; D. Miller 1987; Moore 1994; Schöttler 1995). The crucial role of the material world and of people's action in the construction of meaning, identity, and memory leads me to conclude that ignoring such a substantial material and social domain puts one at risk of overlooking one of the most fruitful and rich contexts of social action, objectification, and reproduction, a context in which people become "both objects of history and its subjects" (Lüdtke 1995:6).

THE SEMIOTIC HOUSE

Homes have been called "memory machines" (Douglas 1993:268) because one's house is a familiar place that "essentially does the remembering" for us (Hirst and Manier 1995:107). To appreciate how houses become implicated in memory, we must consider the everyday in some spatial and relational context. Daniel Miller comments that if we pay too much attention to categories such as household or sociological house that we have abstracted from the ongoing reality of social life, we risk being distracted from "the materiality of the home and its attendant material culture" and prevented from engaging with "material culture in trying to understand the social relations that pertain to the home" (D. Miller 2001:12). In this chapter and the two that follow I apply the semiotic and practical complex introduced in chapter 2 to the materiality of life as lived in houses in southeastern Mesoamerica. In order to focus on the communities of practice based in residential places and on dwellings as memory machines, I consider how social relations are created through the confluence of space, people, and material culture, always mindful that relations are not just between people but also between people and the places they inhabit and the material culture they deploy (Gell 1998; D. Miller 1987, 1998b, 2005). Domestic places are meaningful backgrounds because they are physical and social spaces that actively contribute to the development of identity and memory from which local and localized histories grow. If places are indeed dynamic and constitutive locations and if the social is also spatial, then we need to know what those places were like and how they were contributors to and agents of the production and reproduction of social life, including identity, memory, and history. This allows us to understand how domestic places make that history perceptible and palpable, material and monumental, and seemingly immutable.

Several kinds of buildings have been identified in the sites listed in table 1 (see Fung 1995, 1996; Gonlin 1993; Hendon 1987, 1991; Joyce 1985, 1991). Cooking, food preparation, and storing of goods were the activities most often kept apart spatially, either by building a separate building as a kitchen or designating some part of a residence for this purpose. Some Copanecos living around the Main Group, like many of the people at Cerro Palenque, went to the trouble of constructing a separate building in their compound for religious purposes. Judging by the distribution of censers, figurines, and other objects, however, temples or shrines were not required for the enactment of such ritualized action. Residences have one or more rooms, usually with built-in platforms called benches. Some rooms have ledges or niches in the walls that could be used to hold or store things, or they have cord holders flanking the doorway to secure a removable door or curtain. Rooms with benches in the same building rarely connect with one another so that each room has a separate entrance onto the raised foundation platform. This was usually much larger than the footprint of the residence, creating an elevated, flat outdoor area where people could sit, stand, work, gossip, and keep an eye on things. Sometimes this area was improved by the construction of outdoor benches, giving a permanent seating or working area. In some cases, the foundation platforms of different buildings connected to one another, making it possible to walk from one residence to another without descending to the courtyard itself. The practical benefits of this are debatable—getting to the building opposite you via the connected platforms would be taking the long way around, although it might be preferable in a

14. Residential compounds are often arranged around a central patio with most of the buildings facing onto this open area. Patio D of Group 9N-8, Copan, looking east, with Structure 9N-105 in the foreground and Structure 9N-63 in the rear. Photograph by Julia A. Hendon.

heavy rain. It does suggest close ties between people living in the different houses. Much of everyday life took place inside residences, in the courtyard, and on the terraces and their extensions.

Benches serve as a good example of how the materiality of the built environment shapes people's interactions. A built-in platform in a room offers certain possibilities but also creates constraints on how it is used. Possibilities and constraints are determined by the properties of the object (Knappett 2005) as well as by the context in which its use occurs, the relations it is part of, and the kinds of actions that it contributes to. Were benches used as seats, beds, work areas, play areas? As many a hot and tired modern-day tourist has discovered, the well-preserved ones at Copan afford an excellent place to sit, change film, survey the patio, eat lunch, or take a nap.[1] Benches thus present the potential to be used as seats or places to recline or lie down. That this potential was recognized by the people who built them is indicated by visual imagery. Paintings on pottery, clay figurines, and stone sculpture show a variety of kinds of beings—people, deities, supernatural creatures, animals—sitting or lying on benches (see, e.g., Kerr 1989; Schele 1997; Schele and Miller 1986). These images further suggest

15. Structure 9N-71 on the west side of Patio C of Group 9N-8. This building, which has been reconstructed, exemplifies two common features of Copan houses: the large bench inside the main room and the wide terraces outside of it. Photograph by Julia A. Hendon.

that benches provided these beings with opportunities for social interaction while dressing, eating, listening to music, exchanging goods, and engaging in other activities. Benches also reinforce social difference by placing their occupants above those standing or sitting on the floor.

THE SPATIALITY OF SOCIAL LIFE

Places where people live constitute a significant spatial and material domain where "space is socially constructed, and contested, in practice" (Rodman 2003:212). In thinking about the relationship between practice and location, I focus on space and spatiality in order to consider both "substantial forms (concrete spatialities) and . . . a set of relations between humans and groups" (Soja 1985:92). This makes it possible to immerse oneself in the lived actuality and the meaning created through this actuality.

Residences are *places* that are spatially and socially constructed through nondiscursive practices that create embodied spaces that provide the active background to daily life. Buildings and open areas are not merely a container for everyday life, the stage on which it is played out, or the setting. They are part of the "concrete circumstances in which [people] live" (Pred 1990:5; see also Low and Lawrence-Zúñiga 2003). From a phenomenological perspective, they are a background that actively but nonconceptually contributes to people's understanding of their identities and their relations to others. Drawing on phenomenology's emphasis on the inseparability of figure and ground in the construction of meaning helps overcome the "somewhat unexpected capacity of objects to fade out of focus and remain peripheral to our vision and yet determinant of our behavior and identity" (D. Miller 2005:5). Places are both polysemic, in that they have multiple meanings, and multivocal, in that they engage with multiple people (Rodman 2003).

The spatial and material domains of life lived at home also provide insight into differences in power that emerge not only from control of material resources, time, and labor but also through the identities that are defined and inscribed through routinized daily and periodic action. Sociological houses are usually stratified, and communities of practice are not anodyne. They are not necessarily harmonious, egalitarian, or equitable. In fact, some communities of practice may be able to exist as such only through conflict, inequity, and hierarchy (Wenger 1998). The agendas and interests of people differentiated by age, gender, role, and the ability to impose their wishes do not always coincide (Hart 1992; McKie, Bowlby, and Gregory 1999; Moore 1992). Domestic action and relations are of larger political and economic significance precisely because they are not separable from the relationships and processes that make up the so-called public domain. Life at home is neither isolated from society as a whole nor a passive reflection of changes imposed from outside. The production of appropriate kinds of persons is part of the recreation and redefinition of difference (Bourdieu 1998) and the production of and resistance to relations and structures of power (Sawicki 1994; Weedon 1997, 1999). Claims that only certain members of society cause things to happen or are powerful are in fact an attempt by the very people promulgating them to make a particular narrative hegemonic. This narrative attempts to argue that only certain people—those holding certain titles, able to trace or claim a particular genealogy, doing specific kinds of things, or of a specified gender—are historical actors in ways that others are not (Comaroff and Comaroff 1992).

THE MATERIALIZATION OF SOCIAL DIFFERENCE

Houses as a part of a semiotic and practical complex also play an important role in the construction and expression of social difference. I mentioned earlier that the area around the Main Group, including the Sepulturas zone, is frequently referred to as an elite, urban area. This is a convenient short-hand on the part of Copan researchers that sums up the fact that, on the whole, the houses there are larger and better built, there is more sculpture, some spectacularly well-furnished burials have been found here, and the residents were better endowed with worldly goods. It does certainly seem to be the case that social difference existed at Copan during the Late to Termi-nal Classic (and earlier). There is also evidence suggesting an increasing degree of social difference at Cerro Palenque during the Terminal Classic, as the residents of the ballcourt residential group used a greater variety of imported materials and objects. Even in the Cuyumapa valley, where no class of elites is discernible, residents of neighboring residential areas still found ways to distinguish themselves from one another (see chapter 2).

Based on the Copan valley, which has the widest range of information available, status affiliation or attribution turns out to be more slippery than one might expect, however. The attempt to define clear-cut social groups on the basis of a set of characteristics such as treatment in death, energetics of housing, permanent modification of the body, depiction in sculpture, me-morialization in text, or access to resources results in conflicting patterns. Studies of diet and health based on various subsets of the large sample of burials excavated in the valley over the last century demonstrate that the social, biological, and ecological stresses that could result in high infant mortality, disrupted growth patterns in childhood, and diseases like anemia and tooth decay were widespread among men and women, rural and urban dwellers, people buried in elaborate tombs and in simple graves during the period of peak occupation (Gerry and Chesson 2000; Gerry and Krueger 1997; Lee 1995; Padgett 1996; Reed 1998, 1999; Storey 1992, 1997, 1998, 1999, 2005; Whittington 1999; Whittington and Reed 1997), such that "dur-ing periods of childhood and adulthood all individuals had impaired nutri-tional status" (Storey 1999:178). Individuals believed to be of higher status on the basis of how they were buried may have eaten a somewhat better diet, but their bodies still show evidence of disease. Even rulers were not immune from the stresses of life at Copan. Examination of the bodies from tombs under the Acropolis, believed to be those of members of the Copan dynasty, exhibit similar patterns of childhood malnutrition and diseases, although these individuals seem to have been somewhat healthier and better nour-ished as adults (Storey 2005). At perhaps the most fundamental level, that of childhood nutrition and health, ancient Copanecos were not so different from one another.

The study of the occurrence of dental inlays, circular pieces of jade or other green colored stone, hematite, or other material set into a person's front teeth, of dental filing, and of notching of teeth or otherwise physical altering their shape indicates that these forms of beautification were not restricted to residents of large residential compounds or to those buried in elaborate graves or even to those living in the urban area (Rhoads 2002:74, 225–34). While it is true that richly endowed burials have been found in Sepulturas and other areas around the Main Group, not everyone buried there was given the same treatment. Some are buried in stone-walled, vaulted tombs with niches that look very much like ones in the Main Group. Some of the deceased were placed in smaller, unvaulted, stone-lined crypts inside building platforms or below the paved floor of the central patio. In other cases, a grave was dug in building fill, subsoil below the courtyard along the fronts and sides of buildings, or in the middens behind the residential structures. Other individuals were buried in the middens or building fill with no evidence of formal placement. Tombs and crypts contain a similar range of offerings, including polished brown ware (Surlo) and polychrome vessels, objects for personal adornment made of shell or jade/ greenstone as well as stingray spines, obsidian blades, clay figurine whistles, and Spondylus shells. The burials in graves usually lack pottery or more elaborate sorts of jewelry but do include ceramic beads, bone tools, and obsidian blades as well as figurine whistles (Hendon 1991, 2003d).

Distribution of resources based on archaeological remains also suggests that the use of valued materials was not restricted to elites. Obsidian, for example, brought from Guatemala and other parts of Honduras, is the material of choice throughout the valley to make sharp cutting implements but also objects of adornment (Aoyama 2001; Freter 1988; Mallory 1984). I excavated a beautifully made earspool made out of obsidian from one of the buildings in Patio B of Group 9N-8 (Hendon, Fash, and Aguilar P. 1990:151–55, 185). The locally produced polychrome pottery types, the most common of which is Copador, are used everywhere (Beaudry 1984; Bishop, Beaudry, Leventhal, and Sharer 1986; Viel 1993a, 1993b; Webster, Freter, and Storey 2004). Even imported Ulua polychromes found their way into rural household inventories in small quantities (W. Fash 1983b; Freter 1988). Jade and shell, also imported, were used for jewelry and for embellishing clothing. Objects made of these materials have been found in the Main Group and Sepulturas excavations but also in some rural sites (W. Fash 2001; Hendon 1991; Gonlin 1993). As is true of the Cuyumapa metates mentioned in chapter 2, the variability in differences among burial offerings, or houses, or imported goods, or people's health, or in what they do to their body reinforces Bourdieu's point that we are dealing with categories that are not fixed and moreover cannot be fixed because they are the material reflections of relational processes.

Social relations are the product of common activity and practices through which the continuity of communities of practice, such as the sociological house or the coresident group, is reproduced over time. The material domain of the sociological house is often centered on a physical house that may be a dwelling for the living or a ceremonial residence of the dead (Fox 1993; Joyce 2000c; Waterson 1997). The importance of a physical house as a focus for identity of a sociological house may explain why the most consistent marker of social difference at Copan is the elaboration of buildings or clusters of buildings. It is the size, material, and scale of residences and, by implication, the amount of energy needed to build, renovate, and maintain them that have proved to be the most visible, enduring, and culturally meaningful forms of social differentiation, and the ones that allow us most easily to differentiate social groups over time (Abrams 1987, 1994; W. Fash 2005; Hendon 1991, 1992, 2002c; see also Carrelli 2004). Domestic places lend themselves to elaboration through differences in the size and design of houses, construction materials, and the ways people embellish them (Blier 1987; Oliver 1990; Waterson 1997). Houses in Cerro Palenque and Cuyumapa display less architectural variation, but it is evident that people living in these areas also used home construction as a way to make assertions about difference. Even though the particular markers of distinction cannot remain stable, stability or its appearance is one way to make such processes and relations seem immutable and enduring over time.

Although sites in Cuyumapa, many at Cerro Palenque, and most rural sites in the Copan valley do not match the inner zone Copan residences in size, whether measured in terms of height, area, or volume of material used, they have a common architectural vocabulary and range of construction materials. These materials include carefully cut and dressed rectangular blocks, river cobbles not much modified from their original shape and size with the possible exception of a vertical facing on one side, and a combination of wooden frame and clay covering known as wattle and daub. Wattle-and-daub buildings, roofed with thatch, often have wall bases made of cobbles. Stone houses might have a thatch roof, but at Copan some urban residences had a flat roof made from wooden beams covered with a thick

16. The proximity of the patios in Group 9N-8 at Copan is illustrated here, with Patio B in the foreground and Patio A behind. The building on the left, Structure 9N-74, illustrates another feature of some high-status residences, namely, the construction of benches on the terraces outside of the building, which would have provided places to sit, work, and visit. The thatch roof on the structure at the far end of Patio A was put there by the restorers to protect the sculptured façade of building. Photograph by Julia A. Hendon.

layer of plaster. Rainspouts carved from stone projected from these roofs to carry water off during the rainy season. A few buildings had a raised roof created by a corbel arch. All of these materials were used at Copan and at Cerro Palenque, where cut-stone architecture is associated with the site's earlier occupation. Cuyumapa architecture is cobble and clay, although much less of the settlement has been excavated in this region.

Plaster made from limestone was widely used in Sepulturas to coat court-yard floors and walls and the floors, benches, and other surfaces of the residences (Hendon 1987, 1991). The earlier occupation at Cerro Palenque also made much use of plaster; in the Terminal Classic, its residential use was restricted to the ballcourt residential group where at least one wattle-and-daub building had a coat of plaster over the clay (Hendon 2005; Joyce 1985, 1991). Little to no plaster is reported from Cuyumapa or rural Copan, although the presence of a gravel paving in some courtyards (called *cascajo*) may indicate its former presence (Gonlin 1993). A few cases of good preservation establish that at least some plastered surfaces were also painted.

These are confined to interiors of rooms that are protected. I excavated a room in Patio B of Group 9N-8 at Copan that had traces of red paint on the plaster of the bench and wall niche (Hendon 1991); Richard Agurcia's work in the neighboring Patio C revealed a spectacularly painted bench covered with sparkling red paint made with specular hematite (Hendon, Agurcia, Fash, and Aguilar P. 1990).

Noticeable differences may exist within a single compound in terms of building materials. In urban Copan, there is a greater, more consistent use of block masonry in certain residential groups than in others, specifically, in the ones that were occupied longer and by wealthier people (Hendon 1991). Furthermore, residents made a consistent set of choices when deciding which parts of the building should be built out of blocks and which of cobbles. Better quality masonry is used more frequently for the front wall of the foundation, the staircase, the doorjambs into the main room of the residence, and the stone bench built inside those rooms. Residents of small rural dwellings also recognized the distinction implicit in block and cobble masonry. Site 11D11–2, the largest of the seven, and Site 7D6–2 made use of the same construction materials as those of the inner zone (Gonlin 1993). Even those rural sites that lack dressed stone masonry make use of cobbles and wattle and daub to create solid platforms and walls.

Cerro Palenque residential groups differ most obviously in their architectural mass and use of less common construction materials. Group 1, for example, includes a structure with a well-built cobblestone bench, elevated on the highest terrace in this group. Buried within the bench was a complete, unused basalt mano. The doorway into this building has a single stair made of a cut and faced block of vesicular basalt, available across the river from the site and otherwise used only for sculpture in the ballcourt and on another nonresidential structure. The significance of the use of this exotic material is reinforced by the fact that a second structure in this group included a slab of schist. The closest outcrop is 15 kilometers northwest of the site. Like the basalt, schist has otherwise been documented only as part of nonresidential structures at the site (Hendon 2007; Joyce 1985, 1991).

Cuyumapa residences as represented by Groups 5–2 and 6–2 are much alike in building materials, construction methods, and size of buildings or other elements despite the differences in their arrangement and in their use of other kinds of material culture, such as the raw materials for metates discussed earlier. Here architecture serves to create similarity rather than difference (Fung 1995). The variation in the size between the small resi-

dences and the large, tall mounds, at least some of which were also residences, suggests differences in the amount of time and energy invested
in dwellings. My excavation of one of these larger residences at the site
of PACO 15 demonstrated that it had a main room with a bench and cobble
wall bases.

The people living in these compounds in all three societies at any particular moment were enmeshed in repeated acts of commensality, ritual, and
cooperation that would have created a sense of common or shared identity.
At the same time, they were constantly reminded of the ways in which they
differed from one another in status, wealth, role, gender, age, and so on.
Most patios studied in Copan's inner zone and at Cerro Palenque have one
residence that stands out from the other buildings in its patio owing to its
higher quality of construction and height (Hendon 1991, 2007). Such dominant or focal structures are not present in the small rural sites, although they
probably are in the much larger residential groups in the foothills (Gonlin
1993). Nor do Groups 5–2 or 6–2 at PACO 2 possess such a structure.

CONTROL OF SPACE: INTIMACY AND SEPARATION

One way to explore the semiotic house is to think about how domestic
space is managed by its residents and how it in turn manages them through
such physical attributes as lines of sight and means of access. It is tempting
to consider the settings in residential areas as private and those associated
with monumental areas as public. This temptation is strengthened by the
way archaeologists refer to monumental buildings and spaces as public
architecture. Whether one takes public to refer to works directed by governmental authority or to more communal enterprises, the underlying implication is that the achievement required labor above what could be provided by
the household as well as coordination and leadership sufficiently coercive or
persuasive to overcome the independence or antagonism of domestic units
(Trigger 1990).

Differences in the energetic requirements of residential and monumental
construction have been well documented for Copan (Abrams 1994; Carrelli
2004; Gonlin 1993). There is no question that the larger scale and more
monumental architecture required more labor, more materials, and the development of social mechanisms for providing that labor. At the same time,
such investment does not therefore make such spaces accessible to the
public except under certain socially determined circumstances. Privacy is
better thought of in terms of control: spaces, such as houses or court-

yards, that are more connected to and controllable by some group of people (Birdwell-Pheasant and Lawrence-Zúñiga 1999).

The design of the built environment allows for different degrees of separation and intimacy among larger and smaller groups. Spatial arrangements that affect access, movement, relative position to others, what is seen, and who interacts with whom are means of controlling space and people. They contribute to intersubjective relations and social differentiation and are thus connected to the realization of such abstractions as gender, class, seniority, and solidarity that we commonly invoke when discussing social identity. These spaces are not merely representations or symbols of the ideas people have in their minds about the way the world works and society is ordered, however. The distinctive features of the architectural setting help determine such ideas through the possibilities they create for action and interaction; and the other possibilities they foreclose on or make more difficult. Different groups of people, both in terms of composition and size, would be encountered habitually or frequently in these spaces. Such encounters would be experientially different because of their location. Thus interactions or activities that might seem of the same type, such as preparing a meal or gathering to commemorate some significant event, are in fact not the same, not only because of their different scale or personnel but also because of where they take place.

A roughly square arrangement of structures is considered to be typical of residential sites among the Maya and, more broadly, in southeastern Mesoamerica (Ashmore 1981; Willey and Bullard 1965). This is generally true of the three areas studied here, although in reality many residential sites lack a neatly quadrilateral arrangement, either because they were not constructed so symmetrically, there are not enough buildings, or the topography must be accommodated. A more consistent characteristic—one I think expresses better the important spatial relationship—is that of orientation: structures, particularly residences, are built so that they face onto a central area, often paved or at least with the earth tamped down. The buildings demarcate this patio or courtyard even if they do not completely enclose it. The inner zone at Copan and sections of Cerro Palenque, especially around the Great Plaza and in the area of the oldest settlement, approach most consistently a true quadrilateral arrangement and, as a result, the clearest separation between inside (courtyard) and outside space. It is this greater degree of enclosure that makes these areas look urban to us. Because each patio group maintains its inward orientation, the sense is that of a set of separate units joined together but each retaining its internal cohesion, both spatially and functionally, even in the largest compounds.

In Copan's inner area, the foundation platforms of many of the buildings actually connect. This tighter arrangement has a pragmatic connection to density and length of occupation, but the resulting spatial enclosure is no less capable of being meaningful because it is to some extent dictated by circumstances. The fact that these compounds had relatively few points of entry and that most houses were raised on platforms and were built of stone resulted in an exterior view of mostly plain back walls rising high above the passerby. The close spacing and high walls of these residences would impede unobstructed views into the courtyards, at least from ground level. The Acropolis in the Main Group provides a different line of sight. Although distance would obscure the details of daily life, the view from above was the more intrusive one, allowing political leaders the opportunity to observe comings and goings not easily seen by the residents themselves. This possible surveillance may further explain the inward focus of the compounds in Sepulturas (Hendon 2002c). At its peak occupation, Group 9N-8 was made up of many contiguous courtyards, two of which were higher because they were built on a raised platform. Movement between the adjoining compounds was limited by the location of buildings. Anyone wishing to visit Patio D, for example, would have to pass through at least one other courtyard or go all the way around to the rear at the northern end of the cluster of buildings, passing close to several substantial trash middens. To get to Patio H from Patio B, one would have to walk out into the paved walkway between Patios A and B, then down a set of stairs at the southwestern corner of Patio H and between two of that courtyard's structures. Walls and other barriers were built between buildings in Group 9M-22, making it similarly inaccessible over time (Sheehy 1991).

Rural residents of the Copan valley rebuilt their living areas, sometimes renovating existing buildings, sometimes adding new ones and abandoning old ones (Gonlin 1993). Unlike those living in and around the Main Group, rural dwellers in the small sites considered here were less likely to build over an existing structure and more likely to add on to it or to leave it standing as they expanded the size of the residential group with the addition of new structures. The more spread out nature of settlement outside the inner zone makes a more expansive building pattern possible, but these rebuilding episodes maintain the orientation toward the patio space.

Long occupation does not explain Cerro Palenque's concentration of settlement. The hilly terrain was no doubt a factor. But neither time nor terrain fully accounts for the degree of enclosure here. Cerro Palenque's residents placed their groups of houses so that the oldest part of the settlement, abandoned after 850 CE and on the highest ground, was visible from the Great Plaza and all of the ridges used for building (Joyce and Hendon 2000). The residential compounds are more open to view from the old area than was the case between Main Group and urban Copan because of the generally lower platforms and more spread out arrangement of buildings. Whereas the rulers of Copan allocated to themselves the prerogative of overlooking their polity, everyone at Cerro Palenque allowed themselves to be overlooked by a place no longer occupied (Hendon 2002c). We might understand this as the equivalent of a one-way kind of gaze—later residents left a part of the site's history visible by not building over the older area or otherwise incorporating it into new construction but made sure that no one had a privileged ability to observe others. This assumes, though, that it is only the living who see. Mesoamerican belief systems recognize other entities as animate forces who are able to observe and who may be persuaded or inclined to intervene in people's lives, including ancestors and deceased members of the community (Gillespie 2001; McAnany 1995; Monaghan 1998b).

Groups 5–2 and 6–2 in Cuyumapa differ in their arrangement, one being tightly quadrilateral, the other more of an open U-shape. The Copan limitations of space did not apply at PACO 2: the occupation is about as long as that of Cerro Palenque, and the area where these compounds are found is relatively flat. In other words, there seem to be few external constraints on settlement layout, suggesting that the differences between the two groups result from decisions made by the inhabitants in response to social factors. The contrast in structure size in Cuyumapa leads to multiple places with notably larger buildings, including seven ballcourts. Only six of these were in active use during the Late and Terminal Classic periods, but all were visible. Excavations at the nearby sites of PACO 14 and 15 indicate that both locations have Late to Terminal Classic houses and both have a ballcourt. The ballcourt at PACO 14 dates from the same time period as the houses. The PACO 15 ballcourt was active much earlier, beginning around 150 BCE. These two ballcourts are less than half a kilometer apart but are separated in time by roughly eight hundred years. Although they have different orientations, the later one resembles the earlier one in size and form (Fox 1994:130, 180–81; Joyce, Hendon, and Lopipario 2009). The PACO 15 one was not

17. View of the highest peak at Cerro Palenque from the Great Plaza. CR-44, the earlier settlement, is up on the peak. The expanded occupation in the Terminal Classic period was built at the lower level from which the photograph was taken. Photograph by Julia A. Hendon.

razed after it fell out of active use. It continued to be a visible element on the landscape for its later inhabitants and their neighbors.

Like Cerro Palenque, Cuyumapa was a place in which history was both visible and tangible. Past places could be walked through and touched, not just seen. This was much less so for the people living near Copan's Main Group, where older buildings tended to be covered up by later constructions, but it would have been true to some extent in the rural areas of Copan. Structure 1 at the late site of 7D6−2 was built in part out of cut stone blocks that Gonlin (1993:134−38) suggests were taken from a monumental site nearby known as Rio Amarillo or La Canteada, after it was abandoned (see also Saturno 2000). Even though the houses built of more perishable materials would not remain intact for as long, traces of them, such as the stone wall bases and platforms, would endure beyond their abandonment. Long enough, in fact, to allow archaeologists working some centuries later to make maps of ancient settlement based only on architectural remains still standing above ground.

In the residential compounds themselves, spaces inside buildings are more intimate than the patio area or wide exterior terraces. This would also be mediated by construction materials. Stone walls are less permeable to sound and light, confining what is said or done inside them more effectively than walls of wood or clay, but also limiting the occupants' observation of people's comings and goings to what can be seen through the doorway (if not closed off by a mat or curtain). The porosity of wattle-and-daub walls changes the experience of inside and outside and affords greater opportunity for the continuation of interaction between people working outside and inside the house (Robin 2002). People inside the wattle-and-daub houses in rural and urban Copan, Cerro Palenque, and Cuyumapa would have been able to note what was happening outside more readily than their neighbors in stone buildings. Differences in the ability to observe, hear, see, and conceal exist in all places.

CONCEALMENT, MEMORY, AND KNOWLEDGE

Storage of goods, caching of valuable objects, and the burial of the dead all took place in ancient Honduran domestic places. These actions, which span the range from the most pragmatic to the most conventionally ritual, nevertheless are alike in that they index social relations that endure over time and create opportunities for differentiating people in terms of what they know. Comparing these aspects of domestic life provides further insight into the semiotic nature of the house.

Patterns of Practical Storage In the urban core of Copan, goods were stored in two kinds of spaces. Based on the distribution of clay storage containers, such as jars of various sizes, large basins, and *tecomates*, or bowls with necks that curve in, some people used side rooms while others preferred free-standing structures (Hendon 1987, 1988, 1991). In Group 9N-8, the items to be stored were consigned to small, narrow rooms off the main one and include tools and equipment for food preparation and cooking as well as containers. These side rooms lack benches and cannot be entered from the outside. Individual residences thus included areas for storage as well as for living in their interior.

People living in the other two compounds relied more on buildings built on platforms near their dwellings that often combined the roles of kitchen and storehouse. They are small, not much bigger than many of the rooms with benches in the dwellings. Groups 9M-24 and 9M-22 were occupied by people with less wealth, as measured by the diversity and nature of their possessions and by the size, scale, and energetic investment of their architecture. Belonging to less powerful sociological houses, they put the bulk of their stored resources outside of their dwellings in small buildings. Those dwelling in Group 9N-8, not only wealthier but also more able to signal their importance through sculpture and hieroglyphic texts (see chapter 5), kept their resources hidden inside their dwellings, where they would have been much less obvious to outsiders.

As in the inner-zone compounds, indicators of storage at the small patio groups in the foothills are often associated with evidence of food preparation and cooking (Gonlin 1993:Chapter 6). Two of the foothill sites, 11D11–2 and 32B-16–1, have concentrations of jars in one of their structures that convinced Gonlin these buildings were storehouses. The other sites certainly contained jars, but they are found in open areas and residences. Most of these (Sites 7D6–2, 7D6–1, 34A-12–2, and 99A-18–2) had one residence which displayed much stronger evidence of storage than others at the site. Unlike Group 9N-8, however, these residences do not have a special kind of room serving as the storage area, and in fact the exterior areas of buildings seem to have been important locations for these activities. Overall, the foothill sites show a lesser degree of spatial segregation and building specialization than the inner zone, but the variation in the spatiality of storage suggests that these households were also engaged in a process of differentiation based on visibility and the degree to which knowledge of a group's resources is shared with others. Only in this case, the distinction being drawn is based on whether the household dedicates a structure to a more limited purpose.

Architectural variation and spatial segregation are even less evident in Groups 5–2 and 6–2 at PACO 2 in Cuyumapa. The two residential groups lack dedicated storage structures, and the people living there seem to have used their residences and the space around them for a variety of purposes (Fung 1995:Chapter 5). This may reflect a different set of ideas about the right way to store goods, a different ethic of storage (Hendon 2000b) but does not mean that storing did not continue to form part of the background against which the occupants of these groups defined themselves as members of a memory community bound together by practice.

This state of affairs applies to Cerro Palenque also, where domestic space demonstrates a more consistent emphasis on different kinds of buildings than at PACO 2 but without manifesting the degree of variation evident at Copan. Joyce (1991:106–11) notes the presence of separate platforms where storage, corn grinding, and the making of chert tools took place in the residential groups farther away from the Great Plaza. In the ballcourt residential group, the greatest concentration of material remains of storage and food preparation came from behind the largest structure at the southern end of the compound. I excavated a trash pit here associated with a stone platform (Hendon 2005). The platform is not as visible as the storage platforms in the other groups but neither is it hidden away inside a residence. It is also at the farthest remove from the ballcourt.

I have stressed the storage of food up to this point because it represents the most fundamental kind of domestic storage and is well represented in the material remains. But other kinds of objects and resources were stored as well, including materials that comprise the wealth of the coresident communities of practice and become part of the estate of the sociological house to which these domestic groups belong. Several pieces of ceremonial regalia associated with the ballgame were found in Patio A of Group 9N-8 at Copan (see chapter 7). They fell from the upper part of the room, near the roof, when Structure 9N-81 collapsed (Webster, Fash, and Abrams 1986). This recalls the incident in the *Popol vuh* when the Hero Twins learn that their father's ballgame equipment has been in the house they have lived in all their lives, stored out of sight in the rafters (Tedlock 1996:111–12). Their grandmother and mother deliberately concealed the equipment to protect the boys from suffering the same fate as their father and uncle, who were sacrificed by the Lords of the Underworld. At the Late Classic site of Ceren in El Salvador, buried by a volcanic eruption about 600 CE, the excavators found that obsidian knives and blades had been tucked into the thatching of the roof of a storehouse (Sheets 1992). People would know that other people have things stored up. This knowledge would enter into their interactions with others, either overtly or as part of the background knowledge informing their relationship. Differences in the location of stored items inside the same structure imply that differences in knowledge and the ability to access materials come into play even among members of the same community of practice—perhaps most obviously between adults and children, but also between women and men or between those whose responsibilities habitually involved them in activities requiring the tools, materials, or other things being stored. People create differences in visibility and knowledge through the way they store things. Variation in more or less visible formal storage space relates to the need to define and validate social status, which is fundamentally unstable. At Copan, where social relations were the most contested, maintaining a stable system of evaluation proved especially difficult.

For two of the small residential groups living in the foothills, the ability to construct a dedicated storehouse renders their material possessions both less visible and yet more marked as a recognizable location in the domestic landscape. At the other foothill sites, storage and food preparation merge with a range of ongoing activities in the multiuse space of the dwelling and often take place outside. Although weather and pests make it unlikely that jars and other storage containers stayed in the patio or on the paved terraces of the dwellings all the time, they were placed there often enough to leave a perceptible trace in the archaeological record. The distinction created between those with and without formal storehouses no longer works among inner-zone houses. There the less wealthy in Groups 9M-24 and 9M-22 continue the practice of putting their material resources on display by making their location, albeit not their quantity or type, obvious. This practice is not reciprocated by those living in Group 9N-8, however, who seem most concerned to control what kinds of information they share with others. By making their storage more visible, people in Groups 9M-22 and 9M-24 inadvertently gave their higher-status neighbors a kind of knowledge they cannot possess unless they achieve a more intimate acquaintance with the interiors of dwellings in Group 9N-8. Knowledge itself becomes a way of differentiating people and the memory communities to which they belong. Such unevenly shared knowledge is not limited to the esoteric domain of calendars, writing, and religious ritual but includes even the apparently utilitarian activity of household storage. Through storage, past household labor is preserved, the potential of future labor embodied, and the different (and differently valued) contributions of members of the coresident community of practice actualized.

Burying, Renovating, and Remembering Another way coresident communities of practice in Mesoamerica bind themselves together is by participating in rituals of renewal, healing, and remembrance. Some of these rituals create deposits whose contents are intentionally hidden from view, whose location may or may not be marked, and which contribute to localized memories. Like storehouses or side rooms without benches, burials and caches are spots on the landscape which are capable of being remembered and where items, and sometimes people, of material and symbolic value are deposited, guarded, brought into social practice, and changed. Burials and caches represent another form of storage that becomes a hidden dimension of domestic space. By emphasizing the shared social action and meaning involved in these various practices of putting in and taking out people or things, it is possible to define a social domain that emphasizes the features shared by

18. Part of the contents of a cache found near the east structure of the ballcourt residential group at Cerro Palenque. Shown here are one of the two spiny oyster shells (*Spondylus spp.*) found and the wedge of green marble carved from what was once a marble vessel. The marble and this shell were placed in a shallow Ulua Polychrome bowl. Photograph by Julia A. Hendon.

such mundane activities as storing, feeding, and accumulating wealth with religious rituals, events, or actions that we usually bracket off from ordinary life.

The Copan valley is the only area of the three studied here that has yielded burials as well as caches. The material and conceptual overlap between the two practices that has been demonstrated throughout Mesoamerica allows me to discuss caching at Cerro Palenque and Cuyumapa and burying and caching at Copan together. Deposits that archaeologists label burials and others they call caches may contain human remains as well as objects. Both are deliberate and formal in their arrangement, and they are often put in the same kind of location (Becker 1992; Chase and Chase 1998). These similarities suggest that the people who created them did not draw a firm line between the two but rather considered them to be part of the same domain.

One of the first important finds I made at Cerro Palenque was a carefully placed offering near the eastern building of the ballcourt residential group (see Hendon and Lopiparo 2004). The residents of this group set a wedge-shaped piece of green marble and half of a *Spondylus* shell in a shallow bowl, which was then buried in the gravel paving of the patio. The cache originally included another *Spondylus* half, although not from the same shell, which we found in the dirt removed from the excavation unit. The cache dates to the early part of the Terminal Classic period, but the bowl is not, as I first expected, a fine paste type. It is a Santana Ulua Polychrome, a late member of this large class of polychromes that appears in the eighth century CE and continues to be produced in the ninth. Unfortunately its eroded state did not allow me to determine what had been painted on it, but such a bowl links the residents of the Terminal Classic ballcourt residential group with Cerro Palenque's Late Classic past (Hendon 2006b).

The careful placement of offerings was something I already knew about from the results of the first set of excavations at Cerro Palenque by Rosemary Joyce. This work had demonstrated that the placing of valued objects in domestic spaces was something that continued from the Late Classic into the Terminal Classic (Joyce 1985, 1991, 1993b). One of the structures in the Late Classic hilltop center is a small platform used as a focus of intermittent ritualized action. It contained a *Spondylus* shell holding a jade bead as well as two obsidian tools and a set of irregular pebbles placed at different spots in its fill. Other kinds of objects used in caches in dwellings include clay figurines and whistles, obsidian or chert bifaces, grinding stones, and ceramic objects. Among the materials used to make these offerings are those that archaeologists identify as forms of wealth or markers of prestige, such as shell, jade, or obsidian. These are objects that enchant because of their visual and tactile characteristics, their form, their exotic origin, and how they are worked as well as the symbolism they invoke. But Joyce also reports manos placed in the fill of benches and implements made from the abundant local chert which are not so obviously enchanting or, we assume, so symbolically rich. And she found figurines and whistles which are emphatically personlike objects. In other words, we have objects that encompass the everyday and the special purpose. All result from processes of ritualization, meaningful ways of acting that vary in their purpose and participants. Some index domestic labor, especially that of women, while others call to mind the enduring identity of the group and its components: men and women, adults and children. Sometimes these meanings converge. A cache placed in the body of a shrine from Group 1 at Cerro Palenque consists of three clay figures. One is a female figurine holding a water jar. One is a male figurine costumed as a bird and holding a musical instrument. This pair was accompanied by a clay whistle in the shape of an elaborately dressed person. All three were buried as if they were biological persons, flanking a piece of chlorite schist that was set into the platform as a marker or plain stela.

All levels of Copan society, from farmers in the rural areas to wealthy residents of the inner zone to members of the royal family in the Main Group stored their dead and their objects of value. Rural residential sites yielded both burials and caches (Gonlin 1993). At Site 34A-12–2, the graves most likely date from early in the Late Classic period and contained decorated or polychrome pottery and metates. At Site 99A-18–2, the deceased did not have any obvious funerary offerings, but metates were used as part of the stones delimiting the graves. Site 7D3–1 has a cache that looks very much like a burial minus the body. A stone-lined cist constructed in the platform of Structure 1 held two locally made pieces of polychrome tableware, one a large plate for serving food and the other a cylinder suitable for holding liquid, as well as a long chert biface and an ornament made of jade or some other dense green stone (Gonlin 1993:172, 182–86, Figures 3.34, 3.35). An oval arrangement of stones on the surface of the platform marked the cist's location. A similar interest in making the location of a cache visible may be noted at Site 34C-4–2. Two decorated eating and serving vessels, a hemispherical bowl and a semi-necked jar, were placed next to a limestone slab some 20 centimeters taller than the pots (Gonlin 1993:287, 299, Figure 3.73).

Many caches and burials have been found in the inner-zone residential compounds. As previously discussed, burial treatment itself does not correspond with architectural energetics. A complete catalog has not yet been published, but the reports of the excavations in the different compounds attest to the fact that burying the dead and objects, sometimes together and other times separately, was integral to how people living in these places defined their spatial domain and their sense of identity over time (see Diamanti 2000; Hendon, Agurcia, Fash, and Aguilar P. 1990; Hendon, Fash, and Aguilar P. 1990; Gerstle and Webster 1990; Sheehy 1991; Viel and Cheek 1983; Webster, Fash, and Abrams 1986; Willey and Leventhal 1979). The residents of the compounds around the Main Group, like their rural neighbors, frequently placed locally made or imported ceramic vessels designed for eating, serving food, and drinking in caches or graves. It is possible these vessels contained food and drink when first buried. Large incense burners decorated with human faces, cacao pods, and other plant motifs modeled in three dimensions were also considered to be appropriate offerings. Cacao is like corn in that it was esteemed not just as a food used in making beverages and sauces (see chapter 6) but also as an index of cultural

19. A large storage jar (Casaca Striated type) placed as a cache in Structure 9N-75 (Group 9N-8, Patio B) at Copan. Photograph by Julia A. Hendon.

values. The residents of Patio E in Group 9N-8 interred one of these censers below the latest plaster pavement of their central courtyard, cutting through two earlier floors as they dug the hole and covering the cache with a large slab (Diamanti 2000:105). Imported shell, small-scale stone sculpture, obsidian tools, and carved pieces of bone were also included. At least four animals, two of them dogs, were buried in or near buildings as if they were people. Anthropomorphic figures of stone and clay were set in architectural fill.

Substantial storage jars of the sort used to hold water, chicha, and other large amounts of liquids were sometimes placed in the construction fill of a building as it was first erected or expanded. An even more emphatically everyday kind of deposit comes from Structure D of the group CV-20, an inner-zone compound excavated in the 1970s by Gordon Willey and Richard Leventhal. The cache contained manos, a bark beater, and three vessels "of the coarse unslipped variety" (Leventhal 1979:85). This accumulation of objects integral to the domestic production of food and paper was incorporated into the building at an early point in its construction history.

Putting valued objects or people inside buildings or below patio floors can be juxtaposed with actions that remove, rearrange, or add to burials and

20. Excavation of a trench through the central axis of Structure 9N-71 revealed several earlier versions of the building and a tomb, shown here with its capstones still in place. Photograph by Julia A. Hendon.

caches. Directing excavations in Patio C of Group 9N-8 at Copan, I wanted to understand the sequence of construction of Structure 9N-71 before it was restored for the expansion of the tourist park (see fig. 15). I dug a deep trench from front to back through the foundation platform and the building it supported (see Hendon, Agurcia, Fash, and Aguilar P. 1990:31–34, 53–55). From this trench I learned that Structure 9N-71 covered three earlier versions of itself. Not much was left of the original structure or its first renovation except some bits of wall and fragments of plaster floors. The second renovation was better preserved, however, and showed that something new had been added to Structure 9N-71 at this point in its history. The people living there at the time dug a tomb into the foundation they were about to cover up. This tomb was lined with stone and sealed with a row of heavy slabs. The foundation platform of the new structure, third in the construction sequence, enclosed the older structure and tomb.

When it came time to renovate Structure 9N-71 for the last time, the occupants, at least one generation on from those who built the tomb, also did something not done before. This time, they dug into the floor of the main room until they reached the tomb's capstones. They lifted them, breaking one in the process, and removed whatever and whomever had been inside. We did find some human bones, including a mandible and part of the lower body, from an individual who may have been the original occupant of the tomb. The builders then filled the tomb with fine alluvial dirt and put the capstones back in place. On top of the capstones, at one end of the row, they buried another partial skeleton and four painted hemispherical bowls with ring bases. Only then could the final phase of construction continue, resulting in a one-roomed building over the tomb and the more recent burial.

When I first thought about this sequence of events and actions, I assumed that opening up a tomb and changing its contents were acts of desecration and, as such, very different from burying someone. But as I have learned more about ancient Maya funerary practices I have come to realize that my unthinking interpretation was a product of my own cultural circumstances. Reentering burials and adding, removing, or rearranging parts of the body or the material objects they contain turn out to be regular parts of how the dead were transformed into ancestors and incorporated into the domestic landscape, including that created by royalty in their monumental centers (Chase and Chase 1998; Gillespie 2001; Hendon 2003a; McAnany 1998; Weiss-Krejci 2004).

Bones become an enduring reminder of the individual that transcends death and merges the individual into a collective identity that represents the social group as a whole. They provide a focus for remembering even as the person's former role as a living member of the community fades away. I interpreted the changes to the tomb as desecration because I assumed a burial should be a single event of finite duration that is intended to remain inviolate. Treatment of the dead reflects decisions made by the living, however, who are much more interested in carrying out a ritualized form of ongoing management, interaction, and relocation spanning several generations. Copan's royalty shared this desire to manage their dead. The Acropolis tomb labeled Margarita by its excavators, for example, was rebuilt as the buildings above it were renovated to create additional offering space and to allow continued access to the chamber (Bell, Sharer, Traxler, Sedat, Carrelli, and Grant 2004:137). These practices contribute to the construction and reconstruction of identity, place, and memory for members of the memory communities concerned. Removal of the first occupant or occupants of the tomb in Structure 9N-71 includes aspects of both elements central to local histories. It changes what is memorable about the tomb and how it indexes social relations in past and present. By doing so, the people responsible for the renovation may indeed have created a way to forget as well as remember.

The tomb in Structure 9N-71. Photographs by Julia A. Hendon.

21.1: When the capstones were removed, the chamber was full of a fine silt. Resting on the floor of the chamber were a few disarticulated human bones.

21.2: After filling the tomb with dirt and replacing the capstones, people placed several pottery vessels, including a bowl with a ring base, and human bones in the building fill covering the tomb.

DAILY LIFE AS RITUALIZED ACTION

Life at home combines the mundane and the ritual. People and personlike objects, buried in similarly structured ways, are stored in burials and caches the same way that goods, materials, and foodstuffs are kept safe in storehouses. As the Margarita and Structure 9N-71 tombs reveal, bodies and cached objects move in and out of religiously charged storehouses. Knowledge of the presence of ritual offerings or bodies buried inside, behind, or next to dwellings, like that of stores of useful or valuable commodities inside rooms or storehouses, represents an awareness of a hidden dimension of social and physical space. It is knowledge that is more accessible to some than others. Differentially shared, it may become another basis for how memory communities shape their identity around distinct sets of events and their material remains. As a form of storage, burials and caches combine the material with the moral. They are like storehouses in that they are places where items, and sometimes people, of differing material and symbolic value are deposited and guarded. Sequestering valuables in caches or burials removes them from circulation but does not destroy their ability to contribute to memory, identity, and prestige. Such objects acquire their value from their history and their association with valued people, which renders them generative resources for memory making, conferring a kind of inalienability on them (Joyce 2003; Weiner 1992).

Domestic places have histories that are only partly evident to the outsider. Goods inside rooms, tombs below houses, and figurines incorporated into the very fabric of shrines are part of a materiality of hidden knowledge that complements the importance of visibility and status. Both concealment and display contribute to the spatiality of social life. In Mesoamerica, the location of certain burials is often made obvious by the construction of a large structure over or around them (McAnany 1998). At Copan, the architectural complex of the Main Group was well endowed with burials and massive offerings. These richly furnished deposits have received much attention from archaeologists eager to interpret the extent of royal power (see Becker and Cheek 1983; Bell, Sharer, Traxler, Sedat, Carrelli, and Grant 2004; W. Fash 2001; Fash, Williamson, Larios, and Palka 1992; Longyear 1952; Viel and Cheek 1983; Strömsvik 1941). Just as information about the actions of certain people only are recorded in the hieroglyphic texts on Maya public monuments, so only certain graves are marked in this way. But other members of society also remembered and marked the locations of burials and caches of significance to them.

FOUR

Embodied Forms of Knowing

Learning, knowing, and thinking are often treated as distinct from memory (Kirshner and Whitson 1997; Rogoff, Radziszewska, and Masiello 1995). Learning, however, is "the construction of present versions of past experience for several persons acting together" (Lave 1993:8). Like remembering, it is situated and social, not just an individual, intrapsychic phenomenon that resides in the mind. This has been most evident in studies of so-called informal learning and apprenticeship (for example, Chamoux 1986; Greenfield 1984, 2004; Lave 1988) that have looked at how novices and newcomers become "full participants in a sociocultural practice" (Lave and Wenger 1991:29). Everyday life at home provides the opportunity to connect past and present through participation in events and practices that are productive of knowledge and memory. It serves as a context for situated learning in which an individual undergoes a series of apprenticeships that are both cognitive and embodied, resulting in the development of nonconscious knowledge that is engrained in the body as well as conscious, analytical understandings.

Continuing my examination of daily life as ritualized action and the house as a semiotic memory machine, I turn to remembering as an embodied process. Given that "there is hardly any technique of the body that does not incorporate a given materiality" (Warnier 2001:10), doing and making things involve forms of knowledge that intersect with learning and memory to construct communities of practice in domestic places. In this chapter I discuss repeated practices, including cooking and crafting of textiles, pottery, paper, and shell ornaments. Archaeologists usually place these activities firmly on the domestic, economic, or practical side of the divide, separating them from ritual. I argue, however, that they are ritualized practices that exemplify "a local theory of production: a set of ideas about how people create and maintain the conditions of their existence" (Monaghan 1998a:48). They are creative acts intended to be efficacious. They merge the practical, such as the grinding of corn or making of a pot, with what anthropologists tend to bracket off as religious actions, such as making offerings, praying, and observing restrictions on behavior. Preparing food and crafting objects are both examples of ritualized actions and interactions that take place in the rooms and courtyards, on the terraces and platforms that people considered to be part of their lived space. These different sets of knowledge include not only specialized skills, such as weaving, potting, making paper, and working shell, but also a mastery of the behavior necessary for successful integration into society itself.

OBJECTS, SUBJECTS, AND EMBODIMENT

Much like the Playa de los Muertos figurines discussed earlier or the beings created by divine action in the *Popol vuh*, the bodies of people in pre-Hispanic Mesoamerica were shaped through deliberately imposed changes as well as those resulting from daily life. Concern with molding the body and its movement to conform to cultural notions of propriety permeates documentary sources on Mesoamerican daily life and is reflected in how the human form is depicted in art. Social status was also linked to embodied ways of being in the pre-Hispanic period. The passage of time and the child's development as a physical and social being are marked by ceremonies that left physical traces on the body. Adults flattened their babies' foreheads, pierced their ears and lips, cut their hair, and provided clothing at socially determined intervals (Berdan and Anawalt 1992; Joyce 1998, 2000b; Meskell and Joyce 2003). Children's bodies were also shaped by their training in productive activities like weaving, in elements of ceremony such as songs and dances, and sometimes in the arts of war as well as by nutrition and disease. Producing an appropriately socialized body is a project undertaken by parents, the coresident community of practice, and society as a whole.

The skeleton, that part of the body that survives into the present day for archaeologists to dig up and physical anthropologists to study, shows that changes were neither limited to skin and hair nor destined to disappear after death (Geller 2004; Rhoads 2002; Tiesler Blos 1999). Discs of hard materials such as hematite or jade set in the teeth have already been mentioned. Teeth may also be filed or notched to change their shape. The head itself may be reshaped to make the forehead less vertical and slope backward, considered a sign of beauty and refinement. These changes are not made to all bodies, though, and connect to other processes of differentiation. Such changes can be read by others—as signs of status, gender, age, ethnicity or as symbols reflecting religious and cosmological beliefs—but they also alter the personal experience of the body and the sense of self.

"The things that people make, make people" (D. Miller 2005:38) in ways that are less intentional or institutionalized as well. Objects, as things with physical properties and a material presence, afford possibilities for action and meaning making that interact with the physical properties and capabilities of the human body and its sensory apparatus. Interaction with objects trains the body, constraining and enabling it while accustoming it to certain kinds of movement and materiality. This is, in effect, another form of apprenticeship. Marcel Mauss (2006:90), in his foundational work on how the body and its movement are culturally constructed, asked, why doesn't a man wearing slippers with no back lose them while running downhill? Jean-Pierre Warnier answers this question by arguing that the person is not just a man but a "man-with-slippers" (2001:7). A woman from Cerro Palenque who is grinding corn is likewise not just a woman or a woman from Cerro Palenque, but a woman-with-metate. A host of material objects and the associated actions they engender come together in this woman, all of which contribute to identity through the development of subjectivity and intersubjectivity (Farnell 1999). "Techniques of the body in a given materiality are thus in fact techniques of the self" (Warnier 2001:10).

The tacit, unexpressed quality of the everyday suggests that all meaningful and meaning-making operations, including those related to memory, involve both implicit and explicit knowledge (Fisette 2003; Keane 1997, 2005). "Things explicitly formulated and understood can 'sink down' into unarticulated know-how [and] our grasp on things can move as well in the other direction, as we articulate what was previously just lived out" (Taylor 2005:36). Embodied and sensory forms of knowing combine with people's experiences of the objects, spaces, and people with which they interact (Merleau-Ponty 1958; Meskell 2002; Tuan 1977; Zahavi 2003). What people know is to some degree implicit and even nonconceptual, expressed in movement as much as articulated in language. Phenomenological studies of embodiment and perception argue that the very orientation of the body as it moves through space engrains a sense of the passage of time and relationships between people and their surroundings in the body (Todes 2001, see also Giard 1998; Wu 2003). William Hanks (1990) makes a similar point through his study of expressions of relational position and spatialized reference (deixis) in Yucatec Maya. Humans' ability to move through space and to adjust their movements in anticipation of some action grows out of a direct bodily understanding or motor intentionality (Kelly 2005; Merleau-Ponty 1958). Such embodied forms of knowing are not something one normally reflects on but are still agential (Carman 2005; Gallagher and Varela 2003).

Traces of embodied action surface in the material objects people produce and use. Buildings in pre-Hispanic Honduras were modeled and remodeled as if they were living bodies and thus retain signs of human action. This is evident in the renovation of residential places and monumental space. Although large-scale renovation projects command attention more easily, finer-scaled forms of action also persist: "The carving [of Temple 22] . . . was done with a skill and sureness of line that evidences a high degree of technical ability and an intimate knowledge of the materials used. . . . In some places, small, delicate chisel marks remain. In spite of this accurate delineation, all surfaces of the sculpture were originally covered with plaster and painted. The frequent renewal of the plaster resulted in almost complete obliteration of some of the details of the carving. In places, where plaster still adhered to the stone, it was noted that a thickness of 2 cm. was attained by the application of as many as 25 coats" (Trik 1939:102).

Embodied memory and knowledge have received less attention as a mode of remembering than they deserve. In part this lack reflects larger issues surrounding how and why the body has been brought back into social scientific discourse as an acting, moving presence (Farnell 1999; Joyce 2005; Meskell 2000; Warnier 2001, 2006) and in part how memory has been studied (Connerton 1989). Bodies have gone from being absent to "static, more or less passive cultural objects of disciplines and representation, separate from the mind" (Farnell 1999:348) to sensing, moving, and acting presences, sites of lived experience, produced and experienced through the intersection of the physical, the social, and the material.

TIME TELLING THROUGH COOKING

Perhaps the most domestic of domestic activities are those connected with preparing and cooking food (Simmel 1997). Most archaeologists consider food preparation as useful evidence that a site was residential in function but otherwise uninteresting unless it can be related to commemorative or ritual events that include feasts. Yet an appreciation of eating and drinking as a sensual experience, as a rich source of metaphor and symbol, and as a deeply significant and ritualized social act permeates Mesoamerican societies (Hendon 2003b, 2003c; Heyden 1983, 1986; Love 1989; Pohl and Pohl 1994; Pyburn 1989; Roys 1965; Sahagún 1953–82; Taube 1989). The preparation, service, and consumption of food become a practical and semiotic complex in its own right. Preparing food may give the appearance of routine, repetitive actions with ephemeral results, tempting some to dismiss these actions as irrelevant to an undertanding of memory and knowledge. Although much of what is done while cooking may be an embodied kind of knowing based on perception and the senses, it requires active involvement, planning, improvisation, and often delegation of tasks among cooks and helpers.

In all three regions, these paradigmatic activities of daily life took place in several kinds of locations, including outdoors on the patio, on terraces, and in roofed areas that were not fully enclosed rooms. Cooking utensils include a brazier with a shallow plate that formed a kind of portable stove for heating food (Fung 1995; Gonlin 1993; Hendon 1987, 1988; Joyce 1991; Viel 1993a:Figure 85), manos and metates for grinding corn, bowls and basins for mixing and cooking, jars for holding water and other ingredients, and obsidian or chert tools for cutting, scraping, sawing, and slicing meat, fruits, and vegetables (Aoyama 1999; Mallory 1984). People living in the inner zone and in small rural sites in the Copan valley also used the *comal*, a large griddle with two handles that was placed over the fire and used to cook tortillas made from corn or to toast or parch seeds (Gonlin 1993:Table 4.7;

Hendon 1988; Viel 1993a:Figure 86). This form is not known from Cuyu-mapa (Fung 1995:172) or Cerro Palenque (Joyce 1985:Chapter 5), suggesting differences in local preferences for how food, especially corn, was prepared.

Cooking and food preparation activities did not necessarily take place simultaneously. Animal butchery or corn grinding might be done at one point in the day, cooking at another. Nor did they have to be done by the same person. Both corn grinding and cooking require water, which would have been carried into the compound in jars from reservoirs or rivers. The taste for eating corn in the form of tortillas suggests that cooks at Copan had more preparation time or assistants at their disposal. Making tortillas is time consuming and is best done just before and during the meal.

The spatial concentration of cooking and food preparation suggests it was somewhat separated from other things people were doing in the course of a day, such as gathering in rooms, eating, or making cloth, pottery, shell ornaments, or other things. Preparing meals on terraces, next to foundation platforms, or on small platforms kept the cooks and their assistants visible to others. As they ground corn, cut up meat, prepared vegetables, and stirred the pot, they were also aware of what others were doing around them. As the most consistently repeated actions several times a day, every day, the sights, sounds, and smells of food preparation plus the movement of people as they went about these tasks construct a temporal rhythm to the day. These neces-sary, repetitive activities are a form of time telling (see the introduction), developing out of the comings and goings of water carriers and of people getting goods out of storage, the rasp and scrape of grinding stones, the aroma of corn and meat as they cooked, and the crescendo of activity before each meal was served.

The implements used regularly to carry out these tasks contribute to the sensory experience of living and lead toward a particular subjectivity through their material presence and the techniques of the body required to use them. Metates, for example, are heavy but not immobile (see fig. 12). They are hard and unyielding. The history of their usage and the grinding practices of their users are evident in the depth and contour of the grinding surface. The metates I study have surfaces that are worn down unevenly, reflecting the difference in how women exerted force through their arms and back to press down on the mano and slide it back and forth over and over. Girl's bodies trained themselves and were trained by more senior women to adopt pos-tures, such as kneeling and leaning the torso forward (see fig. 13). These postures made it possible for women to exert pressure, keep their balance, control or minimize the forward creep or sideways roll of the metate. This is a reflexive and recursive process that also defines the proper way for a woman to hold her body. It is not that these postures are the only ones possible but that they come to seem so as the body shapes itself in response. Grinding corn is an exercise in repetitive motion that places stress on certain parts of the body and has a cumulative effect on a person's health over time (Ballinger 1999; Lee 1995). Part of the process of body shaping, then, is also a process of degeneration that manifests itself in less ease and more pain, another form of widespread, predictable but unstandardized time telling. Such postures intersect with how women interact with other objects and technologies that form part of their everyday life, such as weaving on a backstrap loom.

MEMORY AND IDENTITY THROUGH MAKING THINGS

Subjectivity and materiality come together in what bodies wear and what they make. People spent time making things at home to provide themselves with the tools or materials they needed, to decorate the body and manifest social difference, to exchange with others, and generally to make social interaction possible. I discuss four different crafts: the production of textiles, clay pots and figurines, bark paper, and ornaments made out of shell. The archaeological evidence indicates that, in all cases, people were producing these materials on a part-time basis. Their abilities did not exempt them from fulfilling their other domestic responsibilities, and making these things was integrated into the rhythm of the household. In other words, these crafts were not occupational specializations in the modern sense of the term, but they did help create communities of practice among coresidents and between groups living in different residences.

WEAVING AS ENGENDERED KNOWLEDGE

The textile arts of Mesoamerica past and present are justifiably celebrated. Based on his visit to Yucatan in 1588, the Franciscan friar Alonso Ponce commented that the cotton mantles woven by Maya women were "almost as delicate as fine Dutch linen" (Noyes 1932:313). The colorful woven, brocaded, and embroidered clothing of contemporary and historic Maya in Guatemala and Mexico finds its analogue in how the costumes of men and women are depicted in stone sculpture, painting, and figurines from earlier time periods (Morris 1985; Schele 1997; Taylor 1992; Turok and Morris 1994). A variety of materials and techniques characterized pre-Hispanic weaving. Feathers and animal fur supplemented cotton and maguey fibers to produce diverse kinds of cloth. Dyes derived from plants, shellfish, insects, and minerals added color and complexity of design (Anawalt 1981; Carlsen 1986, 1987; Mahler 1965; Turok 1996).

These textiles can be read by considering what their designs symbolize (Dupiech-Cavaleri 1999; Morris and Foxx 1987; Schevill 1993; Turok 1988), a process facilitated by their display in museums and illustration in publications as stretched out (sometimes with seams unpicked to make both sides visible at once), dissociated from any human body, and flattened like pages in a book. For example, the ceremonial *huipil*, or blouse, woven in the twentieth-century for the statue of the Virgin to wear in the town of Santa Maria Magdalena contains motifs that symbolize the ordering of the cosmos, human settlements, important plants that humans and deities eat (corn and beans for the humans, bromeliads for the gods), other deities such as the Earth Lord, and so on (Turok 1988). These readings, made in consultation with the women who make or wear the clothing, are like the reading of the iconography of Temple 22 discussed in chapter 2—fascinating and instructive but incomplete because they do not consider how making and wearing the huipil create additional layers of meaning. The design of a woman's huipil comes together when she puts it on. The motifs, their arrangement, and the separate pieces of fabric joined together as a whole "describe our universe with me, a fertile and productive woman, at the center" (Turok 1988:43).[1] When the huipil is worn, the wearer has placed herself at the heart of the world rendered with such care in the woven and embroidered designs. As a lived element, the huipil becomes another material element of subjectivity and identity.

Multiple lines of evidence allow one to detect a strong association between individuals gendered female and these particular bodies of knowledge connected with textiles, an association reinforced in practice and symbol. "To the Maya, . . . things related to weaving are quite simply, in and of themselves, female" (Prechtel and Carlsen 1988:123). The people or deities depicted in art or described in documents as weavers and spinners are gendered female, an identity signaled by their appearance, clothing, or what they do, reflecting specific social practices of activity, dress, and embodiment (see Hendon 1999c, 2006c).

The human body is an integral part of the basic technology of weaving. The backstrap loom, the device in use before European contact and still used by some weavers today, cannot retain its shape on its own without the support of a convenient upright at one end and the weaver's body at the other. The weaver controls the tension by the direction in which she moves her body and opens and closes the sheds in which weft threads are inserted by lifting heddles, placing and rotating the wooden batten, and using other hand-held implements as needed (Asturias de Barrios 1998; Prechtel and Carlsen 1988; Sperlich and Sperlich 1980). "The loom itself appears to be a simple device. When the cloth is completed, nothing remains of the loom except a pile of sticks," yet studies of this technology have argued that it is really "a complex device, more responsive to the weaver's creative impulses than the modern treadle loom" (Schevill 1993:55) introduced into the region by the Spanish.

Backstrap looms are human scaled and subject to the limitations of the body. Cloth produced on the loom has the advantage of four finished selvedges but cannot be wider than the weaver's sideways reach since she must insert the batten and pass the weft thread through by hand. The overall length of the fabric is dictated in part by the fact that it is rolled around the end of the loom next to the weaver's body. Once the roll has reached a certain thickness, about five yards for modern weavers, its bulkiness impedes effective use of the loom. Weavers need to coordinate a series of body movements through which they control the weaving itself—leaning the torso backward or forward, lifting the heddle with one hand, and inserting and rotating the batten with the other. They may need to count and pick up specific threads to create a design, as when brocading, following the pattern in their mind but with room for improvisation not possible on the treadle loom (Schevill 1993).

The passing on of the knowledge of how to spin, weave, dye, and design textiles begins at home. Aztec child-rearing practices described in the sixteenth-century Codex Mendoza demonstrate that training began early but was gradual and developmental in approach. At five years old, girls were allowed to hold the spindle, at the age of six they began to learn how to spin, and a few years later they began to weave (Berdan and Anawalt 1992 Vol. 3:57v–6or). The gradual approach, which allows the children's bodies to adapt to the technology, continues to be preferred among contemporary weavers (Chamoux 1986; Greenfield 2004). But the technology can also be adapted to the weaver. Backstrap looms can be scaled down to allow young girls to begin weaving, facilitating the development of the bodily discipline and mental concentration necessary to produce quality textiles. At the same

22. Clay figurine of a high-status woman weaving on a backstrap loom. Photograph © Justin Kerr, K2833.

23. Clay spindle whorls from Copan residential groups. Those on the top
are decorated with birds' heads. Photograph by Julia A. Hendon.

time, such children have to be helped periodically by a more experienced
weaver because of physical or conceptual limitations. A child's arms may be
too short to pass the weft thread through easily, she may not have sufficient
motor control to coordinate all the required body movements, or she may
not have understood fully how to set up the continuous warp of the loom.
Much of this assistance is nonverbal and itself embodied; children are not
lectured on the theory of weaving but guided by means of physical interven-
tions at key moments (Greenfield 1984).

In a longitudinal study of twentieth-century Tzotzil Maya weavers in Mexico, Patricia Greenfield (2004) draws attention to the development of a certain way of holding the body that begins at an early age. This deportment is
characterized by a markedly still and centered upper body with arms held
close to the sides plus the ability to kneel for long periods of time and
maintain excellent balance. This set of body techniques facilitates use of
the backstrap loom but also defines the proper physical comportment for
women. Techniques of a craft and the associated techniques of the body
become techniques of the self through which the shaping of body movement
and action also shapes personhood.

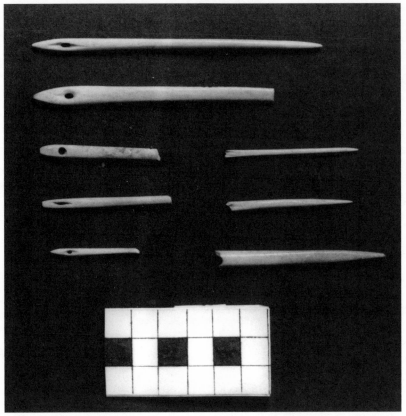

24. Bone needles for sewing and weaving found in Group 9N-8 at Copan. Photograph by Julia A. Hendon.

Girls living at Copan, Cerro Palenque, and Cuyumapa were initiated into this long process of training. Spindle whorls, small weights that sit at one end of the spindle used to spin thread, have been found in all three regions (Gonlin 2000; Hendon 1997, 2005).[2] Spinning thread is one of the most time-consuming steps in textile production and, as the *Codex Mendoza* shows, often involves children still too young to weave. Elderly women can also continue to spin even if they no longer have sufficient manual dexterity or eyesight to weave (O'Neale 1945; Stephen 1993). Bone needles, pins, and weaving picks from residential compounds in the inner zone of Copan demonstrate that women living there wove finely decorated cloth with brocaded or embroidered designs (Hendon 1997, 1999c). Brocading, in which supplementary weft (horizontal) yarns are inserted by the weaver into the warp by means of a pick, created cloth favored by royalty and members of the elite. This technique is more difficult than plain weaving, requiring precise counting and the ability to keep track of complicated patterns. Yet contemporary weavers say they enjoy making brocade because of the way it allows them to exercise their creativity and vary the design motifs over the length of the textile (Asturias de Barrios 1998; Chamoux 1993). Excavation of rural sites recovered only spindle whorls (Gonlin 1993, 2000). Given that the occurrence of some animal bone and human burials at several sites indicates that bone can survive in these deposits (Gonlin 1993:Table 4.24), the absence of implements that would allow the use of complicated techniques suggests that inner-zone weavers produced the elaborate textiles desired by rulers and members of noble houses.

POTTERY MAKING AS PARTICIPATORY KNOWLEDGE

My excavations in the ballcourt residential group at Cerro Palenque uncovered two kilns used for making fine paste vessels and figurines (Hendon 2002a, 2005; Hendon and Lopiparo 2004). Both were dome shaped and made of clay and had a wooden framework. Built at ground level on specially prepared stone pavements, they were located at one end of the group. One kiln was in front of the largest structure that closes off the south side of the courtyard. The other was to one side of this building, in an area behind the western building. Nearby trash pits contained broken molds, including one piece that corresponds exactly to the design on a piece of a fine paste vessel from the same deposit. A few badly burned pieces of pottery were found in association with one of the kilns, indicative of the problems sometimes encountered when firing pottery. Test pits excavated south of the kilns, into the area outside of the residential group's patio but still on the same raised terrace that supports the group and the ballcourt, suggest the presence of a third kiln or at least a work area with more production debris.

The trash deposit makes clear that molds were used to form the vessels to the desired shape, such as small bowls or jars. The kilns also fired three-dimensional clay figures made from molds (see chapter 5). Fine paste vessels, especially those classified by archaeologists as belonging to the Tacamiche group, connect to these figures through the use of the same raw material, similar means of preparation of that material, and the manufacturing techniques (Lopiparo, Joyce, and Hendon 2005). These small, flat-bottomed, straight-sided bowls receive much of their surface relief and

Three figurines from the residential group south of the ballcourt at Cerro Palenque.
Photographs by Julia A. Hendon.

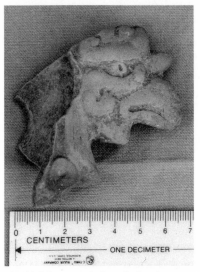

25.1. This bird decorates the hat of a figurine whistle that most likely was in the shape of a woman.

25.2. The torso of a figure with the left hand grasping a strap that runs diagonally across the chest.

25.3. This female figurine is wearing a short, netted cape clasped at the neck.

decoration from the mold, just as the detail of the figurines comes from the way in which the mold is prepared. Despite the adoption of molds, with all that method implies in terms of standardization and increased speed or efficiency of production, the vessels and figurines produced are not all alike. And a shift to molding did not eliminate other kinds of manipulation, including hand modeling of certain parts, the addition of pieces of clay to the molded form, and selective incision or punctation.

Manufacture of clay objects was dispersed among a number of communities in the lower Ulua valley. As at Cerro Palenque, evidence for production, such as kilns, molds, and clay-processing areas, is located in domestic space at these contemporaneous settlements, indicating that this was a part-time activity carried out by people also engaged in the activities of daily life and other forms of production. No single community monopolized manufacture or distribution (Hendon and Lopiparo 2004; Lopiparo 2003, 2007; Lopiparo and Hendon 2009). Although locally made, fine paste pottery and figurines connect these communities to a larger regional network of exchange of ideas and objects that included Cuyumapa to the east and extended west and north into Guatemala, Belize, and the Yucatan.

As part of a local theory of production at Cerro Palenque and in the lower Ulua valley more generally, molds may have facilitated the participation of a larger number of people, including children, in the making of fine paste vessels and figures while maintaining a complexity of design and precision in the reproduction of the image (Lopiparo 2006). The skill needed to use a mold is less than that needed to make one or to prepare the clay or to fire the objects, all actions that can be done by different people. This involves more people than just the craft specialist in the production of objects important to continuing the conditions of existence over time that form a coresident community of practice. The crafting of mold-made figurine whistles and fine paste vessels offers an opportunity for a heightening of social interaction and the display of embodied skills that turn the process into a kind of performance situated in domestic space rather than a strictly economic or practical activity (Mitchell 2006). Molds allow these performances to include both people trained in pottery production, who have a solid understanding of the craft and the properties of the materials, and those less skilled or perhaps even those ordinarily unconcerned with the manufacture of pottery altogether.

Unlike spinning and weaving, which were ongoing, even daily, activities, the production of pottery in the ballcourt residential group, judging by the scale of the features and the number of artifacts recovered, was not something that went on all the time. In fact, I would suggest that the use of the kilns was deliberately intermittent and tied to the celebration of events such as ballgames and feasts that brought outsiders into the monumental and residential space (see chapters 6 and 7). When the Cerro Palenque kilns were in use, the process would have attracted attention through the smells, heat, and noise that it produced. Even when not loaded and heated, the kilns would have impinged on the residents' awareness, embodying the memory of past events and the promise of future ones by their presence. Other signs of present or future action, such as the accumulation of clay, firewood, water, and objects in various stages of manufacture near one end of the patio, would affect how people moved through the area. My excavations in the open space of the patio did not reveal any concentration of artifacts indicative of a work area; in fact the patio was almost devoid of artifact deposits. I conclude from this that people, whether potting or doing other things, did not engage in these activities with any frequency away from the buildings of the group. The presence of trash deposits off to the side of the western building, mentioned above, as well as other deposits behind the southern building indicate that people were preparing food, cooking, and doing a number of other things, including making pottery. But if they were using the open space of the patio, they were carefully cleaning up after themselves.

Pottery production in the ballcourt residential group is a more visible event, perceptible to all present in the compound and even to those outside it, as the kiln gave off smoke and heat. The placement of one kiln directly in front of a building and the other close by creates greater opportunities for people living in or visiting the ballcourt residential group at Cerro Palenque to see and interact with the potters as they prepared clay, shaped the vessels and figurines in the molds, checked others to see if they were ready for firing, and did related tasks connected with the craft. The kilns' location contributes to the crafting of pottery as performance. At the same time, pottery production is also a private event in the sense that it occurs within a particular domestic space under the control of its residents, who were of sufficient social standing to live in the complex made up of the ballcourt and Great Plaza.

Contributing to the distinctive smell of the kilns being fired up was the scent of tobacco. Analysis of the flotation samples collected during my excavations by Shanti Morell-Hart identified four *Nicotiana spp.* seeds mixed in with the collapsed burned clay of the kiln behind the western structure. Tobacco was a precious substance to Mesoamerican peoples. Its smoke was believed to have curative and communicative powers (Chapman 1985:197–98). Dried tobacco leaves may have been placed in the kiln's firebox as it was heated. The occurrence of two fragments of what may be clay pipestems in the trash deposit behind the southern mound suggests that people smoked tobacco as well. In either case, the end result would have been smoke that formed part of the ritualization of making pottery and the sense of participating in a significant event.

PAPER MAKING AS KNOWLEDGE THAT
IS HEARD BUT NOT SEEN

PACO 2 affords another example of craft production in a residential setting. In his excavations of Groups 5–2 and 6–2, Fung (1995, 1996) found evidence that bark paper was made in both areas. A paved area behind the buildings at the southern end of Group 6–2 served as one location. Behind the eastern building of Group 5–2, again outside of the main patio area, is the second spot. No paper was preserved at PACO 2, but analysis of the paper in pre-Columbian codices indicates that it was made from the inner bark of plants in the Moraceae family, many species of which are native to the region and widely distributed (Nelson Sutherland 1986; von Hagen 1977). The same raw material may have been used for clothing (von Hagen 1943).

Barkbeaters, the distinctive tool used to make bark paper, have also been found at Copan and Cerro Palenque (Doonan 1996; Hendon 1987; Joyce 1985). Fung (1995:266) argues that proportional differences in the presence of barkbeaters between PACO 2 and both Copan and Cerro Palenque indicate that paper making was a more significant activity in Cuyumapa. The PACO 2 barkbeaters are made of fine-grained stone (Fung 1995:147). They are rectangular, with two flat faces, one of which is incised with parallel grooves that help distribute the force of the blow evenly across the bark and prevent holes or thin spots from developing as it is pounded and flattened (Leonard and Terrell 1980:14). A larger groove runs around the tool. This groove can be used to attach a handle, although the implement may also be grasped in the hand directly (Christensen and Martí 1979; Lenz 1961). Several other tools and containers are associated with the barkbeaters. Fung (1995:215–16, Figure 5.30) reports finding the remains of jars suitable for storing water, bowls, and quartzite cores. After the inner bark is stripped

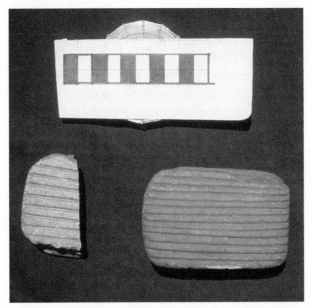

26. Two barkbeaters from PACO 2. Photograph by Christopher D. Fung, reproduced with permission.

from the outer and the sticky residue is washed off, the strips of bark must be kept moist. The jars provide a way to store water nearby, and the bowls would allow the strips to soak until they were needed. Sharp flakes for cutting and trimming can be easily and quickly knocked off the cores as needed to separate the outer and inner bark.

The bark paper work areas in Groups 6–2 and 5–2 of PACO 2 in Cuyu-mapa are entirely off the patio and behind buildings, although, as with the Cerro Palenque kilns, it is likely that at least some paraphernalia and facilities remained in place. Anvils, for example, are needed to support the bark while it is being pounded. These may have been made of wood and may not have been very portable depending on their size and weight (Bell 1983; von Hagen 1943; Woda and Zeller 2008). Unlike the kilns in the ballcourt residential group, no aspect of the process seems to have intruded physically onto the courtyard surrounded by the buildings themselves. People working on bark paper preparation may have been less visible because of their location behind buildings, but their work would have been audible over some distance. An account of paper making in Mexico records that "on our first trip to San Pablito . . . our attention was attracted by a clapping sound. We could hear that it was not the familiar sound of women making tortillas, and we were surprised when our guide told us that the sound came from women making paper" (Christensen and Martí 1979:12). Pounding is done cooperatively using the same anvil (Woda and Zeller 2008). Descriptions of bark cloth made in Polynesia emphasize its sonorous aspect and the pleasure the beaters get from creating rhythmic sequences during communal work sessions. Differences in the sound of anvils allow them to be identified and connected to the women who use them (Leonard and Terrell 1980). The musical sensibility of Mesoamerican peoples suggests that the aural aspect of the process may have been similarly related to community and identity.

The lack of preserved paper, a result of the perishability of its material, makes it like textiles in that researchers must use multiple lines of evidence to assess its purpose and meaning in Late to Terminal Classic Cuyumapa. At the time of the Spanish conquest, some groups, such as the Aztecs, Maya, and Mixtecs, used paper as a record-keeping medium. Most of these books or codices were burned, victims of Spanish missionary zeal (e.g., Tozzer 1978). The few that survived as well as others reproduced during the colonial period contain religious, political, astronomical, and calendrical information conveyed through a combination of numbers, words, and images (Sandstrom and Sandstrom 1986). I have no evidence that people in Cuyumapa used writing of the sort found at Copan. The lack of permanent texts may be as much a product of diverse social and political relations as of anything else. This does not rule out some kind of record keeping since visual imagery is an effective mnemonic device in many Mesoamerican societies and numerical notation is both widespread and ancient. Something like the semasiographic system of the Aztec and Mixtec, for example, in which meaning develops from visual conventions, placement, and methods of use, is possible (see Boone 1994b).

What interests me more as a likely reason for paper making at PACO 2 is the much wider use in Mesoamerica of bark paper to make costumes, ornaments, banners, figures, and other objects to be deployed in large-scale religious ceremonies that might involve an entire community or be state sponsored. Paper objects may have been used as well in more intimate offerings designed to address the concerns of individuals, families, and coresident groups. "It is difficult to exaggerate the importance of paper in the religious life of pre-Hispanic peoples" (Sandstrom 2001:442). Recognizing paper's central role, the Spanish forbade its manufacture and use after the conquest. Participants in ceremonies dressed in paper regalia, houses and temples were decorated with paper banners and other objects, things made from paper were burned or buried as offerings. People used paper to catch drops of their blood and then burned the strips, transforming the sacred bodily substance of their self-sacrifice into smoke as an offering to noncorporeal beings. Images of deities were made out of paper, and a body made from wood, clay, dough, *copal*, or other materials was dressed in paper clothes and ornaments. Paper also played a role in the treatment of illness. It was (and for some contemporary groups in Mexico still is), a medium with which to communicate with ancestors, deities, and other entities and forces that are not human, animate, or corporeal (Barrera Rivera, Gallardo Parrodi, and Montúfar López 2001; Dow 1982; Lenz 1961; Sahagún 1953–82; Sandstrom 1978, 2003; Sandstrom and Sandstrom 1986; Schele and Miller 1986; Seler 1991). Paper was something that all coresident communities of practice needed in order to participate in these religious practices.

WORKING SHELL AS HIDDEN KNOWLEDGE

The making of useful and decorative objects from shell and bone has been documented from several areas of urban Copan. The most complete contexts come from two patios (D and H) of the large multipatio complex of Group 9N-8. Structure 110B on the western side of Patio H is a building with four rooms. Three of them (Rooms 1–3) form a suite, the only door to the outside being in Room 1. A range of tools, objects, and raw materials were recovered from inside Room 2, at least some of which were used for making shell ornaments (Widmer 1997; see also Hendon 1987:227–32, 389–90). These include obsidian blades, cut and drilled pieces of marine shell, and stone work tablets. Some of these artifacts had been stored inside pottery vessels or on a shelf. One of the pots contained a broken star-shaped ornament, more pieces of which were found on the floor along with other pieces of shell. Two other vessels were full of dirt and burned material. Room 4 of the same structure as well as rooms in Structure 9N-115A and Structure 9N-61A (in Patio D) contained raw materials and finished objects of shell or bone (Gerstle and Webster 1990:62–71, 114–21, 168–70; Hendon 1987:184–87, 221–23, 389–90). All of these rooms can be entered from the outside directly through a doorway that gives access to the large terraces of the foundation platform. In addition, shell and bone that had been worked, whether by cutting, drilling, scraping, or other means, have been found in other Sepulturas patios and at Cerro Palenque in contexts suggesting that the working had been done on terraces and platforms (see Hendon 1987, 2005).

Shell working also took place in the Main Group during the Late Classic period, as indicated by a deposit of marine shell ornaments, obsidian tools, animal bone, and pieces of broken pottery vessels at the base of Temple 16 in the West Court of the Acropolis. Analysis of the marks and polish on the stone tools indicates that they were used to cut, groove, whittle, and drill shell, bone, and antler; the prevalence of marine shell in association with the tools suggests that this was the primary material worked. At the same time, the stone tools had also been used quite heavily to cut, scrape, and pierce meat or hide and wood or other vegetable material (Aoyama 1999:169).

The shell working in Structure 9N-110B Room 2 at Copan takes place in the most enclosed and least visible of the locations considered here. It is the most private, in the sense of most controllable by the participants and least subject to intrusion by others. This privacy, which suggests a desire to keep hidden what was being produced or the process of production itself, comes at a cost: the only natural light enters through the doorway into Room 1, which in turn has only one doorway onto the terrace. Artificial light may have been provided by what was burning in the two pots, but the amount of illumination would not have been great. It was not easy to cut, scrape, and shape brittle shells into complicated shapes and objects in this place. The other rooms, having direct access to the outside, would have been better lit and still fairly private if the workers stayed inside and did not take advantage of the large terrace. But they were not nearly as conducive to secrecy as Room 2. One wonders, in fact, if shell ornaments were actually being made in Room 2 or if the archaeological features there are better interpreted as evidence for the storage of tools and materials that would have been brought into Room 1 or even onto the terrace for working. I would agree that some of the objects found there may have been in storage; certainly not all of them were connected to the production of shell objects. It is the presence of fragments of shell and incompletely worked pieces in the floor area that is most indicative of actual processing in the room. These fragments had been cut or scraped off in the process of shaping the material and would not be present if all working took place elsewhere.

The activities that took place in front of Temple 16 are also restricted by its location since the courtyards on top of the Acropolis are among the most inaccessible areas of the Main Group. This deposit differs from the one in

Room 2 in that it also shows evidence of food processing. The manufacturing of shell items occurred in conjunction with preparing, and possibly eating, meat in front of one of the most important architectural symbols of royal power. Once again, as at Cerro Palenque, the performatory aspect of specialized production comes to the fore. This contrasts noticeably with the evident desire for concealment on the part of the shell workers in Patio H of Group 9N-8, offering another instance of the emphasis on controlling access, visibility, and information built into the design of inner-zone compounds at Copan and reflective of the contentious relationships among different memory communities

THE MORALITY OF KNOWLEDGE

Each of these crafts represents a form of knowledge that is transmitted across generations within communities of practice and among adults and children brought together through marriage, coresidence, proximity, trade, feasting, work exchanges, and other formal and informal mechanisms. This is an embodied and often tacit knowledge that is enacted through the mastery of the tangible and the abstract. It is learned through experience, repetition, and engagement of the senses. This knowledge is preserved in products of labor that are worn, used in daily tasks, presented as gifts, and offered as tribute to political leaders. Equipment, techniques, and materials come together to create systems of value and ways of defining people. These people become enmeshed in ongoing relations with certain other people, materials, and objects in the course of their everyday life. Such practices engender intersubjective relations between people and between people and objects that reflect culturally specific beliefs, the social context, and the influence of the materiality of the technology and its end products (Dobres 2000; Meskell 2004). The sampling of domestic tasks presented in this chapter reveals the spatiality of activities central to social reproduction. These spatialized tasks and the interactions they require among people and between people and objects become an important component of social identity.

The intersubjective identities that develop through people's responsibility for these and other actions of daily life are overlapping and to a certain extent situational, given that people did not devote all their time to making things like shell ornaments, pottery vessels, and bark paper. Set against particular backgrounds, these practices are contexts in which the social production of memory takes place by emphasizing certain relationships and events over others. The participation in multiple intersubjective identities shaped around different kinds of interactions that may occur in spatially distinct settings results in more than one community of practice. The decision that bark paper production at PACO 2 would be best done behind buildings was based no doubt on a wide range of factors, some of which one might characterize as pragmatic, others as symbolic. The result was some degree of spatial separation between some residents while they were making the paper and other residents who occupied themselves with other tasks. Identities built around action and what one does now include this particular kind of action and the awareness of the temporary separation it requires. The interaction of paper makers or weavers or potters or cooks or shell workers with one another and with their materials becomes a locus of memory that perpetuates their craft and allows the possibility of its continuation. Processes of remembering and continuity are sedimented in the body of expert and novice, as much a matter of perception and sensation, of the look, feel, smell, and shape of things, as of rules and measurements.

Actions that are based in and productive of a local history are an important part of this process. The residential compounds themselves and the consistent occurrence of such actions as making meals, shaping and firing pottery, spinning thread, pounding bark, and cutting shell in particular locations help turn these places into Douglas's memory machines by assisting in the construction of a sense of coherence and longevity in the experience of daily life. Preparing meals depends on memory, including a mnemonics of gesture and the senses: "From the moment one becomes interested in the process of culinary production, one notices that it requires a multiple memory: a memory of apprenticeship, of witnessed gestures, and of consistencies [of the food itself]" (Giard 1998:157). Like the impermanence of the ephemeral monuments discussed by Küchler (2002) and Forty (1999), that of any single meal makes it a generative resource for remembering and forgetting, for remembering at selected moments in time certain kinds of connections and suppressing or ignoring others.

Learning to master cotton, clay, bark, or shell marks the passage of time as children mature and become more adept. The textiles themselves create a record of the weaver's increasing skill and her ability to produce more complex pieces. One could say the same for pots, paper, and ornaments. Although this record may not have been deliberately saved as an archive of a child's development, many pieces would survive past their initial manufacture. This would be a perishable record made up of absence as well as presence as the objects broke, wore out, were given away, or entered into new domains of practice such as burials or caches. Even items used for everyday, mundane tasks, such as griddles for cooking tortillas or cloth for wrapping them, constitute a tangible entity around which remembering coalesces.

Diego de Landa, a sixteenth-century bishop of Yucatan, describes one public ceremony that endorsed the connection between social identity and productive action. During these rituals, "all the appliances of all their pursuits, from the priest to the spindles of the women" (Tozzer 1978:159) are rubbed with blue bitumen. Boys and girls are brought to the temple, where they are struck gently nine times on the backs of their hands to make sure that "they might become skillful workmen in the professions of their fathers and mothers" (Tozzer 1978:159). A daily task becomes part of a large-scale performance. But one doesn't have to search for evidence of special events or symbols to apply the concept of ritualization to weaving, making pottery, bark paper, or shell ornaments. All of these activities are ritualized in the sense that they involve specific ways of acting and engage people in actions that set them apart from others, at least temporarily. These specific ways of doing things involve techniques, "material resources, tools, operational sequences and skills, verbal and nonverbal knowledge, and specific modes of work coordination" (Pfaffenberger 1992:497) that support a set of social processes involving materials, equipment, ways of using that equipment, and knowledge (Dobres 2000).

The shaping or governing of a certain sense of self over another cannot be divorced from how people experience their own body and the world through that body (Connerton 1989; Hanks 1990; Rowlands 2005; Warnier 2001, 2006). An intimate connection exists between the body, materiality, the historical construction of subjectivity, and relations of power. This helps explain why not all possible subjectivities may be adopted in a particular social and historical context (Moore 1994; Sawicki 1994; Warnier 2001; Weedon 1997, 1999). It is not a matter of a failure to exercise free will or of an unconscious subjugation to structure but of the intersections of "the subjective expression of identity, the physical fact of being an embodied subject and the historical continuity of the subject" (Moore 1994:55). These are social processes both because they are shaped in the context of social relations and because they are subject to the constraints and influences of others encountered through those relations that govern the development of subjectivity.

The knowledge acquired through apprenticeship and performative action is part of a practice that defines men and women as weavers, potters, paper makers, and shell workers because of what they do. The *Florentine Codex* contains many comparisons between good and bad kinds of people. A good potter is "a judge of clay—thoughtful, deliberating . . . a knowing man, an artist," but a bad potter is "silly, stupid, torpid" (Sahagún 1953–82 Book 10:42). A good weaver makes her cloth "tight, [she] compresses it, beats it down; she warps . . . she puts the weft in place . . . she twists the thread," whereas the bad weaver does not merely turn out poorly woven cloth but is "lazy, indolent—a nonchalant, sullen worker; a deceiver," (Sahagún 1953–82 Book 10:36). Good weavers and potters are not just good, that is to say, skilled, at their craft. They are also good people. Even cooks are differentiated on the basis of ability and character: "The good cook is honest, discrete . . . an epicure. . . . The bad cook is dishonest, detestable" as well as someone who ruins the food (Sahagún 1953–82 Book 10:53). Knowledge is neither abstract nor detached from character and feeling. Underlying a Mesoamerican theory of production is an understanding that what a person comes to know helps define that person's identity (Zambrano and Greenfield 2004). This theory of knowledge emphasizes interaction with the tools and techniques integral to productive or habitual action. The acquisition of knowledge is more than the accumulation of facts or ideas. It is central to the moral growth of the individual, who is believed to be building her moral and spiritual character (her soul or heart) and thus turning into a more fully formed human being (Chamoux 1986). Rather than assume that girls should be ready to weave by a certain age, their parents feel that they will begin to learn when they are ready, when their soul or heart has developed sufficiently to enable them to learn (Greenfield 2004). Increased mastery of what people today would consider a practical skill becomes a critical component of the incorporation of children into a moral universe.

The rhythms and requirements of daily life ensure a certain repetition over time of particular combinations of action and interactions that implant an embodied identity over the course of a person's life. Memory and identity are intersubjective and reworked over time through action and relationships. Objects, even the unassuming grinding stone, contribute to the development of an embodied, nonconceptual understanding that shapes a sense of the body and of the self. The combination of particular kinds of places, as meaningful backgrounds, and actions produces communities of practice.

FIVE

Relational Identities and Material Domains

In this chapter I explore further the interaction between material objects, identity, and memory in particular spatial contexts through the concepts of the relational self and distributed personhood. A relational self is constituted through relationships not only with other people but with objects that are treated like persons. These objects, whether enchanting or humble, are personlike in part because they do enter into relationships. They also become a source of inference and interpretation. These qualities render such objects generative resources for remembering and forgetting because they are part of a process that extends the self beyond the individual biological organism, distributing it across time and space. The relational self contributes to a distributed personhood, in which "a person and a person's mind are not confined to particular spatio-temporal coordinates but consist of a spread of biographical events and memories of events, and a dispersed category of material objects, traces, and leavings" (Gell 1998:222).

The relational self can be contrasted with a view of the self as unitary and coterminous with the individual. Some scholars have argued that people in other places, cultures, and time periods do not experience the self as autonomous, isomorphic with the biological body, unique, strategic, and governed by a sense of maximizing individualism (Bulbeck 1998; Gell 1998; Graeber 2001; Moore 1994; Piot 1999). They contend that it is inappropriate to generalize a historically specific definition of the self, that of "Western individualism" or the "Western individual." Marilyn Strathern's study of personhood in Papua New Guinea, in which she identified the "dividual" as central to the Melanesian cultural construction of the self, has been influential in anthropological rethinking, although I do not apply her terminology in this book (Strathern 1988; see also Gell 1999a). The transcendent individual is often presented as a particularly Western conception, although, as LiPuma (1998) makes clear, to contrast Western individuals with non-Western dividuals is really to contrast an ideology to a set of practices; the self is more relational even in the West than philosophy has allowed historically. The contrast also poses the same problem of dichotomization and reification inherent in the premodern/modern or memory/history oppositions already discussed.

My interest in applying the idea of the self as relational and personhood as distributed across time and space and thus not bound to the life span or corporeal limits of any single person develops from my approach to social identity as being historically constituted. Given that the person cannot be separated from "the relationships of which it is constituted" (Piot 1999:18), the nature of those relationships becomes of central importance. I have already presented some that loom large in the development of the relational self in the context of domestic places, including those that develop out of the effort to sustain a community of practice over time. Practices of everyday life, such as preparing meals and engaging in creative acts of production or of political commemoration, such as the remembering (at Quirigua) and forgetting (at Copan) of Quirigua's capture of Copan Ruler 13, perpetuate certain kinds of connections. Relations occur not merely between people (living human beings) but also between people and animals and plants, material objects, and beings or entities that may not be alive (in a biological sense) or corporeal.

Such beings may be deceased members of the sociological house who have become ancestors and are assumed to be still vitally interested in its preservation (Gillespie 2000c, 2001; McAnany 1995). Or they may be beings that Spanish conquerors and modern scholars call gods. Sixteenth-century Europeans commentators on Mesoamerican religions assumed the existence of a series of individual and distinct deities (e.g., Tozzer 1978:108–11; Mendieta 1945 Vol. 1:94–96; see Proskouriakoff 1978; Marcus 1978; Klor de Alva 1989:26). The indigenous conception does not endorse this assumption of a pantheon of individual and individualistic "gods"; rather, it concerns itself with the interaction between natural forces, abstract principles, and lived experience (Burkhart 1989; Spores 1984; Thompson 1970). They represent "clusters of ideas, with a logical order. . . . Since the divine reality was multiple, fluid, encompassing the whole, its aspects were changing images, dynamic, never frozen, but constantly being recreated, redefined" (Hunt 1977:55; see also Klor de Alva 1993). Language, visual representation, and ritualized practices become ways to engage in this process of recreation and redefinition, processes that also recreate and maintain relations between this divine reality and people living on earth.

Two concepts that may be translated as "destiny" and "coessence" form the core of the Mesoamerican version of relational personhood (Monaghan 1998b). Both of these connect to Mesoamerican ideas about the spatial and temporal ordering of existence. A person's destiny is tied to the temporal system because it is shaped, although not determined, by his or her day of birth. Dates (both the named day and its coefficient) carry with them implications for profession, character, and what one might call fortune but do not entirely determine the realization of that destiny (see Durán 1971). People must work to achieve or mitigate their destiny through appropriate behavior. Personhood is developed through participation in social interactions and relations that make up a local theory of production and sustain a "shared 'way of being' " (Watanabe 1992:90). Participation provides evidence of one's moral status and social identity. This shared understanding of the consequences of temporal positioning forms part of how Mesoamerican peoples define themselves in both space and time.

The daily movement of the sun makes visible the passage of time and provides a way of orienting the body. The sun becomes responsible for and linked to the destinies associated with the diurnal periods defined through its movements. The interaction between temporality and human action means that destiny is both "part of the body *and* subject to an outside power—the internal and external complexly intersecting" (Monaghan 1998b:139). Possessing a destiny, and thus being a person, are not automatic, however, because certain moments in time are in a sense outside of time. The 365-day calendar, as noted, divides the year into 18 months of 20 days each plus 5 days at the end. Being born during this 5-day period leaves one without a name, a character, or a social identity.

A Mesoamerican perspective on the self as relational also considers it to have multiple parts or elements, not all of which are circumscribed by the physical body or are an innate characteristic of the mind. Such features are often referred to as coessences or souls (Gossen 1996; Meskell and Joyce 2003; Monaghan 1998b; Watanabe 1992). As Gary Gossen writes, "Meso-american souls are fragile essences that link individuals to the forces of the earth, the cosmos, and the divine. They provide this link because they origi-nate or reside outside the body of their human counterpart" (1996:81–82). As extrasomatic essences, souls may be shared, linking an individual with other beings, not all of which are human, animate, or alive. Something of a person's coessence is said to enter into material objects, such as tools, or nonhuman entities, such as agricultural crops, that people use or produce or engage with as part of their daily lives (Laughlin and Karasik 1988). Bark-paper figures used in curing rites make visible the intangible essence of powerful entities or deities (Dow 1982). An important coessence often takes the form of an animal but may also be a natural force or a plant. It can be encountered in visions and dreams, during which souls may share a con-sciousness. Although separable, the experiences of this coessence and of the embodied person affect one another, damage to one often resulting in ill-ness in the other (Gossen 1996).

Coessences matter to the issues of destiny and the spatiotemporal order. They connect entities that seem to be completely separate because they belong to different phenomenal categories or states of existence: human, animal, or vegetable, for example, or alive or dead. These entities can, how-ever, be linked through a shared temporal position determined by when they were born or came into existence. It might be assumed that personhood defined in this way necessarily restricts itself to biological beings that come into existence through an actual birthing process, but Mesoamerican ideas about the self are not so literal. Coessences may be such natural phenomena as rain or lightning. This, coupled with the fact that material objects such as images—what the Spanish refer to as idols—and buildings can be ani-mated through their production, treatment, or use in the context of the same shared spatiotemporal order, indicates that birth encompasses a larger range of actions and events and characterizes a broader range of beings.

Attempts by Spanish religious authorities in the sixteenth and seventeenth centuries to define personhood as a property of individuals possessed of an integral body, mind, and soul continually run up against the native willingness to apply the same words to and to conceptualize as similar all these supposedly separate phenomenal classes: "Individual selves are only partial expressions of humanity [and] the coessence phenomenon indicates that such a conception need not be based on an absolute assumption of human uniqueness" (Monaghan 1998b:144). These shared features make people, buildings, and material objects indexes and sometimes icons of one another.

DISTRIBUTED PERSONHOOD AND PERSONLIKE OBJECTS

Mesoamerican concepts of coessences and relational personhood jeopardize any attempt to deny agency to things one might assume are inert, inanimate, deceased, nonbiological, or intangible. The ability of such things to enter into relationships stems directly from their status as persons or parts of persons. Here I consider objects that are literally personlike in that they look like human bodies. These objects may be placed in the category of coessences because they can be set in time and space, are defined through the social relations and actions of which they are part, contribute to the framing of a moral discourse about appropriate personhood, and can share animating substances as a result of how people interact with them. They are born through human action in a particular moment and location. They possess a humanlike bodily orientation, which allows them to be placed within the spatiotemporal order that humans inhabit and through which persons are defined. These sets of objects include stone sculpture and clay figurines, elements of the extensive object repertoire associated with domestic places in pre-Columbian Honduras. Sculpture and figurines lend themselves to the process of stretching identities across time and space because they are both icons of the embodied and corporeal aspect of the self and indexes, indicative of a range of connections that support the creation of relational identities through their form, material, appeal to the senses, and methods of use.

Sculpture and figurines that look like people are only part of the representational repertoire created by sculpting images out of stone or modeling them out of clay. This repertoire includes images of plants, animals, fantastical creatures such as the reptilian embodiment of mountains decorating

27.1. A whistle depicting a couple embracing, imported into Copan from central Honduras. Found below a child's grave in Patio D of Group 9N-8, it epitomizes the personlike nature of these objects. Photograph by Julia A. Hendon.

27.2. The side view shows the whistle mouthpiece projecting from the rear of the figure. Photograph by Julia A. Hendon.

Temple 22 on the Acropolis, and hybrids, such as the personification of the corn plant as a beautiful young man with corn stalks growing out of his head, also found on this building. In fact, hybridity runs through the visual imagery discussed here, reinforcing the "disjunction between a contemporary notion of species boundaries and the extension of personhood across apparent natural disjunctures, including those between animals and plants" (Meskell and Joyce 2003:89) and underscoring how Mesoamerican concepts of personhood do not privilege the biological human over other forms or classes of coessences.

INTIMATE REPRESENTATIONS:
FIGURINES AND WHISTLES

Most of the figurines and whistles excavated in these regions were found in trash deposits behind the residential buildings or, in the case of Cuyumapa, near ballcourts. This suggests that figurine whistles were used by residents and then discarded at some point afterward. Residents of Cerro Palenque and of the inner zone of Copan sometimes placed figurines in ritual caches (Joyce 1991, 1993a; Gerstle and Webster 1990). In Copan, the region where researchers have burials to study, one does sometimes see figurines or whistles placed in graves, but ceramic vessels and items of personal adornment that were worn on the body are much more common funerary offerings (Hendon 1991).

As noted in chapter 4, lower Ulua valley figurine whistles are made from molds. This is also the case for many of the Cuyumapa examples. The collection from excavations in Groups 9N-8, 9M-22, and 9M-24 in Copan's inner zone contains a mix of molded and hand-modeled objects. Most of the molded ones are made from clay not found in the Copan valley, and only one mold was found, in Patio D of 9N-8. The clay and design of the Copan mold-made ones resemble closely those used in north-central Honduras, including the lower Ulua valley, demonstrating that a good part of the figurine whistles used at Copan were imported from societies living east of the Copan valley in the Naco, Comayagua, or lower Ulua valleys (Hendon 2003d).

I refer to these objects as figurine whistles because at least some of them were musical instruments, with a mouthpiece extending from the figure's back or tail. In some cases, extra sound chambers inside the body or additional holes have been pierced through the clay back to allow a person to modulate the tone of the whistle and produce notes on the scale. Such objects have been labeled ocarinas, but I have not tried to distinguish between

28. A whistle in the form of a howling animal from Group 9N-8 at Copan.
Photograph by Julia A. Hendon.

whistles, capable of producing a single note, and ocarinas since the degree
of elaboration of the musical instrument can be difficult to determine when
the piece is fragmentary. In fact, it can be difficult even to distinguish between objects that were intended to make music and those that were intended to be effigies alone.

These clay men, women, children, owls, bats, coatimundis, monkeys,
jaguars, dogs, turtles, and other forms of birds and animals are among the
most engaging of objects to the modern eye, which explains their popular-
ity with private collectors. They exemplify the enchanting quality that Gell
writes of, in which an object's complexity draws in the eye and holds the
attention as the viewer tries to grasp the full range of the design. As three-
dimensional objects, they have uneven surfaces with a tactile presence (see
MacGregor 1999). This tactility and their miniaturization produce a sensory
impression that recalls the sensations experienced when touching small
people, that is to say, children, or small animals, such as the young deer or
rabbits that Maya women raised for sacrifice or to serve at feasts, or the birds
they raised for their feathers (Hendon 2006c; Pohl and Feldman 1982).

Figurine whistles resist the usual kind of archaeological analysis. Their visual richness has made them difficult to force into the standard sorts of typologies that archaeologists like to construct to facilitate comparison and quantification (see Butler 1935; Doonan 1996; Lopiparo 2003; Rands and Rands 1965; Schlosser 1978; Tercero 1996; Willey 1972, 1978). In this, they exemplify how people's abilities to perceive and compare physical objects are much more sophisticated than their capacity for putting those discriminations into words (D. Miller 1987). This sort of analysis becomes even harder because any attempt to define a separate class of objects proves difficult. The items researchers want to identity as figurines or whistles often cannot, when broken, be discriminated from other kinds of objects made out of the same sorts of clay that are also icons and indexes of the natural, the human, or the supernatural world. Not all three-dimensional objects made from clay are called figurines. Masks, pendants, and other sorts of objects, some of uncertain use, share similar processes of molding, modeling, incising, and shaping but are not all effigies of humans or animals (see Lopiparo 2003 for a range of examples). Sometimes much larger three-dimensional figures of humans or animals are found. These are not usually labeled figurines because of their size, such as the example from Patio C of Group 9N-8 excavated in 1981 according to unpublished excavation records on file with the Instituto Hondureño de Antropología e Historia.

If one detaches oneself from the archaeological obsession with classification, however, and thinks about these objects as part of a living system of signification, materiality, and knowledge that people regularly engaged with, a new perspective emerges. This view argues that figurine whistles are part of a larger material domain that involves taking that most plastic of substances, clay, and shaping it into images that may be free-standing, may be added to some kind of container or other sort of object, or may be worn on the body as a pendant or other kind of ornament. They index the transformative manipulation of a substance through the addition of other substances, such as water or grit, shaping, adding and removing, sometimes painting, polishing, or slipping (technically, adding a clay-based wash often of a different color), and subjecting to heat. The process of manipulation and transformation is essentially identical to that used to produce pottery vessels, just as these objects' capacity to be images of something else parallels the ways in which vessels become fields for imagery produced by incising, painting, modeling, appliquéing, and other techniques. It is also reminiscent of the way living creatures were first created from water or blood and corn and parallels how the human body is shaped through the modification of teeth and bone and adorned through the incorporation of earspools, labrets, and other objects. Like the early period figurines from Playa de los Muertos discussed in chapter 2, these later examples connect with pottery vessels because their emulation of living bodies, whether human or not, indexes the body's status as a container of material and intangible substances that may be held, dispensed, and shared. These connections lead me to suggest that much of what I argue about the personlike status of figurine whistles could be extended to these other manifestations of the manipulation and transformation of clay. Nevertheless, I want to limit my discussion here to figurine whistles because I think the combination of their small size, three-dimensionality, and anthropomorphism makes them especially personlike.

Many of the human figures look young but are not children. To me, they look like people in the prime of life, old enough to be full-fledged, active, vigorous adult members of society. Some of these young adults have teeth that look like they have been filed or artificially reshaped, mimicking the fashion among many people. In a study of patterns of dental modification at Copan, Rhoads (2002) noted identical kinds of notching and filing (see also Tiesler Blos 1999). Older faces are also depicted, with many wrinkles and the sunken cheeks of a person who has lost some teeth. These old people, who have open, twisted mouths or faces, seem to be in some pain or at least more troubled than their young counterparts. (Hendon 2003d). An unusual head from PACO 2 has heavy cheeks and a protruding lower jaw (Fung 1995:Figure 4.10).

Although female figures predominate in the time of Playa de los Muertos tradition, Late Classic figurine traditions depict both men and women as well as some figures of indeterminate or possibly alternative gender. Cultural beliefs about gender among the Maya, Aztec, and other groups are not rigidly binary. Natural forces are sometimes personified as beings that are both male and female or neither or that change genders. Spanish condemnation of behavior, including but not limited to sexual practices, further supports the presence of people of other genders in society (Hunt 1977; Joyce 2000a; Klein 2001; Looper 2002; Sigal 2000). Analysis of Burial XXXVII-8, an early (ca. fifth century CE), high-status interment from Copan's Main Group reveals that the individual's morphology combines male and female traits, leading Storey (2005:331) to conclude that the person was "what is called an 'intersexed' or 'transgendered' person, an individual with both male and female characteristics." In social terms, gender is developed through dress and participation in certain kinds of productive action, such as weaving, all of which are highlighted in the figurines (Hendon 1997, 1999a, 2002b, 2006c).

On the whole, the human figures are simply dressed. Headdresses and hairstyles are varied. Some are quite elaborate, taking the form of bird, jaguar, or other animal heads, and suggest some kind of costume for dancing or other kind of ritualized performance. Working with objects from several smaller settlements on the valley floor north of Cerro Palenque, Jeanne Lopiparo (2003) has found that some headdresses are restricted to one site or another, while others are more widely distributed. Although I have fewer heads in the Cerro Palenque sample and often the headdresses are too fragmentary to determine their shape, I can detect an emphasis on birds. One partial figurine wears a hat with an oversized bird's head and neck rising up from the side of the hat, and several others wear costumes of feathers with a bird's head headdress.

The most common form of head covering is a cloth turban, however. The various ways in which the cloth is folded, decorated, and tied create a range of intricate designs. Some people wear headbands, the clay incised to indicate the texture or pattern of the cloth. Feathers may be attached to the front of headbands. Women bind most of their hair tightly to their head with the band but allow one lock to hang loose. A fancier headband, with three beads attached to the front, is used to tie up short hair, which rises up above the headband. Another headdress, usually worn by women, is a wide-brimmed hat with a big bow in the front. The hair, when shown, is carefully cut and very neat.

Like many other tangible coessences, especially humans and animals, figurines and whistles have an embodied spatial orientation that defines front and back. This orientation implies movement through space, which helps create a temporal orientation of past behind and present or future ahead (Todes 2001). They are "rigidly frontal" (Schlosser 1978:51) in their design, which makes them look quite different when viewed from different angles. The backs are often much less detailed and may in fact present mostly a smoothed, somewhat undulating clay surface with perhaps a mouthpiece and holes. These simple backs, which may be modeled by hand, further facilitate the participation of less skilled people in the manufacture of figurines at Cerro Palenque discussed in the previous chapter. The greater design complexity of the front, coupled with the fact that when viewed from this angle one is always staring directly into the face of a human figure (and often so with animals), resonates with the emphasis on the head, vision, and angles of view that makes sight one of the most important senses in the Mesoamerican sensorium and an embodiment of interest in and control over the actions of others (Houston and Taube 2000; Howes 1991; Meskell and Joyce 2003).

The poses of the human and animal figures may strike one as being rather static. Figures stand, sit, or sometimes recline, always maintaining their frontal orientation. As in the Copan and Quirigua monuments, action is implied by what the figures hold or wear or by the positions of their arms and hands. The pair of figurines from the cache in Group 1 at Cerro Palenque (see chapter 3) illustrates this. Dressed in a skirt and necklace, the woman stands with her left arm raised and her hand clasping her hair. Balanced on her head is a jar with two handles that looks like the actual jars used to carry water found at the site. The male figurine wears a helmet in the shape of a bird's head and a costume made of feathers. He holds a musical instrument, a conch-shell trumpet, again referring to the real-life activities of the communities of practice based in the residential place. An almost complete figurine from Patio E of Copan's Group 9N-8 depicts a seated adult of indeterminate sex holding a smaller figure on its lap, who sits with its hands under its chin. This smaller figure has a humanlike body but an animal head, possibly that of a rabbit. The pair makes a relationship of coessence visible. The head of the larger figure is missing, so it's impossible to tell if it too was a hybrid creature like its smaller companion.

Study of figurine whistles from other Late Classic to Terminal Classic sites in the lower Ulua valley expands the repertoire of implied action to include women holding infants or young animals, sometimes suckling them, and women carrying ceramic pots under one arm or holding them in their lap. The contents of the bowl may be indicated by a set of small balls of clay that resembles the way corn tamales are depicted in other forms of Maya art. In other cases, the vessel looks like the fine paste ones made and used at these sites for ritualized actions connected to feasts. Other figures carry a bag or pot on their back (Joyce 1993b; Lopiparo 2003).

These small clay images have been found in all three areas I discuss here but with some interesting differences in abundance. Fung (1995:136–45, 176–78) recovered several figurine whistles in his excavations of Groups 5–2 and 6–2 at PACO 2 in Cuyumapa, and the more limited test pitting at other sites in the valley indicates that they were in use more generally. Their presence was not confined to residential areas. John Fox (1994:201, 210, 217, 223, Figure 45) unearthed figurine fragments in the trash deposits associated with the ballcourts at PACO 2, 14, and 15. Use of figurine whistles spans the Late to Terminal Classic occupation at Cerro Palenque (Joyce 1985:329–30, Figures 69, 70). The distribution of figurine whistles after the community grew so large was not uniform among the different residential groups, however. I found many more pieces in my excavations of the ballcourt residential group than were found in the other residential groups excavated previously, on the order of ninety fragments to fewer than ten. People living in the inner zone around Copan's Main Group possessed many figurine whistles. In 1984, I reviewed all the objects made of clay that were not obviously containers, placed in the catchall category of "other ceramic artifacts," from the excavations of Groups 9N-8, 9M-22, and 9M-24. I found over five hundred whole or fragmentary figurine whistles (Hendon 1987, 1991, 2003d; see also Gerstle 1987, 1988). Studies of other inner-zone residential compounds and of the area south of the Acropolis where the last ruler lived report the presence of these objects (Doonan 1996; Willey, Leventhal, Demarest, and Fash 1994). But only sites 11D11–2 and 34C-4-2, the two largest of the Copan foothill sites examined by Gonlin (1993:386, Table 4.11), yielded figurines, and they numbered far fewer than in the inner-zone residences.

Any claim for differences in occurrence must remain only loosely quantitative owing to variations in the size of excavations and the possibility that in some cases the less diagnostic fragments may have been counted as pieces of broken vessels. However, I do feel comfortable arguing that two patterns may be discerned. One, found in Cuyumapa, argues for the use of figurine whistles in both the private activities (in the sense of more controlled and involving fewer participants) taking place where people live and the public activities (in the sense of incorporating larger numbers of people from more diverse locations) associated with ballgames. The occurrence of approximately equal numbers of figurine whistles in Groups 5–2 and 6–2, the two most thoroughly excavated residential spaces in Cuyumapa, leads me to conclude that similar levels and types of use prevailed here. The other pattern, characteristic of Copan and Cerro Palenque, suggests a more uneven distribution of figurine whistles. In the case of Cerro Palenque, it would be the memory community living near the ballcourt that has more; in the Copan valley, those living around the Main Group.

One explanation for the disparities in abundance of figurine whistles at Cerro Palenque is that the people living in the large group near the ballcourt were responsible for making such objects not only for their own use but also for distribution to others in their community and to other communities in the valley, including those manufacturing figurine whistles of their own. The difference in the abundance of figurine whistles between the inner zone and the small rural households in the Copan valley cannot be explained in the same way since little to no production took place in either location. The variation here brings one's attention more firmly to bear on the issue of why people living in the inner zone around the Main Group and in the two more substantial rural residences, as well as in all Cerro Palenque and Cuyumapa residences investigated, wished to interact with figurines and whistles and what forms that interaction may have taken, a question I address in the next chapter. To understand these desires, however, I must look beyond the intimately scaled personlike objects of clay to consider the larger-scale personlike objects sculpted in stone.

PUBLIC VISIONS: ARCHITECTONIC AND FREE-STANDING SCULPTURE

Carved stone images are less common than figurines or whistles in the three areas I discuss and less evenly distributed, suggesting differences in the ability and the desire to deploy them. The people living at PACO 2 did not decorate their houses with sculpture, and test pitting of other residential sites did not reveal any. Instead, Cuyumapans placed sculpture in ballcourts (table 2). The ballcourts at PACO 14 and PACO 5 both have markers, specially shaped pieces of stone placed in the sloping side walls of the court and used as part of the game (Fox 1994:143–44, 155, Figure 12). The marker at PACO 14 has an oval shape. Although not conventionally representational, it stands out from the rest of the building material of the ballcourt by its shape. The marker at PACO 5 takes a more unusual form. It looks like two truncated triangles joined together. It is broken, and the pattern may have continued for at least one more triangle. The ballcourt at PACO 2 was too poorly preserved to determine if a stone marker had been present, but Fox (1994:172–76, Figure 32) did find an unusual arrangement in association with a low platform west of the ballcourt itself. Two long stones placed parallel to one another, like the flanking structures of a ballcourt, and a third, smaller stone placed between them lay on a surface made of orange-brown sand. Fox suggests that the stones form a model or effigy of a ballcourt and notes that the longer ones were placed at the same orientation as that of the court at PACO 2 even though the platform itself is oriented differently. When the platform was enlarged, a new surface buried the ballcourt effigy.

TABLE 2. Cuyumapa Sculpture

LOCATION	DESCRIPTION
PACO 2 platform west of ballcourt	Ballcourt effigy on platform surface
PACO 5 ballcourt	Ballcourt marker in the shape of two truncated triangles set into the slanted side wall of the court
PACO 14 ballcourt	Oval ballcourt marker set into slanted side wall of the court

The architecture of the earlier occupation at Cerro Palenque is marked by a much more substantial use of sculpture that was built into the exterior façades of several buildings in the residential area of CR-44 Group 2 (table 3). At least one of these buildings also had sculpture decorating the interior walls of its room (Joyce 1985:403–4). Although many pieces were too small or broken to determine the motif, three elements may be discerned (Joyce 1985:360–62, Figure 74, 1991:101–2). Rectangular blocks carved with rings are the first element. These may be eyes. The second element is represented by a carved head that would have projected from the wall, held in place by its tenon. The head is that of a bird and is reminiscent of birds painted on some Ulua polychromes (Joyce, personal communication) and further underscores the preference for bird imagery at the site. The third is a schematically rendered humanlike figure that may have been part of a group set on the roof of one of the buildings of Group 2. The overall shape is triangular, widest at the top, where two eyes are carved, with a central and lower section defined by indentations. The central area, or torso, wears a pectoral. The lower segment, suggestive of the legs, has a circular indentation. The form of these beings bears a striking resemblance to the ballcourt marker of PACO 5, although the marker has a plain surface with no suggestion of features or clothing. Similar figures come from Travesia, another large center contemporaneous with Late Classic Cerro Palenque located to its north (Stone 1941:Figure 49), although the Travesia examples are made more overtly anthropomorphic by the addition of a nose and mouth. Several free-standing large stone vessels in a private collection in La Lima, Honduras, are also reported to have come from Cerro Palenque.

During the Terminal Classic, the addition of sculpture to buildings be-

TABLE 3. Cerro Palenque Sculpture

LOCATION	DESCRIPTION
CR-44 Group 2	Many fragments associated with three buildings
	Most are part of the exterior decoration, but at least some came from a room. These include:
	• Schematic anthropomorphic figures
	• Rectangular blocks with rings that may be eyes
	• Bird's head
	Free-standing large stone vessels
CR-157 Group 1	Plain stela
Great Plaza Ballcourt residential group, western structure	Rectangular- to ovoid-shaped piece with tenon associated with an earlier version of the structure
Great Plaza Ballcourt residential group, southern structure	Fragment whose shape could not be determined
Great Plaza Ballcourt	Ballcourt marker
Isolated mound north of the Great Plaza	Squared column with rounded end found near this mound, although original location unknown

came less common but is found in residential and monumental locations. One example from a domestic context comes from the ballcourt residential group where I excavated a tenoned piece from the collapsed wall debris of the front of the western structure. The part that would have projected from the wall is broken. What is left is roughly rectangular to oval in shape. A curved line and a small circle were pecked into the surface near the broken end, suggesting the beginnings of some sort of design. A second find that may be a piece of sculpture comes from excavations near the large southern structure, although it is too fragmentary to allow determination of its shape (Hendon 2005). Excavations in the low patio platform of Group 1 revealed that a large slab of green chlorite schist formed part of a line of stones on the platform's summit, suggesting to Joyce (1991:48) that it may have served as a plain stela. A plain, round ballcourt marker is made from volcanic stone rather than from the limestone used to build the ballcourt. A squared column with a rounded end was found near the isolated mound that sits

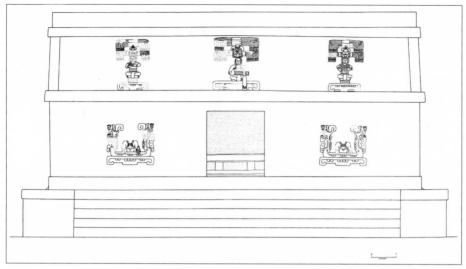

29. The layout of the sculptural elements forming the façade of Structure 9N-82 (Group 9N-8, Patio A) can be clearly seen in this reconstruction. Drawing by Barbara Fash, reproduced courtesy of Dumbarton Oaks Research Library and Collection, Trustees for Harvard University, Washington, D.C.

north of the Great Plaza and is connected to it by raised walkways. The original location of the column is unclear, but it may have been associated with the large structure (Joyce 1991:101–2).

Copan is well known for its sculpture, which has been heavily studied as examples of a distinctive stylistic tradition, as visual texts rich with symbolism, and as political documents manifesting royal authority (see Ashmore 1991; Baudez 1994; B. Fash 1992; W. Fash 2001; Schele and Miller 1986; Webster 1989). Most of these works come from the Main Group and take the form of architectonic decoration or large free-standing monuments such as stelae or altars. Some residences in the inner zone of settlement also feature sculpted elements as part of their exterior façade or interior walls. Tables 4 and 5 summarize the architectural and free-standing sculpture from Groups 9N-8 and 9M-22 (Group 9M-24 has no sculpture). When outside, decoration is found in two registers, a lower one flanking or surrounding the main doorway and an upper one. Although most often found on the front of the building's exterior, decoration sometimes continues around onto the sides or even the back of the building. Even in the dense settlement created by the press of buildings, figures in the upper register would have been visible from

TABLE 4. Sculpture from Group 9N-8 in the Inner Zone at Copan

LOCATION	DESCRIPTION
PATIO A, STRUCTURE 9N-80	
Building exterior, position unknown	Three blocks, two carved with a spiral and one not identifiable
In courtyard in front of building's stairs	Altar (stone cylinder with no decoration)
PATIO A, STRUCTURE 9N-81	
Lower register of front exterior wall	Two heads of a monkey or jaguar with bat headdresses
PATIO A, STRUCTURE 9N-82	
Upper register of all four exterior walls of the center structure	Eight seated anthropomorphic figures
Lower register of front exterior wall of the center structure	Two torsos of anthropomorphic figures set in the open mouth of a reptilian creature. More fully preserved figure holds half of a conch shell like those used by scribes for paint or ink.
Interior of main room of the center structure	Bench with hieroglyphic inscription. Two anthropomorphic figures support the bench. Two more figures are carved on the plinths at each end of the bench.
Construction fill of final version, dates to earlier version of the center structure	Anthropomorphic figure with simian face holding a shell paint pot and writing stylus
Stairs of the foundation platform, which were plastered over during final phase	Blocks carved with hieroglyphs
PATIO A, STRUCTURE 9N-83	
Lower register of front exterior wall	Frieze of T-shaped blocks
Courtyard in front of building's stairs	Altar
PATIO B, STRUCTURE 9N-67	
Lower register of front exterior wall	Frieze of blocks set diagonally on either side of a notched square. Repeats on both sides of the entrance to the main room
Behind the building in the collapsed fill of the foundation, may have decorated an earlier version of the building	Bird's head and L-shaped piece
PATIO B, STRUCTURE 9N-74	
Main room of northern building	Square blocks found in wall collapse that probably formed a frieze on the room walls

PATIO B, STRUCTURE 9N-74 OR STRUCTURE 9N-67

Mixed in with the rubble from collapsed walls on the terrace between these two buildings, which share a common platform   Seated human figure

PATIO C, STRUCTURE 9N-69

Lower register of front exterior wall	Blocks carved with the date of 8 Ahau
Upper register of front exterior wall	Short hieroglyphic inscription
Rear wall of main room	Frieze of blocks representing a serpent

PATIO D, STRUCTURE 9N-60A

Lower register of front exterior wall	Frieze of T-shaped blocks
On the bench of the main room. May have been set in an interior wall or may have been moved from somewhere else	Jaguar's head

PATIO H, STRUCTURE 9N-110C

Mixed in the collapse of an exterior wall   Block carved with a mat design

---

at least some vantage points outside the confines of the compound itself (Hendon 1992).

Some of these elements project from the face of the wall, held in place by stone tenons that fit into the masonry of the wall. The three-dimensionality of these pieces adds to their visual impact and recalls the frontal emphasis of the figurines. In other cases, the builders used specially shaped blocks to create decorative friezes. Free-standing or tenoned sculptures were set in niches, as in the case of the figures on the front façade of the central building of the three structures that share a platform and are known as Structure 9N-82 (Group 9N-8 Patio A). Here the niche itself takes the form of the open mouth of a reptilian creature like that featured on Temples 11 and 22 (W. Fash 1989). A free-standing figure found in Patio B of this same group and a human-monkey hybrid scribe that dates from an earlier version of Structure 9N-82 may also have been set in niches for display, as were four heads from Group 9M-22 (Hendon, Fash, and Aguilar P. 1990; Sheehy 1991).

The kinds of things depicted in the sculpture of Groups 9N-8 and 9M-22 vary, but an emphasis on anthropomorphic figures and animals, especially jaguars, monkeys, and bats, is apparent. Some of these creatures combine animal and human attributes. Of particular interest to my consideration of object agency and memory is the practice of placing anthropomorphic

TABLE 5. Sculpture from Group 9M-22 in the Inner Zone at Copan

LOCATION	DESCRIPTION
PATIO A[a]	
Center of courtyard	Cylindrical plain altar
PATIO A, STRUCTURE 9M-194B	
Exterior walls, possibly all four sides	Nine round, flat-surfaced blocks
Upper register of all four exterior walls	Eight hybrid figures with jaguar faces and anthropomorphic hands and arms
Upper register of all four exterior walls	Sixteen macaw heads placed near the hybrid figures
Lower register of front and side exterior walls	Two free-standing fantastical animal heads and one anthropomorphic head. May have been set in niches in the walls
PATIO B, STRUCTURE 9M-189	
Courtyard floor in front of the building[b]	Free-standing head of an anthropomorphic figure

[a] Several pieces of sculpture are reported from a room of Structure 9M-193B, the platform of Structure 9M-196, and in the courtyard that may have been moved from their original location during the final phase of occupation of the group.

[b] The excavator of Group 9M-22, Patio A has argued that this head was originally part of the architectonic decoration of Structure 9M-195B, where it was set in a niche in the lower register of the building's exterior wall (Sheehy 1991).

figures on the upper register of important buildings. This is the case for Structure 9N-82 of Patio A in Group 9N-8 as well as in another inner-zone group, 8N-11, and in Ruler 16's residential compound behind the Acropolis, Group 10L-2. The residents of these places invested time and energy in the creation of permanent, idealized human figures on houses.

The central building of Structure 9N-82 was decorated with eight seated human figures: three on the front, three on the back, and one on each side (W. Fash 1989). Carved almost in the round, the figures project beyond the plane of the wall and are placed more than five meters above the level of the patio. Structure 10L-32 also features seated figures, three on the front and three on the back (Andrews and Fash 1992). The figures on Structure 8N-66s do not include the lower body. Eight figures, with heads, arms, and torsos only, are arranged on the upper façade like the Group 9N-8 full figures but here placed in niches. Their arms are folded as if they are leaning on the niche, and the palms of their hands face each other in front of their chest (Webster, Fash, Widmer, and Zeleznik 1998).

Structure 9M-195B of Group 9M-22 presents a somewhat different design. The same figure repeats on all four sides of the building. It depicts a fusion of animal and human features unlike the other three examples just described. No definitive reconstruction of these figures has been put forward, but they combine eminently human hands and arms with an animal face (see Sheehy 1991:Figure 6). The face is that of a jaguar with the addition of other features such as feathers that signal its status as a supernatural creature. The presence of the human limbs has led archaeologists to refer to the faces as masks worn by the human figure whose arms and hands are visible. But really this is a hybrid that makes visible diverse components of this creature's identity and represents the coming together of coessences.

In the Main Group, hieroglyphic inscriptions and carved images often occur together on the same monument or building. This is less common in the rest of the valley. A few examples of hieroglyphic writing are found set into the exterior walls of especially well-built inner-zone residences. On one building in Group 9N-8, Structure 9N-69 in Patio C, the builders divided the text between the two registers, placing an abbreviated form of a date in the upper and a short text dedicating the building itself in the lower (Hendon 2002c). The separation of the glyph blocks for the date from those for the subject and event portion of the text means that the date would be the most visible part and what one would see first. Most hieroglyphic texts in the inner zone are found inside buildings, however. Such inscriptions generally take the form of long, detailed texts carved on the face of benches in the main room of the dominant residence in the compound. Patio A in Group 9N-8 possesses one of these benches, inside the main room of Structure 9N-82. Carved benches have been found in at least three other inner-zone groups (see W. Fash 1983b; Webster, Fash, Widmer, and Zeleznik 1998; Willey, Leventhal, and Fash 1978). Their location makes them difficult to see unless one lives in the residence or is invited inside. The fact that they are less visible and thus likely to be seen by few people makes them comparable to many of the inscriptions on buildings (as opposed to stelae) in the Main Group. Most of these buildings are in the courtyards on the Acropolis and take the form of interior wall panels or bench facings or interior steps (see Baudez 1994; B. Fash 1992; Hohmann and Vogrin 1982; Trik 1939).

The seven rural groups in the Copan foothills did not have any architec-

TABLE 6. Sculpture from Small Rural Sites

LOCATION	DESCRIPTION
SITE IID-II-2, STRUCTURE I-SUB	
Near or on the foundation platform	Free-standing frog, 18 cm (7.2 in) tall
SITE 7D-3-I, STRUCTURE 2	
Off the northwest corner of the building in the fill of the paved courtyard	Free-standing frog, 9 cm (3.6 in) tall; its head is missing
SITE 34C-4-2, STRUCTURE 3	
In front of the building in courtyard fill	Free-standing house effigy, 17 cm (6.8 in) tall

tural sculpture, but Gonlin (1993:123–24, 186–87, 297, 305, Figures 3.15, 3.36, 3.75) reports pieces of free-standing sculpture at three different sites (table 6). These include two effigies of a frog or toad sitting upright in a rather human manner. Gonlin cannot decide if the third example is an effigy of a house, a bench, or a metate with legs. If a house, then it has walls, roof, and doorway; if a bench, it has the legs and the seat they support. I myself incline toward the house since Copan benches rarely have separate legs, and the metates have three or four legs. In a sense, though, benches and metates are aspects of the same concept as the house in that all are central to what makes a building a dwelling. Benches are indexes of houses, and both are indexes of the multigenerational sociological house and the coresident group (Gillespie 2000b). Even the humble metate shares in this relationship through its role in the preparation of food that ties people together through shared action and commensality.

These three sculpture pieces are small. The broken frog and the house effigy were found in the fill of the courtyard of their respective sites. They do not seem to have been formally arranged like the figurine cache at Cerro Palenque, but they were nevertheless concealed within the material used to construct part of the living area. The context of the complete frog is less clear. It was found on or near the edge of the foundation platform of Structure 1-sub along with an intact mano. This is the first version of this building; the excavators reserved the designation Structure 1 for the final version, in which the original foundation platform was partly covered over by a new residence. The portion of the platform where the frog was found, however, was not covered up by this renovation, which means it was still in use. I cannot tell from the description of the find whether the excavators thought it and the mano were deliberately buried by the inhabitants of the site.

DISTRIBUTED PERSONHOOD AND MEMORY

Objects made of stone and clay undergo the same processes and changes that people do: they come into being at some point in time through human action, their natural shape is modified through physical manipulation and the addition of other objects or materials. They are disposed of in similar places and contexts in domestic space as those used for human graves, including inside buildings, under courtyards, or even in trash deposits. Treated like persons, sculpture and figurine whistles enter into relationships with people and with other objects. They have a temporal as well as spatial existence. They participate in events and practices, not merely as props but as points of reference and as agents of memory that affirm identities across time and space. As generative resources, these objects become integral to the development of the kinds of relational identities that define personhood as distributed among multiple entities and phenomena. Their contribution to the formation of relational identities, however, does not take the same form because their different material characteristics and the different ways people engage with them distribute personhood differently.

DISPERSING THE RELATIONAL PERSON: FIGURINE WHISTLES AND DOMAINS OF PRACTICE

Figurines and whistles can be held in the hand, carried from place to place, and passed from one person to another. The movement of figurine whistles, whether among the lower Ulua valley communities, or from residences to ballcourts in Cuyumapa, or to Copan from its eastern neighbors, makes it possible to extend personhood outside of the domestic area or the coresident community of practice. As points of recall, these figurines and whistles serve as a focus for remembering sets of relationships with local and more distant groups. The ways in which people received these objects as gifts or exchanges at ballgames and ritualized feasts become part of the significant events around which they build the history of their own memory community. Since these events and interactions engage members of multiple memory communities, opportunities abound for the construction of different histories around the same happenings.

These small clay objects depict many different animals and hybrid creatures as well as humans. The human figures represent a range of ages, including children, active adults, and the aged. Furthermore, they are shaped into people that are identifiably male and female as well as some that may be neither. This contrasts with the anthropomorphic sculpture that is generally male and young, as at Copan, or indeterminate, as at Cerro Palenque. Some figurines and whistles emphasize productive actions of daily life. The figures carry water jars or bowls of food, hold small children or hybrid creatures, or embrace one another. Others allude to more infrequent events through their dress or by holding objects such as shell trumpets or shields. They span areas of performance that are often assumed to be quite separate, the realms of the everyday and that of the religious, reinforcing the way these analytical distinctions merge in the reality of Mesoamerican philosophy and practice.

The connections between figurine whistles and other things made from clay underscore how these objects link the daily practice and the periodic special events that together make up the experience of everyday life at home in these societies. This is particularly the case with pottery vessels, suggesting once again how corporeal bodies and those made of clay share the quality of being containers for vital substances and coessences that may be dispersed beyond their confines. The distribution of personhood implied by this shared ability to contain, dispense, and thus intermingle with substances and coessences from other entities is reinforced by the tendency to make some vessels personlike through their form and decoration. Partial or whole animal, human, fantastical, and hybrid figures are commonly painted or incised on vessel surfaces (Hendon 2006b; Joyce 1993a; Longyear 1952). In addition, Copador and Ulua polychromes may have jaguar, monkey, frog, and other animal heads projecting from the sides of cylindrical vases or jars in place of conventional handles (Beaudry-Corbett, Caputi, Henderson, Joyce, Robinson, and Wonderly 1993; Joyce 1985, 1993a; Viel 1993b:Figures 70a-b, 73a,c,d, 80d). Squat, round-bellied jars from Copan have eyes, nose, mouth, and a pair of arms appliquéd to the body just where it narrows to form the neck (Viel 1993b:Figure 84d-e). Handles or legs may take the shape of animal heads or have parts of animals, usually a face or a tail, applied to them (Beaudry-Corbett, Caputi, Henderson, Joyce, Robinson, and Wonderly 1993; Viel 1993b:Figure 65j).

Censers, flat-bottomed, straight-sided containers with lids and holes for the dispersal of smoke, may have human faces with fancy headdresses, cacao pods, human bones, or other elements projecting from their sides or built into their lids (Hendon 2005; Viel 1993b:Figures 88–90). Ladle

30. Ulua polychrome vessel with a monkey design. Courtesy, National Museum of the American Indian, Smithsonian Institution (247041.000). Photo by N M A I Photo Services Staff.

censers, which combine a small, flattish receptacle with a long handle, may be shaped into the form of an animal head, like the one I excavated at PACO I in Cuyumapa that looks like a crocodilian creature. Excavations inside the Hieroglyphic Staircase at Copan discovered twelve censers with lids associated with an elaborate tomb (Burial XXXVII-4). On each lid was seated a very detailed, in-the-round representation of a human figure, which the excavators have argued represent the previous rulers of Copan (W. Fash 2001:Figures 61–64, Plate VI). Their incorporation into the lids of vessels renders them members of a different class of objects to the archaeologist, but their conceptual and formal connection to figurines cannot be ignored.

The combination of the portability of figurine whistles, their widespread distribution, and their means of manufacture further underscores how the performatory acts around which memory coalesces are ritualized but not necessarily limited to the conventionally religious or ritual. In chapter 4

I illustrated how the process of manufacture itself could be incorporated into ritualized acts of group solidarity. The use of some of these objects as musical instruments provides another kind of opportunity for shared performance that distributes the separable elements of personhood among humans and other entities. When a whistle is held up to the mouth to be played, it is the front that is presented to view. Several intact whistles recovered from Patio D of Group 9N-8 at Copan give an idea of size. One, in the shape of an owl, stands 10.3 cm tall and 7.4 cm wide (4.1 inches by 2.96). Another, in the shape of a dog with its head tilted back, as if howling, is 10.5 cm tall and 4.3 cm wide (4.2 inches by 1.7). A third shows a man and a woman standing side by side, arms clasped. The feathers in the man's headdress make this one even taller, 12.5 cm in height and 8 cm wide (or 5 inches by 3.2). Although not large enough to cover the entire face of the musician, these whistles would obscure most of the person's features, replacing a human face, one that might be well known to the other participants, with something else. A composite being made up of musician and instrument comes into existence during the performance as the musician sends her or his breath into the chamber of the whistle, sharing his or her vital animating substance and receiving back a similarly animating substance from the whistle. This mingling of coessences distributes the personhood of musician and instrument across the physical boundary between the two, sharing aspects of musician's and instrument's soul between person and object and those others who might also play the whistle or retain it after the event.

FIXING THE DISTRIBUTED PERSON:
SCULPTURE AND THE EMBODIMENT OF HOUSES

The sculpture placed on or in buildings in residential compounds draws people and personlike objects into domestic space by creating an immobile locus of personhood. The preponderance of these images at Copan suggests an emphasis on how social relations were maintained over time and on the nature of those relationships different from that in Cuyumapa and Cerro Palenque. Images carved out of stone are generally too large to be held. Even when small enough, their weight makes them unwieldy and difficult to hold and move around with ease. Much of the sculpture is attached to buildings, making it as immobile as the structure itself, although equally subject to change and renovation. At the same time, the size and placement of sculpted images make them more visible and thus more public.

These features imply a greater sense of permanency than figurines or whistles. In this they fulfill the same role that monuments do. In chapter 2, I discussed how monuments contribute to memory and identity by providing a focus of attention for intermittent moments of remembering by particular memory communities in which performatory actions make recall possible. Using the example of royal ritualized events such as the periodic insistence by the Quirigua ruler of his capture of Ruler 13 of Copan, I noted that such occasions afford an opportunity to reinvigorate identities, relationships, and events important to the political economy of memory for that memory community. Carved images attached to houses also function as remembrancers but for a different set of rememberers, those who live in the domestic compound and those who live elsewhere but who participate in those periodic performative actions through which the relations which define identity are reconstituted. I don't intend this to be a perfect opposition since pieces of sculpture were relocated to some extent at both Copan and Cerro Palenque, although often long after their original installation. What I am suggesting is that figurines and whistles were explicitly created as things to be moved around just as people do, whereas the architectonic sculpture and even the free-standing pieces were designed to be a fixed point, like the domestic place itself, on which people and personlike objects such as figurines converge.

The multiple and varied nature of coessences that distribute the person beyond the human body and develop relations between living humans and a range of other entities and phenomena helps one make sense of the many images and elements in architectonic sculpture, only some of which I have described in detail here. What I would like to discuss further are those figures that are personlike in appearance. By concentrating on these anthropomorphic figures I am not implying that the animal heads or hybrid creatures such as those on Structure 9M-195B are less central to the construction of relational personhood in the context of domestic space. But I do feel that the few cases in which the images are explicitly humanlike, even if they do not represent actual individuals or living beings, represent a strengthening of the semiotics of personhood that suggests that these houses were especially important in the attempt to continue identity over time (see Bachand, Joyce, and Hendon 2003; Hendon 2002c, 2007).

The anthropomorphic figures on the Copan Structures 9N-82, 8N-66s, and 10L-32 share certain characteristics. They are all male, young, and beautiful and display the large, high-bridged noses, sloping foreheads, rounded limbs, and graceful posture the Maya admired. Young male figures are presented as the ideal human form not only here at Copan but in sculpture and other visual media associated with royal courts, such as painted polychrome vases, at a variety of Maya sites. Presentation of young male figures as the ideal human form singles out young men as subjects of desire and admiration (Joyce 2000d, 2002). Dressed and ornamented as people of high rank, they also wear regalia that associate them with supernatural forces, creatures, and concepts ("deities") or sacred materials such as corn. They are thus hybrids in the sense that they combine features of living humans with those associated with ancestors or deities.

The full-figure carvings show people sitting cross-legged or with one leg folded under and the other hanging down. They and the torsos on Structure 8N-66s hold their arms out in front of their bodies and gesture with their hands, transcending the static nature of their raw material. Even as these figures evoke the movement of the body in space through their gestures, they also freeze that body at a point in its own movement through time. These young, fit bodies replicate in stone an intrinsically transitory moment in the experience of embodiment, a moment that only some of the people moving through the domestic spaces below would have been able to approximate in their own embodied being.

The figures on these buildings also communicate a subtle but important sense of social difference beyond that created by singling out a particular point in the life of a living human body or by showing only a single gender. Although at first glance all the figures on these three buildings possess an overall similarity and convey a sense of repetition, implying the importance of the whole or the collective rather than its individual parts, they also speak to hierarchy because the central figure on each building has different regalia and body ornaments. Scholarly opinion differs as to who these male figures are supposed to be. Baudez (1989) has argued that those on Structure 9N-82 are apotheosized ancestors. According to Andrews and Fash (1992), the figures on Structure 10L-32 represent the most important person living in the compound, the sixteenth ruler. A similar argument has been made that the central figures on Structure 8N-66s represent the head of the sociological house living there (Webster, Fash, Widmer, and Zeleznik 1998). The biographical specifics of these readings of the iconography have in common a recognition that the male figures should be connected to the memory community living in the compounds. Their headdresses, ornaments, clothing, and surrounding elements embed them in a set of ritual and metaphoric

Reconstructed examples of the human figures on Structures 8N-66s (Group 8N-11) and 9N-82 (Group 9N-8, Patio A) that illustrate the differences in body position and costume. Photographs by Julia A. Hendon.

31.1. The central figure of the upper façade on the front of Structure 8N-66s.

31.2. The central figure of the upper façade on the front of Structure 9N-82.

31.3. One of the figures placed next to the central figure of Structure 9N-82.

associations that transcend the world of day-to-day activities taking place in the patio compounds below them. At the same time, they index the people who live or have lived in the compound who are members of the sociological house for whom these buildings are an important part of their estate. In this sense, they result from practices similar to those evident in the sculpture of the Main Group associated with the royal memory community.

Copan rulers invested considerable energy in the construction of permanent, monumental images incorporated into architectural settings. They too placed idealized images of themselves and their ancestors on and in buildings. Perhaps the most salient example is the Hieroglyphic Staircase, where the dynastic history of Copan is embodied in statues of rulers seated in the midst of the selective documentation of their accomplishments and bowdlerized accounts of their lives (B. Fash 1992; Fash, Williamson, Larios, and Palka 1992; Stuart 2005). The Copan dynasty also detached imagery of these ideal versions of themselves from buildings and especially from houses by placing stelae in the plaza of the Main Group. By merging images with inscriptions that specify individual identities engaged in actions set in time, these stelae bring to the fore the actions of the ruler in ways that the images of exemplary bodies bound to houses do not.

The rare cases of hieroglyphic texts outside of the Main Group, in the form of inscriptions on benches or on building façades, include some temporal reference which fixes the events they describe in time. The house itself becomes anchored to that particular moment and to the people mentioned in the texts. Yet these dates by no means encompass the life span of the building or its occupants or sum up the length of time people have lived in it or its earlier versions. Instead, they memorialize a particular moment in the history of the place. Such seats of authority (Gillespie 1999) affiliate the residents of these residential compounds with the centralized political structure, but, because the emphasis is on recording temporally fixed action by certain local residents, they memorialize events of significance to the resident memory community and only indirectly to the polity as a whole.

As opposed to the separation of image and structure, the practice of attaching sculpture to domestic buildings characteristic of Cerro Palenque and Copan focuses attention on the houses themselves. Houses are like human bodies, figurine whistles, and pottery vessels in being containers for precious entities and substances. They enter into relationships with other entities. The terms of reference for their constituent parts equate them with living bodies, as does their spatial orientation (Hanks 1990). At least some houses have names, and house construction rituals have been widely documented (see W. Fash 2001; Stuart 1998; Vogt 1969, 1998). The building, renovation, and destruction of houses entails the same blurring of the practical and religious as the production of figurines. The enactment of a local theory of production can also be traced in the very existence of the house itself, in its form, its materials, and the construction techniques used to build or dismantle it.

The personification of houses seems most obvious for those buildings with the anthropomorphic decoration, namely, Structures 8N-66C, 9N-82, 10L-32, and 9M-195B as well as the building in Group 2 at Cerro Palenque with the more schematic human representations. But thinking in terms of a local theory of production requires one to recognize that the placement of images of humanlike beings or of other coessences does not carry out this process of personification. Instead, these images make more specific the identification between particular dwellings and particular persons. This is comparable to the example of Temple 22 I discussed in chapter 2, in which the inclusion of personified mountain and corn symbols on that structure takes its general quality of mountain-ness and makes it more precise by indexing the corn mountain of creation. In other words, all houses are embodied and contribute to the distribution of personhood among multiple beings, but certain houses have their anthropomorphic quality enhanced and reinforced through large-scale imagery.

The restricted occurrence of anthropomorphic sculpture may be a sign of a particularly close relationship with royalty and of an important political role for the sociological house that owned the building (W. Fash 2001; Fash and Stuart 1991). But one must keep in mind that royal favor can be expressed in many ways. In fact, turning this idea around, one can see that the presence of human sculpture in domestic space doesn't merely imitate royal practice but also sets up an alternative set of idealized images that challenge the status of the Main Group as the source of monumental touchstones for memory. As enchanting objects in their own right, these human figures and torsos as well as all the other sculptural elements provide multiple locations where personlike objects become agents of social memory and identity that contribute to the significance of the productive and performative action that takes place there. They form part of the background I introduced in chapter 1 that takes an active role in how people give meaning to their interactions and activities in a particular spatial context. Thus, despite the obvious shared stylistic, formal, and iconographic features of Main Group and inner-zone

sculpture, the latter is more than a scaled-down version of the former because it is housed in a different spatial setting and enters into relations with
a different group of people.

The effort to distinguish domestic compounds from one another through
architecture and sculpture may also be discerned at Cerro Palenque but,
especially in the Terminal Classic, on a much less grand scale. It is even less
evident in Cuyumapa. Yet the distribution of other elements of the material
culture of these two societies belies any assumption that coresident memory
communities were uninterested or unable to construct a social and physical
space in which differentiation and connections could be made manifest.

SIX

Special Events at Home

Special events punctuated life at home in ancient Honduras. Although intended to celebrate different achievements and changes to the coresident group or sociological house, the events have one thing in common, eating and drinking on as lavish a scale as possible. Even as it contributes to the meaning of domestic places as a participatory, phenomenological background, the practice of feasting also expands the spatial and social setting for memory work by bringing outsiders into domestic space, changing temporarily but periodically the experience of places where people live. Residents play host to guests who may be relatives, neighbors, or members of the same sociological house but also may be of different social standing. They may be from far enough away to be outside the usual realm of frequent contact. This might mean no more than from across the valley or the next river drainage but could extend to more distant societies that were politically, culturally, and linguistically distinct. In all cases, the occasions become a moment in which the coresident community of practice must define itself not just through its internal intersubjective relations but in its interactions with others. The network through which social memory is created by means of selective remembering and forgetting expands as diverse communities of memory come into contact with one another even as it may be challenged by the presence of more than one local history.

FEASTING: A TOTAL SOCIAL PHENOMENON

Feasts are social occasions bringing together hosts and guests at a set place and time to celebrate some achievement or event through, in part, the provision, display, and consumption of large quantities and special types of food and drink. They draw on the inherent sociality of eating together, an act, according to Simmel (1997:131), of "immense socializing power" because of the way it transcends "the mere naturalism of eating" (1997:135). Feasts, as an amplification of commensality, express cultural notions of style, behavior, and aesthetics, notions that are both the cause and effect of efforts to promote claims for social difference and distinction (Bourdieu 1998:3–9). Feasts are not merely about social, in the limited sense of personal, relationships. Feasting is, in fact, a "total social phenomenon," in the broadest sense as laid out by Mauss (1990:3) in his discussion of gift giving and receiving. The process of feasting, like that of gifting, encompasses the religious, economic, political, moral, aesthetic, and social (see also Dietler 2003; Hayden 1996; Kan 1989). It is a process that requires an intense engagement between people and the most humble and most enchanting of objects, many of which are personlike in nature and agential in role.

Celebration of memorable moments of transition in the life of the individual and the group—birth, coming of age, marriage, death—is part of the social life of coresident communities of practice and sociological houses at all levels of society, rich and poor, small farming families and powerful extended noble ones. Landa notes that the Maya he encountered "have strong friendships and they remember for a long time these invitations although they are far apart from one another" (Tozzer 1978:92). Hospitality should, whenever possible, be reciprocated: "If one of the guests should die, his household or his relations are obliged to repay the invitation" (Tozzer 1978:92). Wealthy, prominent people incorporated this expectation more fully into their personal definition of their social and political prominence. As a result, the ability to host substantial feasts or to be invited to them serves as a way that social differences is created through practice.

Perhaps because of this, sponsoring a feast becomes a source of tension, bringing with it the possibility of social disaster or political betrayal. Feasts are times when there was supposed to be enough food for all (Roys 1967:137). Guests could shame their hosts by disdaining their hospitality or finding it wanting in some way. If guests "were not well satisfied, nor happy, nor content, with the chocolate, the food, the flowers, and the tobacco . . . they . . . ran away angry. . . . Thus, oppressed and troubled, they went to seat themselves . . . in their [own] houses," and it was up to the host to try to make amends and entice the aggrieved guests back to the feast (Sahagún 1953–82, Book 4:118). Violation of the norms of hospitality plays a role in two important collections of Maya historical accounts. Mistreatment of guests is central to the parallel episodes in the *Popol vuh* in which two pairs of twins are invited by the Lords of Xibalba (the Underworld) to come into their realm and compete against them in a ballgame. In both cases the Lords fail to behave like proper hosts, resulting in the death of one pair of twins followed by the destruction of the Lords' power by the second pair (Tedlock 1996). Several versions of the Book of Chilam Balam, texts written by Maya authors after the conquest, attribute the fall of the city of Chichen Itza to the treachery of a nobleman from the rival city of Mayapan. The betrayal takes place during a banquet, and it is clear the behavior violated social and political expectations (Roys 1967:137, Appendix C).

SOCIAL COHESION AND DISTINCTION

The recurring nature of feasting is often structured by an ordered temporal framework, such as a religious calendar or the human life cycle. However, the true impetus for its repetition is the reciprocal nature of the social relations created and reinforced through these events—one cannot be just a guest but must also be a host at some later time (Kan 1989; Mauss 1990). Probably the best-known cycles involving feasts in Mesoamerica are the elaborate state-sponsored festivals tied to the 365-day calendar or to the chronology of a particular ruler's reign (see Durán 1971; Tozzer 1978; Martin and Grube 2000; Sahagún 1953–82, Book 2; Stuart 1998). But important events in the lives of people at all levels of society also required feasts to mark the occasion (Hendon 2003b; Pohl and Pohl 1994). The remains of the dead stored in the foundations of Copan houses and below courtyard floors are a reminder of ceremonies during which hospitality needed to be extended to family, friends, and acquaintances. Although archaeologists tend to focus on what a burial reveals about the deceased, it reflects as much about the decisions of the survivors responsible for carrying out the funeral rites (Hendon 2003a). It is the living members of the social group who must incorporate the commemoration of the dead into their social memory and identity.

The personlike status of houses signals that the renovation of buildings and placement of caches would require similar kinds of celebration. One significant moment in the local history of the ballcourt residential group at Cerro Palenque demonstrates how objects, houses, and people's actions come together to celebrate events that may be recalled over time. Excavation of the western structure revealed a complex sequence of construction starting with a pavement that preceded the building itself (Hendon 2002a, 2003a, 2006b). The people living there at the time got together to eat, drink, and burn incense prior to the raising of the structure's foundation platform. They ended their feast by smashing censers and fine paste serving and eating vessels on the pavement. As I excavated the deposit over a millennium later, I found pieces that fit together from these vessels strewn across the surface. The most striking is a censer decorated with a design of bones tied with rope, appliquéd in high relief on the surface of the vessel.

The next step was to cover the pavement and the broken vessels lying on it with a fill of gravel and dirt which itself had a large amount of stuff mixed in it. Careful excavation determined that the fill was deposited in a series of fine lenses. Again, I found sherds from the same vessel in the same lens. The lack of weathering of the artifacts argues for a rapid depositional process that did not leave any of these temporary surfaces exposed for very long. The fill was created especially for the construction process from the implements used at the feast itself. It is made up of trash, in the sense of objects that have been discarded, but these vessels, censers, figurine whistles, and other items had their useful life deliberately and prematurely cut short by people's decision to break them and leave them behind in this place.

The burial of the pavement was complete after about 16 centimeters of fill had been laid down. At this point a human femur from the body of a young, healthy adult was carefully placed on a bed made from large sherds broken from various pottery vessels. The stairs of the building covered the bone. It shows little signs of weathering, suggesting it was either removed from the body of someone who had recently died or had been conserved in a protected

32. Part of the incense burner from Cerro Palenque decorated with a motif of human bones bound with rope. Photograph by Julia A. Hendon.

location until the people living there were ready to construct the building that would house it. Human bones thus mark the beginning and end of the ritualized interment of the pavement and the birth of the western structure. Using and then breaking the censer with its motif of bound human long bones initiates the process; placement of the actual ancestor brings it to a close. Bones and binding are elements of creation mythology, metaphors for building construction, and symbols of the ties across generations that define social groups (Tedlock 1996; Vogt 1998).

The presence of human bone and its representation in clay distributes the identity of the coresident group beyond the immediate moment in time. Burials are associated with many urban and rural residences in the Copan valley. Like the caches at Cerro Palenque, including this one and the one containing the male and female figurines discussed in previous chapters, many human burials are hidden inside the fabric of the building itself. As containers of a precious coessence, residential buildings index certain

33. Human femur placed as a cache below the stairs of a building on the west side of the ballcourt residential group at Cerro Palenque. The bone projects from underneath one of the steps to the left of the north arrow. Photograph by Julia A. Hendon.

qualities also associated with people, becoming more personlike through this connection. Houses provide permanent markers of events such as the dedicatory feasts that can be recalled at later ceremonies.

At Copan, feasting emerges as an important way in which noble houses and the royal house of the sixteenth ruler worked to reiterate their claims to status and importance. Evidence from the area south of the Acropolis where the royal family lived indicates that the king was committed to hosting feasts (Andrews and Bill 2005). As noted in chapter 4, obsidian tools deposited in front of Temple 16 have wear patterns consistent with both food processing and shell working. This plus the presence of animal bones suggests that such events may have taken place here as well. Materials recovered in and around Structure 22A, next to Temple 22, indicate the preparation of food in the East Court of the Acropolis late in its history (Aoyama 1995; Joyce 1986; Longyear 1952).

The basic suite of pottery vessels from Sepulturas residences includes small, medium, and large jars, large basins, comals, portable braziers, bowls of different shapes and sizes, large plates, some with feet, censers, and "cylinders," the sides of which run straight from base to rim (Hendon

1987:314–53, 1988). Locally produced and imported vessels intended for use as tableware are frequently decorated in ways that, as noted in chapter 5, make them like figurine whistles.

In a study of the distribution of grinding stones, figurine whistles, and the pottery vessels found in Groups 9N-8, 9M-22, and 9M-24, I merged the objects into four broad functional categories: food serving, food preparing, storage, and ritual. I found that the dominant structure, or the most elaborate dwelling in a patio, was a focus of feasting activity in the inner zone (Hendon 2003b). The difference between this dwelling and others in the same patio is one of degree rather than absolutes. In other words, dominant structures do not monopolize ritual or food serving and preparation for their compound. But they are the setting for preparing and serving food to the exclusion of other activities practiced elsewhere in the compound, such as crafting.

The distribution of serving vessels and implements used for food preparation, including metates as well as containers, leads me to conclude that residents of small residential compounds, such as Group 9M-22, were as eager to participate in status-enhancing feasting activities as residents of Group 9N-8, who were potential rivals and allies but were also wealthier and of higher rank, making direct competition difficult. A raised paved walkway runs eastward from the Main Group into the Sepulturas area, terminating in a large, walled courtyard that forms part of Group 8N-11, the elaborate residential compound with sculpture and a carved bench mentioned in chapter 5. A small spur leads toward Group 9M-22. This physical connection may be indicative of the social ties between this sociological house and that of Group 8N-11. Such ties could have included the provision of food to support the noble house of Group 8N-11 in its feasting of important rivals such as Group 9N-8, participation in such feasts, and the hosting of return feasts back in the Group 9M-22 compound.

People living in Group 9N-8 had the advantage of a wider circle of coresidents to supply food and materials and to help with the preparations, but the distribution of serving vessels, censers, figurines, and other related material indicates that no one patio within that complex enjoyed exclusive rights to the role of host. Reciprocal feasting within this large compound may have been important not only as a way for the sociological house as a whole to compete with other houses in the potentially fluid and unstable domain of social status but also to maintain local cohesion. Having so many patios, the Group 9N-8 house was both larger and more diverse than most of the other high-ranking houses living around the Main Group, making the retention of group solidarity especially challenging. Sponsoring feasts in celebration of life-cycle events or as part of a temporal religious cycle may therefore have been equally important for the renewal of internal social ties.

Rural dwellers also used fancy serving vessels and ritual objects such as censers (Gonlin 1993:Tables 4.6, 4.8, 4.14). The surface of many vessel fragments is eroded, making precise identification of their decoration impossible. However, both the locally made types (for example, Copador or Gualpopa polychromes or Surlo brown ware, often carved or incised) and the most commonly imported ones of the Ulua polychrome group have distinctive pastes, making it possible to note their presence in a more general way (Gonlin 1993:371–72). Locally produced types are present at all seven of the sites discussed here. Four sites, 11D11–2, 7D6–2, 34C-4–2, and 99A-18–2, have also yielded Ulua polychromes in small quantities (Gonlin 1993:Table 4.6). The consistent occurrence of local serving vessels and the more limited occurrence of imported ones in the domestic assemblage of these sites suggest that ritual and commensal events were not restricted to rich or high-ranking sectors of society. Residents of these small sites may also have been involved in larger-scale feasting events through their social connections to the more substantial residential groups in the foothills or with residents of the inner zone. Although Ulua polychromes are a tiny fraction of the ceramic assemblage of the four sites, they are nevertheless there. Their presence signals that rural families shared with their urban neighbors an appreciation for imported serving and eating vessels.

Fung (1995:236–44) found jars with incised decoration, serving vessels, figurines, and censer fragments at Groups 5–2 and 6–2 at PACO 2 in Cuyumapa. Although so similar in architectural materials and energetic investment, differences in material culture can be observed between these two groups. In chapter 2, I noted that the material of which metates are made is one way Groups 5–2 and 6–2 differentiated themselves, 5–2 preferring basalt and 6–2 rhyolite. Something similar can be seen in the choice of fancy tableware. People living in Group 6–2 possessed polychrome pottery imported from the Sulaco region to the east. They also were more likely to possess locally made pottery decorated in the style of this foreign serving ware. Residents of the other group made greater use of fine paste vessels that correspond to a kind of pottery found at Cerro Palenque and other communities in the Ulua valley where it was manufactured. Fung (1995:243) interprets this variation as evidence that "different residential groups may have had unique ties to ceramic producing areas outside the . . . area." Like the noble sociological houses in Sepulturas and even a few rural families who celebrated their ability to consume elaborate polychrome pottery and figurine whistles acquired from their eastern neighbors in the Ulua, Comayagua, and Naco valleys, the Cuyumapa residents' foreign ties are embodied in the imported objects, or those locally made in a foreign style, that people used during the ceremonies they sponsored in their home. As guests are served with food and drink from jars and bowls, the containers attest to their hosts' connections, even if indirect and on a small scale, with a wider world. Furthermore, this assertion of a more cosmopolitan identity is one that contrasts one group's ties to the larger and more complex societies to the west, in the Ulua valley, with the other group's ties with comparable societies to the east.

The people living in the ballcourt residential group at Cerro Palenque continued to make the western structure a focus of feasting (Hendon 2005). Behind the final version of the building, they dug a large pit and a trench. Both contained lots of broken pottery from a limited range of vessel types, echoing the contents of the earlier fill containing the human bone. The majority of the sherds come from fine paste serving vessels, both locally produced and imported from the Cuyumapa area. Forms include small bowls, often with feet, plates or small jars, used mainly for serving or consuming food and drink. In fact, almost 75 percent of all the fine paste sherds from my excavations came from these two deposits. Other special kinds of ceramics include Ulua Polychrome, imported Las Vegas Polychrome, and censers. Again, these are trash deposits but they result from a special range of activities. In contrast, another sizable trash deposit found behind the large structure at the southern end of the patio contained objects related to food preparation and storage, including large jars, manos, tools made from obsidian, quartz, and chert as well as the remains of the food itself.

DEPOSITING COESSENCES AND DISTRIBUTING IDENTITY

The feasting debris behind the western structure also includes jewelry. A clay earring in the shape of a narrow tube that flares out at one end and a small clay lip stud, roughly L-shaped, are among the items discarded. These are exactly the kinds of objects that were used to mark the maturation of members of the social group, creating an appropriately socialized body. After the initial ear or lip piercing, parents replaced the ornaments worn by their children as they grew older (Joyce 2000b). The obsolete pieces of jewelry, broken pottery containers, and figurine whistle fragments contribute to the special nature of the deposit, making it a concentration of coessences derived from food, breath, and things detached from the body. The only other pieces of jewelry reported from Cerro Palenque date to the earlier occupation. Beads or pendants of greenstone, jade, shell, and animal teeth have been found in the hilltop part of the site (Joyce 1985:362–63). People living in the ballcourt residential group, like their predecessors, differed from their neighbors in their physical appearance as well as in where they lived and what they did.

Objects designed to be incorporated into and then removed from the body occur more widely at Copan, having been found in trash and fill deposits in both rural and urban residences (Gonlin 1993:Table 4.12; Hendon 1987:311–13, 361–77). Gonlin reports a worked piece of jade, tentatively identified as an earspool, and a ground obsidian cylinder, which may be an ear or lip ornament, from Site 11D11–2. Another site, 7D3–1, had a jade or greenstone ornament in a cist. A jade tubular pendant and a bead, beads of other materials, and a clay earspool and labret were recovered from Site 34C-4–2. The Sepulturas deposits yielded ornaments made of clay, jade, obsidian, teeth, bone, and shell in greater quantities and variety but with a similar emphasis on items to be worn on the body or inserted into it.

It has always been something of a puzzle why enchanting, personal objects like these would be in the trash or building fill rather than just in burials or caches. Things do go astray, but a jade bead or an obsidian earspool represent something valued and intimate, worn on (or in) the body. It is hard to imagine how such objects could be repeatedly lost track of. I found a lovely piece of bone carved with a profile face wearing a tall headdress of leaves or feathers inside Structure 9N-74 in Patio B of Group 9N-8 when I dug a trench along the midline of the main room. The lower half is missing. What remains is about 6.2 centimeters (2.4 inches) long and 1.5 centimeters (0.6 inches) wide. Why would one deliberately get rid of it? Or of a similarly long, narrow object carved with two glyphlike figures found in a midden in a cul-de-sac formed by four buildings at the north end of Patio D? Other pieces of bone are carved with geometric designs of lines, chevrons, and curves, while a few depict human or animal figures very much like the images sculpted in stone. They are not common but have been excavated from several patios in Group 9N-8 and 9M-22. I have always suspected that these

Ways of decorating the person. Photographs by Julia A. Hendon.

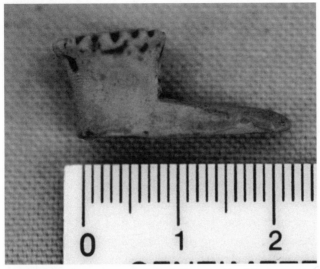

34.1. A clay labret, or lip ornament, from the ballcourt residential group at Cerro Palenque.

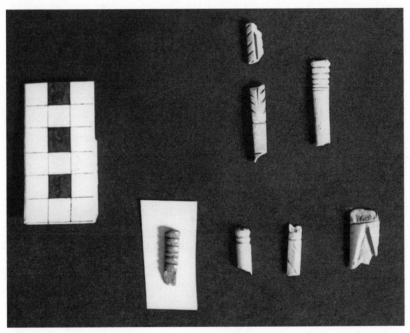

34.2. Decorated fragments of long, slender bone objects found in Group 9N-8 at Copan that may have served as pins to fasten clothing or style hair.

objects were originally used in the hair or to pin together clothing. An intact example from Patio D with a profile human head set atop a long pointed shaft provides some support for my interpretation.

The relationship between people and objects I have presented here suggests a reason archaeologists find these ornaments not just in graves but also seemingly discarded. These are enchanting objects that have become not only signs but agents of individual growth and development and of the renewal of social ties across time and space. They contribute to the personhood of the buildings they are deposited in or near. Like the sculpted figures on certain Copan buildings, body decorations made of bone, shell, clay, and stone help define a personhood that abstracts from the ongoing lived reality of experience an idealization of the group's identity constructed from bits and pieces of objects connected to present and past members of the coresident community of practice and the sociological house. Physical houses concentrate this sense of an enduring entity through their visible attributes and hidden contents without being identified with or as any individual.

The presence of male figures frozen at their moment of greatest physical appeal and strength on certain buildings might be explained as another manifestation of the elite social status of Copan's inner-zone residents. The fact that few houses in the zone are so decorated suggests their significance is not so simply defined. Since status is not a fixed attribute but a relationship with others that is always in a state of becoming, the placement of rows of human sculpture on building façades is better seen as one way that certain sociological houses assert their importance and longevity through an unusual kind of embellishment of a physical house. The presence of these human images does not by itself anthropomorphize these structures because houses are already like people. They contain precious coessences that can be removed and distributed. They come into existence at a moment in time that can be remembered and, like human birth, placed in the spatio-temporal order of things. The addition of sculpture enhances the association between particular people or kinds of people and these particular buildings, creating a permanent and iconic representation of an aesthetic and moral ideal of personhood. Feasts ensure that guests periodically enter domestic space where they would be able to see the sculpture that was normally obscured from view by the height and enclosure of the compounds. Some of these guests would have been relatives enjoying the opportunity to renew their association with the ideals embodied in the sculpture and more generally in the domestic space of the compound. Other guests would have been from unrelated, even rival, memory communities. The physical decorum and understanding of the aesthetics of feasting, including appropriate dress, behavior, and ways of interacting and eating, would be on display for all present.

Monuments such as stelae and the Hieroglyphic Staircase are readily understood as manifestations of a kind of distributed personhood because they seem to reproduce an individual's historical identity over and over through portraits and inscriptions that identify him or her with specific actions carried out at specified moments in time. This assumes that personhood is bounded by the physical limits of the body and defined by an individualistic sense of the self. The Mesoamerican relational self introduced in chapter 5 and the associated concept of coessences that are both of the body and separate from it, corporeal and incorporeal, requires a broader appreciation of how personhood develops, is distributed, and connects the present with the past.

GIVING AND RECEIVING GIFTS

Feasts are also a vehicle for exchange, creating another kind of obligatory reciprocity. Hosts and guests give each other material goods, often in large quantities. Such transactions may be called gifts, but the social obligation created is one that requires a return, either immediately or later (Mauss 1990). The food and other items given away may far surpass the amounts of food consumed at the event. As part of their inaugural feast, Aztec rulers provided rich gifts of clothing and weapons as well as food and drink to all their guests, including their enemies (Sahagún 1953–82, Book 4:118; see also Book 2:passim). Maya nobles "at the end of the repast, were accustomed to give a *manta* [piece of cloth] to each [guest] to wear, and a little stand and vessel, as beautiful as possible" (Tozzer 1978:92). Guests not only received gifts but brought them as well, the quality of which was determined in part by their social status and wealth (Sahagún 1953–82, Book 6:129).

The kinds of craftwork presented in chapter 4 are all examples of the skilled and knowledgeable activities designed to produce the sort of high quality and highly valued things appropriate for giving as gifts. The obligations to give and receive bound up in these occasions are part of how social relations and identities are reproduced. Gifts taken away by guests distribute the personhood of their maker, their giver, and of the group as a whole beyond the spatial setting and the particular moment in time. They become part of the remembering process for both those giving and those attending the event. Objects received are a tangible reminder of one's experience of the feast as a guest. The absence of such objects becomes an intangible marker for the hosts of the success or failure of the event. Body ornaments or pottery vessels placed in burials continue this process of distribution beyond the life span of the individual, endowing the sociological house with heirlooms that form part of its estate (Joyce 2003).

At Cerro Palenque, the production of mold-made figurines and whistles can be seen as a kind of performance situated in the ballcourt residential group. These performances were intermittent and involved people of varying skill levels and training. The shared enterprise of making figurines and whistles helps develop the connections between people necessary to the creation of a community of practice among the residents living near the ballcourt. A consequence of this enterprise is that these residents have a greater ability, by virtue of being producers of these objects as well as the hosts of events in which these objects participated and entered into relations with people beyond the coresidential circle, to distribute their coessences as much as the products of their craft beyond their most immediate and intimate relational nexus. The west mound deposit also contains broken molds which are of the type used to make fine paste vessels. I even found a piece of a mold corresponding exactly to the design on a piece of a fine paste vessel, suggesting that a short amount of time passed between use of the mold, use of the vessel, and the discard of both. The significance of when, why, and how this production takes place is as much social as economic. Cerro Palenque did not dominate or monopolize the production of figurines and whistles in the lower Ulua valley (Lopiparo 2003, 2007; Lopiparo and Hendon 2009). The community was part of a network of exchanges that, by distributing certain objects across the landscape, expanded and reaffirmed the relationships through which people define their own personhood and that of others.

Another more public although not necessarily comparably participatory performance may have occurred in the court facing Temple 16. The conjunction of such activities as processing animal flesh, hide and bone, and plants with carving shell reported by Aoyama is a curious one by conventional standards of what constitutes either craft production or ritual. If these activities were brought together as part of a ceremony hosted by the royal family, then the combination points to the desire to merge the sociability of sharing food with the renewal of royal authority through gift giving and a demonstration of control over valued materials.

This instance of shell working contrasts markedly with the concealed production taking place in the rooms of Structure 9N-110B in Patio H of Group 9N-8. Although the West Court of Copan's Acropolis is not the most accessible of areas, what took place there has at least a greater potential of being observed than in 9N-110B owing to the mere fact that the court is an open area much larger than rooms inside a dwelling. People invited to the West Court would be able to observe the ritualized activities taking place in front of Temple 16, whereas even those living in Patio H would be hard pressed to see the shellworkers at work even though they might be right outside the building. Evidence exists for the crafting of objects from marine shell in other areas of Group 9N-8. This is most definitive for Patio D, where archaeological excavations found remains of manufacture of shell and bone objects in rooms in two buildings, Structures 9N-61A and 9N-115A. Traces in middens and deposits on building terraces imply shell working also took place in other patios, but the location cannot be so precisely identified.

What the difference in setting between the Main Group and the residential compounds suggests is that production intersects with ceremonial events, such as feasting, in more than one way. In other words, productive activities become a flexible and fluid set of practices that can be used to create more or less public kinds of interactions. The approach evidenced by the remains in the West Court has its closest parallel with the production of figurine whistles and fine paste vessels in Cerro Palenque in the ballcourt residential group. In both cases, there is an emphasis on performances that draw in spectators by allowing them to observe what is happening and possibly even taking a hand in the process. This recalls the earlier discussion of the kinds of ritualized events surrounding the dedication of royal monuments such as Stela E at Quirigua and the Hieroglyphic Staircase at Copan, events that would have engaged the senses in different ways through sights, sounds, actions, and smells.

OFFSTAGE AND ON

What happens after the guests arrive is only part of the picture. Ceremonies and feasts are the culmination of a great deal of work. Material resources must be stockpiled and commitments of people's time and labor secured.

"Often they spend on one banquet what they have earned by trading and bargaining many days" (Tozzer 1978:92). Since much of this work must begin well in advance of the event itself, considerable planning is needed as well: "The ashes were prepared, ground cacao was prepared, flowers were secured, smoking tubes were purchased, tubes of tobacco were prepared, sauce bowls and pottery cups and baskets were purchased . . . the maize was ground; leavening was set out in basins. Then tamales were prepared. All night they were occupied; perhaps three days or two days the women made tamales. . . . That which transpired in their presence let them sleep very little" (Sahagún 1953–82 Book 6:129). Activities that are normally part of the routine of daily life or that are carried out by people with no specialized training in the use of the calendar, writing, prayers, or other esoteric forms of knowledge are as crucial to the success of the event as actions conducted by specialists. In a contemporary context, Alan Sandstrom's intensive inter-action with the ritual life of Nahau-speaking people in Veracruz, Mexico, points to the value placed on contributions of time and effort both before and during the ceremonies. Sandstrom writes, "Of equal importance is the labor that participants expend in the sometimes onerous preparations for Nahua rituals. . . . participants deprive themselves of sleep for days on end" (2003:54). Time becomes an important resource. The ability to assert some sort of control over one's own time and those of others is a frequent source of conflict in households (McKie, Bowlby, and Gregory 1999). The men and women, adults, adolescents, and children living together in the large or small house compounds in Copan, Cerro Palenque, and Cuyumapa would have many demands on their time as they prepared for these important events, including producing the textiles, bark paper, offerings, decorations for the house and ornamentation for the people, gifts for guests, and food for all.

There is thus a significant backstage *and* nonprofessional aspect to the ceremonies hosted by domestic groups. I have already mentioned the degree to which responsibility for providing the labor and materials was shared among all the patios of Group 9N-8 and suggested Group 9M-22 had a similar relationship with Group 8N-11. Although evidence for food prepara-tion exists in the ballcourt residential group at Cerro Palenque, it is insuffi-cient to produce the quantity and variety of food and drink necessary for the feasts they hosted. The residents of all of the other house compounds that have been excavated were also regularly engaged in food preparation and production, suggesting that they represent another source of goods and services for the people living close to the Great Plaza.

As noted earlier, both of the excavated Cuyumapa residential groups contained the remains of fancy serving vessels, figurines, and censers (Fung 1995:Chapter 5). Group 5–2 has more evidence of eating and using figurines and censers based on the fact that relevant artifacts are found in more locations within the site and in greater quantities. In contrast, the residents of Group 6–2 were involved in more food preparation and craft working. The difference indicates that the people of Group 5–2 must have had a wider network of support extending beyond their immediate domestic group. This network did not necessarily include Group 6–2 since the living area known as Group 5–2 is in fact part of a multipatio cluster, the remainder of which has not been excavated yet.

Feasting revolves around cooked and prepared food, drawing heavily on the skills, knowledge, time, labor, and equipment of women. Documentary and visual sources on feasting and associated offerings emphasize the presentation and consumption of dishes requiring ingredients that were not eaten every day, such as venison, or which required more work and time to prepare, such as tamales (Bill 1997b; Bricker 1991; Brown and Gerstle 2002; Pohl 1981; Reents-Budet 2006). These sources and the archaeological debris of feasting also underscore the importance of drinking. Such drinks, nowadays often referred to by the generic term, chicha, may be made from many different fruits or vegetables. Writing of corn chicha, Cutler and Cardenas (1947:52) note that "well-made chicha is an attractive drink, clear and sparkling, with a flavor somewhat similar to that of apple cider. Its alcoholic content varies greatly, from about two per cent in new or weak and watered chicha to as high as twelve per cent in a few exceptional samples." Corn chicha was a central component of ceremonies and feasts in indigenous Honduras (Chapman 1985; Fung 1995). Lenca Indians, who made corn chicha into recent times (and may still do so), told the ethnographer Anne Chapman that the beverage produces a pleasant kind of drunkenness without leading to violence or aggressiveness (Chapman 1985:106–7).

Drinks made with cacao, sometimes fermented, sometimes not, were another important part of special meals in Mesoamerica overall and in Honduras in particular. Chemical analysis of residues on pots from the village of Puerto Escondido demonstrate the use of cacao by 1100 BCE in the lower Ulua valley, a region known for its cultivation of the plant at the time of the

Spanish conquest (Henderson, Joyce, Hall, Hurst, and McGovern 2007). Similar studies of the contents of vessels placed in royal tombs at Copan also document cacao as an ingredient in sauces and drinks left as offerings (McNeil, Hurst, and Sharer 2006). During the Late Classic, images of cacao pods decorate Ulua valley cache vessels and figurines (Henderson and Joyce 2006) as well as Copan censers, including the one mentioned in chapter 3 as having been placed in a cache in Patio E of Group 9N-8 (Diamanti 2000:105) as well as another in Patio B of that same group (Hendon, Agurcia F., Fash, and Aguilar P. 1990:182). Although some cacao may have been grown in the Copan valley, it is more likely that most was imported from the east, along with the figurines and Ulua polychrome vessels.

Producing sufficient quantities of these beverages was a laborious, time-consuming process. To make corn chicha, the kernels must be ground and cooked. Fermentation may be achieved either by the addition of saliva or by allowing the corn to sprout. In their detailed study of chicha making in South America, Cutler and Cardenas (1947) refer to the first method as salivation rather than mastication because women do not chew the corn. Instead, they put balls of corn flour in their mouth, working them with their tongue and palate until they are thoroughly impregnated with their saliva. The result are small cakes of dough that can keep for some time—the authors don't specify how long, but they do indicate that such cakes were regularly sold in the marketplace, which implies some shelf life. In the context of Mesoamerican beliefs about coessences, it is possible to see this process as the mingling together of precious substances contained within the human body with those embodied in the corn plant to create a literal sharing of coessences with all participants in the feast.

Achieving a good quality fermented drink requires several days' work because the liquid must be heated and allowed to settle and the solids must then be separated from the liquid several times until sufficiently fermented. After as long as ten days of boiling, the mixture must be allowed to settle and the process of fermentation and boiling repeated. It does not keep well, which means that the cooks cannot prepare the large amount needed for a feast very far in advance. Cutler and Cardenas report that the solids, once removed from the liquid, are often cooked some more to produce a kind of candy. Preparation of cacao chicha also requires several steps and close observation to achieve the proper amount of fermentation without spoilage. If left too long, the liquid becomes a kind of "cacao vinegar" as the alcohol converts to acetic acid (Henderson and Joyce 2006:145).

All this effort did not take place entirely behind the scenes. To achieve an elegant presentation of a cacao drink, the server must produce a froth on the surface of the liquid, one that would be visible above the rim of the drinking cup or bowl. This layer of foam is fugitive and must be created just before or at the moment of passing the container to the guest. Female figures pour liquid from one cylindrical container to another on Maya polychrome vessels and in the illustrations in the *Florentine Codex* watched by all concerned, turning the provision of food and drink into a kind of performance (Henderson and Joyce 2006; Reents-Budet 2006). The women pour from a standing position, which separates the two containers quite a bit. This would facilitate the incorporation of air into the liquid and make for a substantial layer of foam, but it also increases the risk of spilling the liquid onto the recipient or missing the lower container altogether, in other words, of giving a poor performance.

Many of the Ulua polychrome pots found in inner-zone Copan residences take the form of cylinders and come in two sizes, one large enough for pouring cacao and one small enough to serve as a drinking cup. Receiving one's portion of cacao chicha in an imported cup was a particular mark of distinction; being able to offer it in an imported cylinder a triumph of social striving. Passing among the guests with decorated jars in hand to replenish cups with fermented drinks made from corn or cacao, women of the house would enhance the atmosphere of conviviality even as their actions helped underscore the generosity and wealth of the hosts.

All of this recalls those humble objects of domestic life already discussed as indexes and icons of the human body, the social group, and the reproduction of both, grinding stones and pottery vessels or, more specifically, the metate and the jar. Jars are especially interesting because of their size range, varied decoration, and ability to be both humble and enchanting objects depending on their physical properties, contents, and context of use. They may be so small as to suggest service for one. Two that I excavated in Patio B (Group 9N-8) illustrate this well (both are less than six inches high). One is a Copador polychrome jar only 13.5 centimeters in height with a basal diameter of 11.5 centimeters and that of the rim of 11.7 centimeters. Its companion in the same deposit is 12 centimeters tall with almost the same rim diameter (11.5 centimeters) and an even smaller base (8.5 centimeters). This jar belongs to the Surlo group of pottery and has a red-painted neck. Both have animal heads and legs projecting from the body of the vessel. In the case of the Copador jar, the animal is a frog, but I was not able to identify the one on the Surlo jar. Another deposit in Patio B included an even smaller Ulua polychrome jar. As these examples suggest, such individually sized jars at Copan are vividly decorated and are made locally and imported (see descriptions of Features 38 and 73 in Hendon, Agurcia F., Fash, and Aguilar P. 1990:183, 189; Viel 1993b:Figures 69b, 73a,c, d, 79h for more examples).

Others are of such large capacity that they could not have been moved frequently once filled and were used mainly for the long-term storage of food or other materials. In between these two extremes are jars that are well suited in size and shape to being carried around on the head or tucked under the arm, whether to bring water from the river or to dispense drinks at daily meals or feasts. This sort of jar is not painted in the fancy local or foreign polychrome traditions. They are often rather plain by comparison but by no means undecorated and, as discussed in the previous chapter, overlap the most with figurine whistles as personlike because of the way they share properties with the human body. Areas of the jar may be incised, slipped red, or appliquéd with human heads or arms (see especially the descriptions of the types, Reina Incised, Raul Red, and Masica Incised Cruz Variety, in Viel 1993b:112–13, 117–18, Figures 83–84).

The relationship between women and food is celebrated in the female figurine balancing a jar on her head buried in the low central platform of one of the residential groups at Cerro Palenque. Among the artifacts recovered from these platforms are a higher than expected proportion of sherds from decorated serving vessels, including jars painted with red-colored designs, as well as grinding stones. A similar pattern pertains for houses with benches (Joyce 1991:114, 124). The area around the building in the northwest corner of Group 6–2 in Cuyumapa contained a similar pattern of jars, metates, and portable braziers (Fung 1995:175). Comparable jars, often decorated with human faces and arms, are part of the domestic utensils in Copan (Hendon 1988).

Metates and jars thus not only index women's repetitive labor to sustain the household but the contribution of their time and energy to the episodic feasts that expand the coresident community of practice's commensality beyond its immediate social circle and spatial boundary. The very fact that these implements figure prominently in both the most basic activities revolving around food and the most elaborate defines their importance to identity and memory. The construction of intersubjective identities and processes of remembering cannot be separated from the most mundane forms of action and interaction. At the same time, the significance of alimentation and commensality, of eating to sustain the physical body and eating together to define the social body, comes not only from feasts but also from daily meals. Feasts become a moment around which memory coalesces because they are like and unlike ordinary meals. And ordinary meals provide another kind of opportunity for remembering because of their similarity and differences from feasts.

SEVEN

Ballcourts and Houses
Shared Patterns of Monumentality and Domesticity

Momentous life events that involved feasting (see chapter 6) are not the only kinds of special occasions observed in ancient Honduras. Another, common to all three societies, is the ballgame. Like feasting, the ballgame is a constellation of happenings subsumed under the term *special event*. Both kinds of events, feasting and the ballgame, whether taken together or separately, represent further examples of ritualization that incorporate the everyday into the religious and the political. They are part of how memory communities define themselves through remembering and forgetting within particular spatial, temporal, and social frameworks. Feasts and ballgames serve as a vehicle for the shared participation of people and involve repertoires of objects, spaces, actions, and intersubjective interactions that blur the boundaries between modern

35. Ballplayers hit the ball to one another as spectators gossip and make noise in the stands. Roll-out photograph of the design on a Maya polychrome vessel. Photograph © Justin Kerr, κ5435.

categories of private and public, domestic and monumental. The ballgame can be seen as the inverse of ceremonies at home in that it moves residents out of their houses into a different spatial arena, that created by the ballcourt and its environs. Here people encounter members of other memory communities against a different background. Like special events at home, ballgames provide moments of recall around which remembering can coalesce and be brought back into the foreground of group life in diverse social contexts, including not just the large-scale one of the ballgame but the smaller, more intimate one back home as well.

Ballcourts are a kind of monumental construction widely found in Meso-america and in fact often taken as paradigmatic of the cultures in this area (Taladoire 1981). They appear very early in the history of settled life in the region and have been implicated in the development of political authority

(Hill and Clark 2001). Although variable in size and architecture, they share features of form and layout that make them identifiable by archaeologists long after they have gone out of use and been left to decay. The most salient is the presence of two parallel mounds, longer than they are wide and set close together to define a playing alley. Many ancient Honduran societies built ballcourts after 500 CE (Begley 2004; Fox 1994:Table 8). At least three predecessors to this florescence of ballcourts in the Late Classic through Postclassic periods are known. One is the main Copan ballcourt, the first version of which was dedicated in 435 CE (Fash, Fash, and Davis-Salazar 2004:67). Another comes from a site called Los Achiotes, about twenty kilometers (about twelve and a half miles) east of Copan, where a ballcourt was built sometime between 250 BCE and 150 CE (Canuto 2004). The third is the ballcourt at PACO 15. Radiocarbon dates and ceramic comparisons from the excavations in Cuyumapa place its construction and use between 400 BCE and 150 CE (Fox 1994:Table 12; Hendon and Joyce 1993; Joyce, Hendon, and Lopiparo 2009).

At ballcourts some people played and others watched a fast-paced, exciting sporting event. Games played with teams of men or women using a rubber ball have been documented as a feature of many indigenous societies in the Americas (Bradley 2001; Gillespie 1991). People in Mesoamerica were more concerned than people in other areas to build permanent arenas in which to play, although even here such facilities were not always used (Uriarte 2006). The lack of standardization in the design of the courts and what scholars know about the game from visual imagery, Spanish descriptions, and how it was played in modern times indicate that the rules of the Mesoamerican games varied over time and regionally (Cohodas 1991; Leyenaar and Parsons 1988; Taladoire and Colsenet 1991). Representations of the ballgame in Maya art, such as the ceramic vase in figure 35, indicate that the game was played by teams of two players on a side who kept the ball in motion by bouncing it off their bodies, especially the hips and shoulders, without using their hands (M. Miller 2001). The impact of the elastic and dense solid rubber ball, when volleyed back and forth at high speeds, was capable of inflicting severe bruises and even of breaking bones. The players wore protective padding around their torsos, hips, and knees, which reduced but did not eliminate the risk of injury. How the game was scored or a winner determined remains elusive for the time period discussed here, but scholars suspect that the markers, pieces of sculpture set in walls and floors of the court, were important to the process of earning points. Images of ballgames also show the ball as extremely large when compared to the participants, who wear elaborate headdresses and jewelry, suggesting that these representations, like most Maya art, wish to emphasize important elements at the expense of realism and conflate events that occurred at different times. The costumes of the ballplayers, for example, include things that would be worn before or after the game itself. And the match itself, absorbing as it was, did not represent the sum total of what people did at ballcourts or encompass the full social significance of the place (Day 2001). Although sacrificing has been the most commonly mentioned associated event (Schele and Friedel 1991), excavations in the vicinity of ballcourts in Cuyumapa and Cerro Palenque document other kinds of activities.

Ballgames have certain formal characteristics in that the play was governed by rules. In practice, a successful game was predicated on serendipity, athletic skill, human psychology, and political manipulation. It celebrated the beauty of finely tuned, well-trained young bodies in constant motion achieving spectacular feats of coordination at high speed—the same sorts of bodies displayed in arrested motion on certain high-status houses at Copan. Ballgames also offered the vicarious experience of danger. Injury and even death were constant possibilities, whether accidental in the course of play or planned as a sacrificial rite woven into the event. Readings of the ballgame's meaning place greater emphasis on its metaphysical aspect. But there is the physical and experiential aspect as well, which helps explain in part the psychological appeal of the game and why it would have been so compelling a symbolic vehicle.

Neither the players nor the people attending the event conducted themselves with the solemnity and rigidity one might expect when confronted by a reenactment of the cosmic struggle between light and dark. For one thing, ballgames took place in a noisy atmosphere, with musicians playing and spectators shouting (Matos Moctezuma 2001; M. Miller 2001). In colonial-era writings, Spaniards comment on the gambling, eating, drinking, and socializing endemic to ballgames (Leyenaar and Parsons 1988; Scarborough 1991). Clay models of ballgames made by Mesoamerican cultures living in the western part of Mexico depict an excited audience perched on the top of the court's side walls frozen in attitudes suggestive of intense engagement with what goes on below them (Day 2001). In figure 35, a ceramic vase shows two spectators conferring with one another in highly animated fashion. One of the two men talking so intently to his seatmate holds two rattles with which he contributes to the noisy atmosphere. A third man leans forward and flings out his hand as he shouts at a player diving for the ball below (Reents-Budet 1994:Figure 6.37). Mary Miller (2001) identifies this figure as a referee holding a conch shell trumpet with which to help control the play.

BALLCOURTS IN COPAN, CUYUMAPA, AND CERRO PALENQUE

All three of the societies I examine here used monumentality to create places that were separate from and yet connected to domestic or living areas, and all invested in a particular kind of special-purpose structure, a ballcourt (table 7). At Copan and Cerro Palenque, ballcourts are part of the largest cluster of monumental architecture, the Main Group and the Great Plaza. Present in both locations are planned open spaces that could accommodate

TABLE 7. Ballcourt Dimensions

BALLCOURT	LENGTH OF FLANKING MOUNDS (IN METERS)	WIDTH OF PLAYING ALLEY (IN METERS)
CUYUMAPA VALLEY: LATE FORMATIVE PERIOD		
PACO 15	27.04 and 26.76	9.32
CUYUMAPA VALLEY: LATE CLASSIC PERIOD LARGE BALLCOURTS ON MAIN RIVERS		
PACO 5	43.12 and 44.85	22.14
PACO 11	32.38 and 31.66	7.26
PACO 17	30.67 and 30.67	14.81
CUYUMAPA VALLEY: LATE CLASSIC PERIOD SMALL BALLCOURTS ON TRIBUTARY STREAMS		
PACO 2	27.78 and 23.78	10.69
PACO 9	16.45 and 16.16	9.42
PACO 14	28.81 and 28.21	8.84
CERRO PALENQUE		
Great Plaza	35	11
COPAN		
Ballcourt A final version	28.45	7.2
Ballcourt B final version	17	6

Sources: Cuyumapa: Fox 1994:Table 11; Cerro Palenque: Joyce 1991:61; Copan: Strömsvik 1952: 189 (Ballcourt A); Fash and Lane 1983:515, Figure H-3 (Ballcourt B).

large numbers of people, but access to these spaces and the ballcourts they contain is made difficult by their enclosure by massive stone buildings.

The Copan kingdom built two ballcourts, each renovated several times. The main one, Ballcourt A, first constructed during the Early Classic, is centrally located in the Main Group, tucked into a space at the foot of the Hieroglyphic Staircase, the massive monument to dynastic continuity begun by Ruler 13 and renovated by Ruler 15 (Ashmore 1991; W. Fash 2001). The court's final version (A-III) was restored in the 1930s by the Carnegie Institution of Washington. This, plus more recent work exploring the earlier constructions in this part of the Main Group, has made the details of the ballcourt's appearance well known to archaeologist and tourist alike. Ballcourt A-III has a playing alley paved with rectangular stone slabs into which were set three large carved stones, or markers. Badly eroded, they nevertheless retain enough detail to indicate their main theme of an outsized rubber ball and at least one humanlike figure (Baudez 1994). The flanking platforms that enclose the alley have a complex profile. At first they rise vertically to create a low, bench-shaped section. Above this the walls slope backward away from the playing alley before straightening up to vertical again at the very top. Here are set six stone macaw heads, three on a side at the two ends and center of the wall's length. A line of stones carved with hieroglyphs runs from the central macaw head on each side down the slope to the bench (Strömsvik 1952). The playing alley itself extends beyond the ends of the flanking buildings, giving it the shape of the capital letter I. On its southern end, the alley opens directly into the court formed by the Hieroglyphic Staircase and the Acropolis, but to the north it is closed off by a set of steps rising to a terrace supporting the carved monument Stela 2 (W. Fash 2001:Plate II, Figure 7).

The later example, Ballcourt B, is located southwest of the Acropolis and the area occupied by Ruler 16 in the dense residential area surrounding the Main Group, opposite the Sepulturas zone. Rebuilt three times, the earliest phase dates to the Late Classic period. The excavations of the ballcourt found Tohil Plumbate pottery in the upper levels of the excavation, demonstrating that people continued to use Ballcourt B in the Terminal Classic to Early Postclassic period, after the collapse of royal rule. Its profile is similar to that of the main ballcourt but on a smaller scale: the vertical wall is much lower, and the sloping one does not rise as high. Although quite a bit shorter than the one in the Main Group, the playing alley of Ballcourt B is only slightly narrower (see table 7). No ballcourt markers are associated with Ballcourt B. Both ends of the court are enclosed by stone walls, and the playing alley was not paved (Fash and Lane 1983).

The ballcourt at Cerro Palenque is placed at the southern end of the Great Plaza within easy reach of the residential group to its south (Joyce 1991). Built on a raised terrace, it and the nearby houses of the ballcourt residential group sit above the level of the rest of the monumental plaza to the north. The side walls have a more steplike profile than at Copan owing to the presence of a second vertical wall built on the lower bench (Joyce 1985:222–29). The sloping surface typical of ballcourt walls begins at the top of this second wall. The single marker, a basalt circle, was set in the eastern wall and represents the only sculpture associated with the ballcourt (see table 3). The ends of the playing alley are open. To the north, it merges with the

36. Ballcourt A as seen from the top of the Acropolis at Copan. Photograph by Julia A. Hendon.

37. Ballcourt B, the smaller court built outside of the Main Group at Copan. Photograph by Julia A. Hendon.

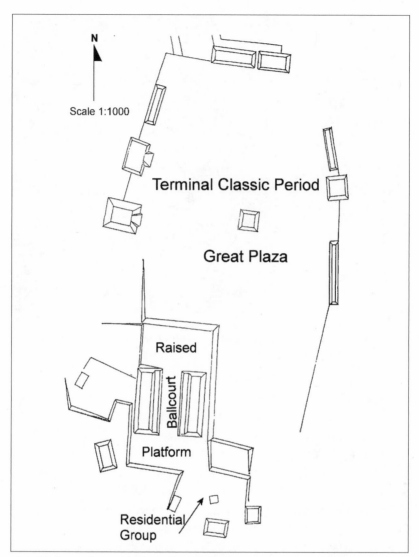

N

Scale 1:1000

Terminal Classic Period

Great Plaza

Raised

Ballcourt

Platform

Residential
Group

38. Plan of the heart of Cerro Palenque's Terminal Classic monumental space that demonstrates
the relationship between the Great Plaza, the ballcourt, and the ballcourt residential group.
Courtesy of the Instituto Hondureño de Antropología e Historia, redrawn from the original
plan by Rosemary A. Joyce, used with permission.

39. Looking down the playing alley of the Cerro Palenque ballcourt from the residential group. One of the two mounds marking the sides of the court is visible in the left rear of the scene. Photograph by Julia A. Hendon.

remainder of the raised terrace. To the south, it turns into a paved walkway that connects to the residential group some 20 meters (65 feet) away (Hendon 2003c, 2005).

People in Cuyumapa effected a significant expansion of their ability to participate in and watch ballgames by building six ballcourts throughout the region that superseded the one at PACO 15 (see chapter 1; Hendon and Joyce 1993; Joyce, Hendon, and Lopiparo 2009). Unlike Copan and Cerro Palenque, where all ballcourts are oriented more or less north–south, the Cuyumapa ones vary in the direction of their playing alleys (table 8). The three largest are located on the main rivers feeding into the Cuyumapa river (PACO 5, 11, and 17). The remaining ones, built near tributaries of these larger rivers, are smaller (PACO 2, 9, and 14). The Cuyumapa ballcourts are in clusters that include houses. The site of PACO 2, for example, contains a small ballcourt, a large-scale residential structure, and many small residences. PACO 5, near the Oloman river, has a larger ballcourt and eight large structures. These houses, despite their proximity, do not align themselves to the monumental architecture in the way seen at Copan or Cerro Palenque.

TABLE 8. Ballcourt Orientations

BALLCOURT	ORIENTATION (DEGREES EAST OF NORTH)
Cuyumapa PACO 15	35.5
Cuyumapa PACO 5	105.5
Cuyumapa PACO 11	163.0
Cuyumapa PACO 17	106.0
Cuyumapa PACO 2	9.5
Cuyumapa PACO 9	88.0
Cuyumapa PACO 14	52.0
Cerro Palenque	0
Copan Ballcourt A (final version)	353
Copan Ballcourt B (final version)	352

Sources: Cuyumapa: Fox 1994:Table 11; Cerro Palenque: Joyce 1991:61, where the orientation is described as "north–south," Figure 5; Copan: Baudez 1994:165 (Ballcourt A); Fash and Lane 1983:507, where the orientation is described as "ligeramente al oeste del norte" (slightly west of north), Figure H-2 (Ballcourt B).

The best-preserved Late to Terminal Classic one, PACO 14, has a clay floor laid over a gravel subflooring. The bench segues to a sloping surface covered in packed gravel. This in turn ends in another vertical wall, which forms the retaining wall for the top of the structure. A line of stones defines one end zone, whereas the other is not demarcated in any permanent fashion (Fox 1994:149–58, Figures 6, 18). As noted in table 2, sculpted pieces were placed in the sloping walls of the PACO 5 and 14 ballcourts.

The difference in the number of ballcourts between Copan, Cerro Palenque, and Cuyumapa during the Late and Terminal Classic periods becomes even more marked when one factors in the disparity in population, as approximated by settlement density and distribution. For most of the time that there was a ballcourt in Copan, there was just one in the entire valley. The distinctive location, much smaller size, and lack of decoration of the second one, built perhaps some two hundred years after Ballcourt A first came into use, render it an unlikely equivalent facility in terms of use or participants. At · Cerro Palenque, a single ballcourt served the whole settlement of around five hundred houses; in Cuyumapa, there was one ballcourt for every seventy-five residential buildings. The fewer number of ballcourts at Copan and Cerro

40. Unexcavated ballcourt in the Cuyumapa valley. The men are positioned to mark the slope
of the structures. The playing alley runs between them. Photograph by John G. Fox,
reproduced with permission

Palenque makes them centralizing places but also suggests a more restricted
use and the exercise of greater control. The fact that all three societies
considered ballgames sufficiently important to merit the building of one or
more permanent facilities indicates that they used a common means of
promoting social interaction and integration. At the same time, the degree
to which social difference among individuals and groups was present and
made visible through material culture and architecture varies between these
three societies, implying that the ballgame's contribution to memory and
identity may also have differed.

THE SOCIAL CONTEXT OF BALLGAMES

The ballgames and associated activities taking place at Copan, Cerro Palenque, and Cuyumapa are examples of ritualization in that they are ways of
acting that are differentiated not only by their content but also by their
location even though the practices by which ritualization is created are not
identical in the three areas and do not have the same consequences. Consid-

ering the role of eating and drinking in connection with the ballgame helps elucidate these differences.

CUYUMAPA: COMMENSALITY AND THE BALLGAME

The many courts in Cuyumapa may be taken as an indicator of the degree of community involvement in a continuing series of games taking place over time and moving through the region. Excavation of the ballcourts at PACO 2, 5, 14, and 15 reinforces this notion by what it reveals about the other things people did at ballcourts. They brought food and jars of chicha to the ballcourt from their homes. They ate and drank, using carefully decorated bowls which they broke and left behind along with fragments of the jars. They burned incense, held figurines, and played whistles (Fox 1994:149–76). In other words, they did some of the same sorts of things they did at home when celebrating important moments in the life of their social group. And they did these things often enough over the life of any individual ballcourt and over the long term, from the beginnings of ballcourt activity at PACO 15 through the Terminal Classic period, to leave perceptible archaeological traces.

The ballcourts at Cuyumapa also contain sculpture (see table 2) and caches. Two round pits below the floor of the PACO 14 ballcourt had been used to burn some kind of material (which the excavator could not identity) as the court came into existence and began to be used. Two small jars, alluding yet again to the centrality of drinking at social events, were buried near an earthen ramp that leads into the playing alley of the PACO 14 ballcourt (Fox 1994:151). The deliberately arranged set of stones that Fox describes as a ballcourt effigy at PACO 2 becomes a cache over the course of its life. The platform adjacent to the ballcourt where the effigy was found has a fill of orange-brown sand. During the time the small representation of a ballcourt was exposed on the surface of this fill, people burned materials that left a layer of carbon on the stones of the effigy itself. Later, after the ballcourt model was covered up by a new layer of sandy fill, people continued to burn incense, leaving behind the broken remains of the censers. They also left behind parts of braziers, an imported Ulua Polychrome bowl, and an unbroken mano, again in a matrix of burned material (Fox 1994:173–75). Two things about this sequence of events are interesting. One is the way the effigy of a ballcourt continues to be a focus of ritualized action even after it has disappeared from view. The other is the nature of the objects found smashed and burned on the second surface. These include bowls and jars, figurine fragments, and a piece of polished greenstone. Many of them are related to making or eating food, the kinds of things usually found at home.

Pieces from another kind of implement are also found in the deposits at PACO 2 and 15. Labeled brazier/censers, they consist of a shallow plate with incising on one side and prongs projecting upward from the rim and an hourglass-shaped base with parts of the side walls cut out to create openings through which air and smoke could pass. The pieces from both ballcourts have smudged and discolored areas, signs of having been exposed repeatedly to heat. A very similar kind of implement was used at Cerro Palenque houses as a portable stove (Joyce 1991:103), and I can add that a comparable implement served this same purpose in the Sepulturas houses (Hendon 1987:335–39, 1988). Fox (1994:Table 19) interprets his examples as incense burners, arguing that food preparation did not occur around ballcourts in Cuyumapa. This apparent distinction leads him to differentiate between domestic and ritual settings as well as actions. However, deposits at both PACO 15 and 2 contain another sign of food preparation in the form of basalt manos, one associated with the PACO 2 platform and two from PACO 15. Furthermore, heating food and burning incense in the same brazier are not mutually incompatible uses. There is nothing in the physical form that precludes doing both, and Mesoamerican local theories of production do not support the separation of ritual and mundane spheres (Monaghan 1998a). The smaller representation of braziers and manos when compared to bowls and jars does suggest that most food and drink arrived at the ballcourts already made, but their presence also implies that some reheating and grinding were incorporated into the ritualized activities taking place there.

CERRO PALENQUE: DOMESTIC SPACE AND THE BALLGAME

I searched diligently for comparable deposits around the Cerro Palenque ballcourt but did not find them. Test pits placed around the back and sides of both ballcourt mounds in 1998 found almost no artifacts at all and quickly encountered the fill of the supporting platform (Hendon 1998), while work in the ballcourt alley and Great Plaza was similarly limited in what it found (Joyce 1991). I did, however, retrieve the remains of several pottery vessels broken on the paved corridor between the ballcourt and the residential group, including a fine paste vessel and an imported jar, possibly from El Salvador (Hendon 2002a, 2005). This leads back to the adjacent living space and the feasting and associated performances of figurine making described in chapters 4 and 5. The connection between one set of houses and the ballcourt is further reinforced by the platform located at the northern end of the ballcourt residential group.

This patio platform, measuring 5 x 4.25 meters (21.25 square meters or almost 230 square feet) and standing 32 centimeters (about 12.6 inches) above the patio, was built entirely of a fill made from mixing medium to very large river cobbles with clay. No evidence was found that it ever supported a building, even one of perishable materials. Although bearing some resemblance to the shrines (small, centrally located platforms) excavated in several other groups (Joyce 1991:48–52, 59–60), it is much larger and lacks their architectural features. As an open, slightly raised surface, it would be well suited to serve as a viewing platform for a small group of favored spectators, especially given the fact that its placement allows an unimpeded view across the open area of the terrace and into the south end of the ballcourt playing alley. Unlike Cuyumapa, where people perambulate through space and use ballcourts of differing sizes, the inhabitants of Cerro Palenque congregate at one spot on the landscape for feasts and ballgames. Given the ballgame's association with diurnal and seasonal periods of time, it is likely that both societies participated in a sequence of ballgames over the course of the year (Gillespie 1991; Joyce, Hendon, and Lopiparo 2009). Cuyumapans sometimes hosted ballgames and at other times were guests. Based on the range of court sizes, the size of the gatherings and the nature of the game varied as well. Both the assignment of the roles of host and guest and the kind of game played were much less flexible at Cerro Palenque. One coresident community of practice, made up of those living closest to the Great Plaza, is in the best position to provide the physical location for associated events and in consequence comes to dominate the proceedings.

COPAN: ROYAL AUTHORITY AND THE BALLGAME

No comparable archaeological deposits that would indicate what people did in and around Copan Ballcourt A have been reported from the various excavations that have investigated the court and its associated buildings (Cheek 1983; Fash and Lane 1983; Strömsvik 1952; Williamson 2003). This probably reflects a real difference in behavior between Copan and the other two societies. It is true that archaeologists from the Carnegie Institution who worked at Copan in the 1930s showed little interest in analyzing artifact deposits they might come across in their excavations of monumental architecture. Even if they saved and described artifacts, they did not pay much attention to deciphering the context of the deposits. When they did come across accumulations of artifacts, however, they often mentioned their presence, and the lack of such reporting bolsters the argument that such deposits were not present.

Fox (1996) points to the very early discovery of a small jar in the building constructed on top of the west platform of Ballcourt A as evidence of an emphasis on drinking similar to that at Cuyumapa (see also Gordon 1970). He extends this interpretation to Ballcourt B on the basis of the fact that the Tohil Plumbate sherds came from jars. The excavators of this ballcourt, however, see their finds, which also include green obsidian implements, stone censers, and carved blocks that once formed part of the sculpted doorjambs of Structure 18, the looted tomb of Ruler 16 in the East Court, as marking activities that took place after a rupture in Copan society and political organization (Fash and Long 1983; Fash, Fash, and Davis-Salazar 2004). This view makes it difficult to know how similar this Terminal Classic/Early Postclassic use of Ballcourt B is to what happened there in the Late Classic period, when it was first built.

What is clear is that Ballcourt A is connected to many symbols of royal authority, such as Stela 2 at its northern end, its proximity to the Hieroglyphic Staircase, and a wealth of architectonic sculpture. In addition to the markers set in the floor of the playing alley and the macaw heads on the walls of the final version, the buildings which sit on top of each of the flanking platforms have façades that continue the macaw theme and elaborate it with visual references to corn, the sun as it passes through the underworld, serpents, and bones (Baudez 1994; B. Fash 1992; W. Fash 2001; Kowalski and Fash 1991). Its builders secreted caches in the body of the ballcourt as it was renovated (Cheek 1983), signaling the substantial and long-term royal investment in having a ballcourt next to the Hieroglyphic Staircase.

The later construction of Ballcourt B in the southern part of the residential area may serve as a sign of expanded involvement in the ballgame and its incorporation into the domestic life of a wider segment of Copan society. Its proximity to residential structures dated to the Terminal Classic and Early Postclassic and the occurrence of pottery from these periods are important for what light they may shed on the dissolution of or change in Copan society after the end of dynastic rule (Fash, Fash, and Davis-Salazar 2004; Manahan 2004). Nevertheless, the evidence provided by its original excavators demonstrates that its construction and much of its use predate these changes. Ballcourt B was built during the apogee of Copan society in a very different spatial setting from that of the main ballcourt and yet not all that far away from Ruler 16's residence. In fact, it is more easily reached from there than is the main ballcourt. Is it possible that Ballcourt B represents an attempt by the high-status families living in this area to augment their involvement in the ballgame and to draw closer to the ruler as a counterweight to the influence gained by the people in Group 9N-8 as a result of the significant role assumed by the residents of Patio A?

ARE BALLCOURTS PUBLIC OR PRIVATE PLACES?

At this point, I want to revisit the issue of public and private space raised in the discussion of the semiotic house in chapter 3. There I suggested that rather than simply conflate private and domestic in opposition to public and political, one should pay attention to who exerted control over the space in question, how, and with what result. From this perspective, the most public space in these three societies emerges as that associated with ballcourts and large mounds in Cuyumapa. The six ballcourts in use during the Late to Terminal Classic are closer to some clusters of small-scale structures (residences) than others. Three are associated with a single large structure, while the remaining three have additional large structures nearby arranged to form a plaza. None is embedded in one particular monumental locus, however, as at Copan and Cerro Palenque, nor do they have the close spatial association with a particular set of dwellings. Multiple contemporaneous ballcourts distributed across the landscape lend themselves less to a monopoly of control than to a system of alternating use and shifting identities as people host events in one ballcourt and visit another over some period of time.

The monumental areas at Cerro Palenque and Copan contain only a small number of residences. The spatial relations created by the design of these places separate the people living there from everyone else to a much greater extent than in Cuyumapa. Why did other members of the Copan polity come into the Main Group? Several reasons have been posited, including consultation between ruler and politically subordinate officeholders (W. Fash 2005), attendance at periodic performances linked to significant dates or events, including ballgames (Baudez 1991; W. Fash 2001; M. Miller 1986), and feasting (Andrews and Bill 2005; Hendon 2003b). Consultation, performance, and feasting are also applicable to Cerro Palenque, where the attendees are put in the position of being invited into one domestic setting for specific reasons and for a limited amount of time (Hendon 2003c). Performance and feasting and, no doubt, consultation pertain to Cuyumapa ballcourts as well, but the ability of one group to assert control consistently over these interactions is absent or reduced.

Monumental space shifts location over time at Cerro Palenque. The earlier, smaller settlement puts monumental architecture in close proximity to well-built residential compounds. As the community expands, several concentrations of more monumental architecture are built in association with clusters of houses. The largest area, the Great Plaza, is most closely connected with only one residential group that is so close to the ballcourt that a misaimed ball might easily have ended up in the patio area. Anyone wishing to participate in the ballgame and its associated festivities would be in close proximity to the people who live there and even inside the residential group itself. The shared foundation platform supporting the Great Plaza–ballcourt complex and the residential group, and the paved walkway that extends from the residential patio into the ballcourt playing alley create a unique spatial relationship between this one living area and the largest complex of monumental, nonresidential architecture at the site.

The Main Group at Copan is also spatially and socially connected with one group of people, those forming the royal house revolving around the person identifying himself as the ruler of a political entity that included the Copan valley and possibly neighboring areas as well. Excavation of the large residences behind the Acropolis, located at the base of its south side, suggests that Ruler 16 lived here (Andrews and Bill 2005; Andrews and Fash 1992; Bill 1997a). Even the large open plazas must be considered part of this royal residential space, however, an association reinforced by royalty's habit of placing personalized statements of authority, such as stelae and other forms of sculpture carrying images of current and past rulers, in these plazas.

CONSTRUCTING A SPATIOTEMPORAL ORDER

Scholars have worked diligently to discern what religious, social, and political beliefs ballcourts and the ballgame communicated in light of regional and temporal variation (Scarborough and Wilcox 1991). The game reenacts mythological episodes by recalling the ballgames played by the Hero Twins against the deities of the underworld and the beneficial consequences of those games and their aftermath for humanity, events recorded in the *Popol vuh* (D. Tedlock 1996). It symbolizes more general beliefs about life, death, regeneration, agricultural fertility, astronomical bodies, and seasonal cycles (Gillespie 1991). It enhances political power by offering a way for individual rulers to celebrate their achievements and to wrap themselves in the mantle of the creation story through sponsorship or actual participation (Baudez 1984; Leyenaar and Parsons 1988). Some Maya monuments show a ruler dressed as a player or playing the game, often with a human skull or body as the ball (Miller and Houston 1987; Schele and Miller 1986). Royal players do not bounce their anthropomorphized ball or human victim against the sloping walls of a ballcourt, however, but against the steps of a monumental staircase. This setting suggests that these images, even if intended as a more or less factual record of royal action, depict something different from the usual ballgame (Cohodas 1991; Schele and Friedel 1991).

These readings of the ballgame's meaning put a heavy emphasis on its symbolism as expressed in such products of the Maya artistic tradition as stone sculpture, painting, and clay figurines. Astronomy, mythology, cycles of life and death, agricultural fertility, and political power all figure as prominent themes. Like Temple 22 and the Acropolis, ballcourts can be decoded to elucidate these more general meanings and those more specific to a particular edifice. This approach has been applied to the main ballcourt at Copan, in its final phase and earlier incarnations, where sculpted motifs and carved ballcourt markers have been interpreted in the context of dynastic consolidation and religious beliefs (Baudez 1994; B. Fash 1992; W. Fash 1998, 2001; Fash, Andrews, and Manahan 2004; Kowalski and Fash 1991). Again, as with the Acropolis, these iconographic and structural studies have been productive of insight but do not fully exploit the ways in which the ballcourt and the ballgame become part of the semiotic and practical complex through which people give meaning to and gain an understanding of their world.

Ballgames have the potential to be significant to remembering and forgetting because they connect important events with places and time. In other words, they are another contributor to the construction of a spatiotemporal system. Partly this results from their association with the passage of time and the movement of the sun, other astronomical bodies, and the seasons of the year, an association marked symbolically in myth and art but also experientially by the celebration of games and events in particular kinds of spaces at different points in the year. Here again the contrast between Cerro Palenque and Cuyumapa is instructive. Cuyumapans achieve their marking of a spatiotemporal order by relocating themselves from house to court and by moving through the valleys and hills they lived in to visit different spots on the landscape (Joyce, Hendon, and Lopiparo 2009). Cerro Palenque's denizens take the opposite approach. They extend one house (or living area) to include the ballcourt and make it a focus of repeated aggregations of people from elsewhere in the community or the valley. These congregations of friends, relatives, and strangers occur in a place that alludes to the past as well as the present by virtue of its location beneath the hilltop center that is no longer inhabited by the living. Of course, the converse is also true in that the ballcourt expands to include the house.

Doubts have been expressed as to whether Maya ballcourts, including the one at Copan, ever housed the kind of athletic ballgame played elsewhere: "The Classic Maya ballgame was [never] a 'spectator sport,' at least when played on ritual occasions in the principal masonry courts. . . . Perhaps only elite members of the royal lineages were privileged to observe what, despite the excitement of the game, was more of a ceremony than a diversion" (Leyenaar and Parsons 1988:87–88). The lack of any trace of substantial participation and plain old fun implied by the chicha jars at Cerro Palenque and Cuyumapa may provide some support to the notion that the Maya game was a "symbolic [one] in which a few heavily costumed nobles took perfunctory shots at an oversize ball in a small exhibition court, perhaps reenacting a cosmogonic myth" (Cohodas 1991:257–59).

Or the absence of trash may merely mean that Copan royalty either demanded a much more thorough cleanup or expected the eating and drinking to take place elsewhere, perhaps as a way of reinforcing social difference between those invited to drink with royalty and those left to their own devices. Furthermore, the claim often made that Maya ballcourts do not "provide much space for massed viewing" (Leyenaar and Parsons 1988:87) can be countered in the case of Copan by the steps at the northern end zone and the presence of the Acropolis with its soaring tier of steps ending in the large paved area that forms the north side of Structure 11 at the top. Although people may have been forbidden to loll on the carved stairs of the Hieroglyphic Staircase, the wide terraces on either side of it could have been used as seats. As vividly imagined in a reconstruction by an artist in the *National Geographic*, one might not be very close to the action, but one would have a panoramic view (W. Fash 2001:Figure 89). Where one sits may become another source of privilege, as some areas, such as the terraces beside the Hieroglyphic Staircase, offer a more obstructed view than others.

Not just royalty played an active role, however, in events connected with the ballgame at Copan. The removal of the collapsed walls and roof of Structure 9N-81, on the west side of Patio A of Group 9N-8, uncovered several objects that can be connected to the ballgame because of their resemblance to images of ballplayer regalia (Webster, Fash, and Abrams 1986:209–10, Figure 46, Plates 65, 72–74). Their position just above the floor below the rubble indicates that they had been stored in the rafters or high up on the wall of the main room, a common way of storing valuable items not for general use, including ballgame equipment (Sheets 1992; Tedlock 1996). The excavators found a stone U-shaped object known as a yoke and a three-dimensional carving, known as an *hacha*, in the main room. This hacha is interpreted as a flattened macaw's head shown in profile, while a second hacha, found in the side storage room, is carved in the form of a human skull, again in profile view. Pieces from another yoke were also found as well as two smashed pottery vessels, a jar and a censer. Ballplayers are sometimes shown wearing objects similar to the yoke around their waist with the hacha projecting from it in the vicinity of the wearer's stomach, although these depictions are more frequently found in other areas of Mesoamerica where this costume seems to have been more common than in the Maya lowlands. Most scholars believe that the stone versions were reserved for ceremonies before or after the game. The actual equipment used in play, it is thought, was constructed from organic materials that would be more comfortable to wear and better than stone at absorbing the force of the rubber ball's impact (Cohodas 1991; Nicholson 1988; Scott 2001).

This same building is supported by a large platform, much larger than the building itself, which leaves quite an expanse of open terrace to its south with some evidence for food processing (Hendon 1987). This in turn connects to the platform supporting the largest building, Structure 9N-82, the one with a hieroglyphic bench and stone male figures attached to the façade (see chapter 5). While previous studies of these figures have identified them as ancestors and possibly scribes, they may also be ballplayers as well.

The yokes and hachas in Structure 9N-81 raise an intriguing thought about the role played by the residents of Patio A in ballgames at the Main Group. I noted earlier that the floor markers of Ballcourt A-III are so badly eroded that little detail remains. The markers for the preceding version, A-IIb, however, are quite well preserved. It has been suggested that these markers were placed by Ruler 13 shortly before he ordered the substantial renovation that resulted in the construction of the final version and its dedication in 738 CE (W. Fash 2001; Martin and Grube 2000:204–5). The central marker depicts two individuals actually playing. The one on the viewer's left has been identified both as Ruler 13 and as one of the Hero Twins who defeated the lords of the underworld in a set of mythic contests recorded in the *Popol vuh*. He is shown at the moment of bouncing the ball off the heavy padding that encircles his torso. Thus he wears the kind of protective gear commonly illustrated in two- and three-dimensional images of ballgame players in the Maya area. His opponent, on the right of the ball, has been identified as the God of the Number Zero, in other words, a supernatural being whose connection to death and the underworld is obvious in the features of his face. The symbolism is plain: Ruler 13 is conflated with one of the Hero Twins and enacts their victory over death (Baudez 1994; W. Fash 2001:Figure 69; Schele 1987).

Unlike the figure of Ruler 13/Hero Twin, the Number Zero deity is not dressed in typical Maya ballplayer costume. Instead, he wears a much narrower belt around his waist with a human head attached to the front that partially covers his stomach and chest. This had been identified as the "yoke-and-hacha complex" (Cohodas 1991:257). Cohodas goes on to note that it is unlikely that actual teams squared off wearing such different protective gear because to do so would "jeopardize the skill of ball players if . . . put into practice." The connection to the objects found in Structure 9N-81 must lie in the realm of the symbolic and semiotic, then.

Although stone yokes and hachas have been found at Maya sites besides Copan, they are nevertheless a later introduction into the region and, more importantly, not considered to be part of the usual Maya uniform (Scott 2001). The noble house in Group 9N-8 Patio A was the custodian of yokes and hachas during the reign of Ruler 16, who took office twenty-five years after Ruler 13 but who continued to use Ballcourt A-III. Some members of the Patio A family may actually have worn the yokes and hachas as part of ceremonies before or after games in Ballcourt A, entering the Main Group from the east along the raised path. By wearing this foreign costume, they may have had the privilege and responsibility of enacting the role of the opposition during these performances in which Ruler 16 took on the same role as his predecessor. I am not saying that Patio A's residents were really foreigners from some other part of Mesoamerica. The biological relatedness of the Copan population alone argues against an overly literal understanding of this role. Rather, by donning these accoutrements, the representatives of Patio A's sociological house serve as a foil to the ruler that reinforces his assumption of the role of victor in the cosmic struggles at the heart of the game.

41. Ballcourt marker A-IIb, Copan. Photograph © Justin Kerr, K2871.

The many readings of ballgame symbolism index a pervasive relationship, that of disjunction (Gillespie 1991). The design of the courts, the nature
of the game itself with its winners and losers, its temporal and astronomical
associations, its role in myth, and the way it is represented in art express
inequalities that are never resolved back into an equilibrium. The ballgame is
thus implicated in the continual recreation of social difference as a relationship rather than a set of fixed categories, just as houses and objects are.
Hachas and yokes, ballgame regalia that are indexical icons of foreignness,
make disjunction visible when put on display in the context of a particular
kind of ritualized performance.

The political co-optation of the ballgame is evident throughout Mesoamerican history, and Maya kings, judging by the kinds of art and text they
commissioned, were no different in subverting the game to their own political ends. It seems perverse, however, to assume that Maya kings were so
blind to the effectiveness of a "non-symbolic" game in riveting the attention
of its spectators (Fash and Fash 2007) and thus providing a focal point for
the promulgation of social memory favorable to their own ends that they

vitiated the sporting and *communitas* aspects of the game—the gambling, the vicarious participation in thrilling athleticism, and the element of chance (or at least its simulacrum). If one thinks in terms of communities of memory, one of which Copan's royal line constitutes, then it is possible to see how such events situated in the specialized place that Ballcourt A represents and in the heart of the monumental space controlled by the king become a powerful reification of a spatiotemporal order defined not by seasons or the movement of astronomical bodies but by the continuity of dynastic succession. At the same time, the Cerro Palenque and Cuyumapa ballcourts demonstrate that the ballgame's indexing of disjunction and its construction of a spatiotemporal order do not depend on the existence of such a centralized political system.

Communities of Memory and Local Histories

The contents of the memory bundle presented for inspection in the introduction have been explored throughout this book through an examination of everyday life and domestic space, crafting and performance, feasting and the ballgame. My perspective on the bundle reveals that remembering and forgetting are both social and individual, the outcome of intersubjective relations stretched across time and space. Starting with collective memory as inherently social (Halbwachs 1992, 1994, 1997), I have incorporated ideas about social memory, commemoration, and identity (Cole 2001; Handler 1994; Hirst and Manier 1995). Social memory is intimately bound up with objects, which, having their own materiality and life histories, may be linked with yet separated physically from individuals, social groups, or places. Objects can transcend the limits of the human life span yet at the same time become so identified with people that they absorb something of a person's identity and history. In a sense, objects are not just personlike but may be perceived as persons in their own right. Mesoamerican concepts of coessences and relational personhood help shape the particular ways in which objects become personlike in pre-Hispanic Honduras. Like people, the lives of houses, ballcourts, figurine whistles, sculpture, textiles, grinding stones, and jars have a trajectory that can be linked to the passage of time and located in space to participate in the same spatiotemporal order that directs human lives and destinies. They are part of the practical and semiotic complex that includes, but is not limited to, signs to be read (Bourdieu 1993; Keane 1997; Preucel 2006). This more inclusive complex encompasses the interrelationship between material properties, practices, and referential inferences from icons and indexes that cross the analytical and perceptual boundaries between such seemingly distinct entities as people, objects, and places. The practical and semiotic complex in Mesoamerica embraces the animate and inert, the corporeal and the disembodied, the quick and the dead.

To close out my archaeological study of social memory and identity in pre-Hispanic Honduras, I want to return to the central questions that prompted this book and that have served as the driving force behind my discussion of daily life, the semiotic house, the relational self and distributed personhood, the humility and enchantment of objects, the embodiment of knowledge, and how these elements become generative resources for remembering and forgetting. At earlier points I have asked, How do objects help people remember? How does everyday life become part of the work of remembering and forgetting? And how do memory communities assert connections between present and past? I end by considering the political and social consequences of multiple memory communities.

The phrases I have adopted to refer to the people I am interested in, coresident community of practice (Wenger 1998), sociological house (Joyce and Gillespie 2000; Lévi-Strauss 1982, 1987), and memory community (Burke 1989), do not exactly trip off the tongue. Their clumsiness notwithstanding, I have found them useful because they capture important relationships. At the same time, these terms free me from having to assume that the people enmeshed in these relations are necessarily biologically related or even kin in any sense. That many of the people who made up communities of practice or memory in ancient Copan, Cerro Palenque, and Cuyumapa, or who saw themselves as members of a sociological house, did consider themselves as kinsmen or women is neither unimportant nor uninteresting for a deeper understanding of intimate relations and social life. Trying to determine social organization, however, whether family, household, clan, lineage, or moiety, to mention just a few of the wealth of kinship categories anthropologists have concerned themselves with, fails to zero in on what is truly significant for the intersubjective construction through historical action of memory and identity.

HOW DO OBJECTS HELP PEOPLE REMEMBER?

Objects may be enchanting through their cognitive stickiness or humble to the point of fading into the background of everyday life (Gell 1998; D. Miller 1987). Either way, they may become agents of memory and identity. The two kinds of enchanting objects to which this study has devoted the greatest attention are small-scale personlike artifacts, clay figurine whistles, and larger-scale ones in the form of stone sculpture attached to houses. Figurine whistles are found in all three areas. Anthropomorphic sculpture is restricted to the hilltop center of Late Classic Cerro Palenque and Copan. In the latter case, it is more specifically associated with certain houses surrounding the Main Group.

I have argued that these two kinds of objects are alike in that they are both icons and indexes of persons (Joyce 2007; Preucel 2006). Their status as icons and their indexicality derive most obviously from their material properties and their form, which give them not only the appearance of humans (or living beings) but suggest that they possess a humanlike gaze and spatial orientation (Todes 2001). A more subtle kind of analogical relationship derives from the fact that they come into being ("are born") through the enactment of a local theory of production that can be tied to particular moments in time (Monaghan 1998a, 1998b). This temporal anchor provides sculpture and figurine whistles, as it does other objects discussed here in somewhat less depth, such as pottery vessels, with a place in the same spatiotemporal order that gives humans their destiny and serves as one framework for time telling (Wu 2003).

At the same time, figurine whistles may be contrasted with sculpture in terms of how they connect with the spatial side of the spatiotemporal order. Unlike architectonic sculpture, figurine whistles are mobile. More precisely, they were made to be moved around, while sculpted images were designed to be integrated into the fabric of buildings. Sculpture is more fixed in place, at least until someone decides to renovate, dismantle, or move even the most massive of building stones, architectural carvings, or free-standing monuments. Figurines and whistles of humans, animals, and hybrid beings contribute to social networks at the local and regional scale through their movement across the landscape. Their involvement in ritualized events and their manner of exchange do more than remind people of events or relationships. They also become part of a relational self, distributing the identity of particular persons or groups beyond their location of origin, their moment of creation, their context of exchange, and the life span of individuals. Like monuments of royal authority such as Stela E at Quirigua and the Hieroglyphic Staircase at Copan, decorated houses are a focal point where people can congregate for the celebration of performatory acts of remembering and forgetting—acts which may in turn rely on figurine whistles for part of their effect.

The involvement of enchanting objects in practices that distribute personhood, reconstitute social identity, and reinforce selective remembering and forgetting is one way that objects contribute to the work of memory. The process of production itself provides another. I have highlighted the manufacture of four kinds of objects—cloth, pottery, bark paper, and shell ornaments—each with its own material properties and techniques of manufacture. By looking at how and where such valued materials were brought into being in Copan (textiles and shell ornaments), Cerro Palenque (pottery), and Cuyumapa (bark paper), I have expanded further the role of objects in social memory and the construction of social identity. The spatial setting and social context in which learning occurs emerge as significant to the process (Lave and Wenger 1991). This expansion is important for a number of reasons, two of which I have emphasized here. First, it demonstrates that learning, knowing, and doing are intimately connected to remembering (Lave 1993). The frameworks that coresident communities of practice contribute to the work of social memory include those stemming from processes that socialize individual members and transmit bodies of knowledge across generations. Second, the expansion directs attention to the way in which remembering is an embodied process reflecting an often implicit bodily understanding and motor intentionality (Mauss 2006; Merleau-Ponty 1958; Warnier 2001). Objects are not only the outcome of this form of remembering but also its material traces.

I have considered these issues of making and using in relation to ephemeral tasks and humble objects as well. Cooking, the quintessential repetitive quotidian act, is another domain with material and experiential properties requiring particular kinds of objects and sets of actions (Giard 1998). I have suggested that the sensory and social aspects of periodic, often daily actions at home that form part of everyday life have a rhythm that is not the un-differentiated repetition so often assumed by those who dismiss the everyday as unmemorable (Lefebvre 2004). As perhaps one of the most intimate and small-scale forms of time telling, cooking may be said to exemplify the distinctive background provided by domestic places. Yet again, however, cooking also becomes a performatory process that not only helps define the rhythm of daily life but is also necessary to the virtuosic provision of food and drink during the special events hosted by coresident groups of practice at home. That most humble of objects, the metate, has also given me insight into how the body becomes a physical locus of memory and how objects like grinding stones become embodiments of human action over time.

THE CONTRIBUTION OF EVERYDAY LIFE
AT HOME TO SOCIAL MEMORY

The domestic and productive actions discussed in much of this book furnish contexts for the construction of memory and identity that are closely tied to a particular spatial setting. I have drawn on phenomenological studies of perception and anthropological discussions of the importance of place to reconfigure the physical location as an active background which gives mean-ing to the actions, events, relations, and interactions that take place there (Kelly 2005; Low and Lawrence-Zúñiga 2003; Rodman 2003; Taylor 2005). The active background provided by residential compounds, the implicit tem-porality of the spatial orientation of the body's movement through this setting, the time telling that develops from preparing and consuming food, the imperfect knowledge of what has been stored or who has been buried, and the embodied abilities required for the manipulation of materials and the manufacture of goods all become part of a local history, identified with the coresident community of practice and the sociological house to which this community belongs.

The special events considered in the previous two chapters, feasting at home and participating in the ballgame, may be thought of as another kind of context because of the different kinds of interactions involved which develop out of events important to the family, the coresidential community of practice, the larger settlement, or the political leadership. The shift in venue associated with the ballgame certainly introduces another active background. At the same time, however, this implicit contrast should not be overdrawn, nor should the two frameworks just enunciated be thought of as dichotomous or in opposition to one another. Everyday life and special events share important features that make them interesting intertwined contexts for remembering and forgetting. People in Mesoamerica used the experience of living daily life, burying the dead and storing things, crafting objects and transmitting knowledge, and exchanging goods and feasting at home to construct their histories, leading to multiple memory communities in society. Domestic places actively contribute to the meaning people give to their actions and interactions with one another and the material world, a process that includes embodied, sensory, and nonconceptual forms of knowing (Carman 2005). Public ritual and commemoration are better seen as an attempt on the part of some to sustain a memory community that binds people together into a larger collective totality rather than as the only source of memory.

The concept of ritualization (Bell 1992) has been helpful in my thinking about the significance of everyday life. Defined as sets of distinctive ways of acting that fulfill some purpose, ritualization dovetails with the idea of local theories of production that, in Mesoamerica, do not distinguish between mundane and religious domains of action or spheres of belief as things that can be separated conceptually or in practice. The semiotic house (D. Miller 2001) becomes just that because the same actions do not have the same meaning when they occur somewhere else. Places where people live—where they sleep, eat, craft, welcome outsiders, host parties, laugh, argue, get married, have sex, give birth, and die—become part of the process of ritualization because residential space is a persistent background imbricated with meaning reproduced over time. Houses are integral to the practical and semiotic complex.

The assertion of difference between sociological houses through material culture is part of the local history of domestic places and their inhabitants. Examples presented here include the difference in the use of raw materials for metates and imported ceramics in Cuyumapa that speaks to participation in diverse social networks, the unequal distribution of obsidian at Cerro Palenque and the performatory production of fine paste vessels and figurines in one part of that community, or the display of imported Ulua polychromes during special events in urban and rural Copan. Rather than assume the existence of fixed social classes or ranks, I have concluded that the lack of congruence among such potential signs of status as health and nutrition, treatment after death, access to imported goods, and the kind of built environment people lived in indicates that social difference could not be easily fixed or signified but needed to be reasserted in multiple ways over time (Bourdieu 1998). It was negotiated through social practices affecting the human body and the places where people lived as well as through periodic events such as feasts and games. The domestic places discussed here vary in size and construction, from the wood and clay houses of rural Copan and Cuyumapa to the painted and plastered, dressed-stone architecture in and around the Main Group. Houses, like monumental architecture, play a central role in the attempt to mark degrees of social difference in a way that appears unassailable because of its apparent permanency.

ASSERTING CONNECTIONS BETWEEN THE PRESENT AND THE PAST

As the study of malanggan intimates, objects may serve as generative resources for remembering through their presence and through their absence (Küchler 1999, 2002). Remembering is as much a process of recall as it is of archiving. Significant points in the history of an individual, a group, or a kingdom are brought forward through ritualized events that use enchanting or humble objects as their focus. In this sense, what is remembered and what is forgotten connect to how knowledge relating to creative processes of production is acquired, shared, or restricted. Remembering and forgetting are thus also part of an embodied sense of self that is engrained in the body through what one does and what kinds of objects and materials one uses. Here is another way in which objects take on a sense of personhood as icons and indexes of the essential features of the Mesoamerican person. Jars, figurines, and houses are all containers of precious materials, including such substances as blood, breath, and saliva as well as dead members of the social group. The presence of these substances or the knowledge that such substances were once contained in these buildings and objects allows these corporeal but inanimate entities to play a role in the forging of relations among people, between people and objects, and between the objects themselves. These relationships are all part of a relational and distributed personhood that links past and present, near and far, and the living and the dead.

Buildings and residential places serve as a focal point for practices that turn these structures into tangible historical referents that span generations and speak to multiple actors. The everyday cannot be outside of history or relevant only at one particular scale because it is central to how members of communities of practice engage with one another as they pursue their joint enterprises, one of which is the production of "persons with particular social identities . . . persons who are appropriately differentiated socially" (Moore 1994:90). These practices help make these dwellings a source of memory and an enduring manifestation of the social group that inhabits them. The treatment of monumental architecture echoes this. It too is the subject of repeated episodes of renovation and expansion that leave older buildings as well as valued people and objects entombed within its architectural mass.

The semiotic house becomes a memory machine (Douglas 1993). Domestic places have the ability to endure beyond the life span or experience of any individual person. Houses can be torn down, but they nevertheless represent a possibility of permanence across generations. Or if not truly permanent, in the sense that a specific building endures forever, at least of continuity. Settlement in Copan and Cuyumapa is notable for the tendency of people to live in the same spot, if not in the same building. Excavation of the residential groups in Copan discussed here reveals a multigenerational presence even in the rural area. The small sets of houses in the foothills possess a spatial stability belied by the perishable nature of their building materials. Artifact deposits from the Acbi phase (ca. 400–600 CE), predating the period of peak occupation, were found at several sites. Even longer continuity or reuse has been documented in the Sepulturas area near the Main Group, where early occupation debris and burials underlie the houses I have discussed at length. Both rural and urban buildings were renovated, added to, or rebuilt. The importance of particular locations may also be seen in Cuyumapa, where, for example, occupation dating as early as 900 BCE and as late as 900 CE was found at the site of PACO 1. Older constructions become part of later landscapes as well. The early ballcourt of PACO 15 remained visible to later residents who built the PACO 14 ballcourt nearby. Cerro Palenque presents a similar pattern of spatial stability. The Terminal Classic expansion left the first occupied area untouched but was designed to incorporate the Classic period area as a central point in the landscape. Furthermore, buildings were rebuilt during the Terminal Classic in the ballcourt residential group.

The rebuilding of the buildings in this group included the deposition of personlike objects, such as figurine whistles and fine paste vessels, of the sort used during ritualized feasts and their associated celebrations of events important to the coresident community of practice, the sociological house, or the ruling dynasty. All of these were broken in place on a paved floor, resulting, I would argue, in the permanent incorporation of the coessences of those members of the community of practice who ate and drank from the vessels or made music with the whistles. Other artifacts, such as spindle whorls, also distribute the personhood of these people by marking the productive action and creative and technical knowledge of the social group. A figural censer decorated with images of human bones bound with rope and an actual bone serve as even more direct reminders of the sociological house and its desire to assert connections between previous incarnations of the structure and its present form.

Rural and urban Copanecos demonstrate a similar interest in turning their residences into storehouses of valued objects and people. Many burials inside foundation platforms, under benches, and beneath patio floors have been excavated from these residential groups. Objects of evident significance were also interred in ways that are comparable to the treatment of the dead. A number of these caches contain polychrome vessels used for serving or eating, but not all cache objects are fancy or made from prestigious materials. Large storage jars, for example, were cached. Cerro Palenque's residents also considered objects of everyday life such as manos and markers of prestige such as jade, marble, and imported shells as appropriate offerings. In Cuyumapa, ballcourts appear to have been the focus of these kinds of deposits more than houses.

Caching significant objects and burying the dead give people a means of concealing some things and making others more visible. Although most caches and burials, like the construction fill and its contents, are hidden with the architectural fabric of domestic places, sometimes they were not. A double burial was placed in Group 9N-8 Patio C in Copan below the patio floor with two rock slabs covering the bodies. Instead of repaving the patio, the mourners left the slabs exposed so that whenever one looked at that corner of the patio one would be reminded of its presence. Metates mark the location of a burial at Site 99A-18-2, while the cache in Site 7D-3-1 was covered by a stone cap that remained visible.

The importance of controlling knowledge, which parallels the importance of controlling physical and visual access to residential groups, may be seen not only in caches and burials but also in storehouses. I have used variation in how and where storage takes place in rural and urban Copan,

Cuymapa, and Cerro Palenque to suggest that knowledge of a group's accumulation of material resources, as much as the resources themselves, represented something that might or might not be shared. The kinds of storage areas that different social groups built for themselves serve as a material marker of wealth that outlives the individual.

POLITICAL AND SOCIAL CONSEQUENCES
OF MULTIPLE MEMORY COMMUNITIES

Comparable practices in Copan, Cerro Palenque, and Cuyumapa that turn domestic space into places of social memory have important consequences for the production of social difference, the entrenchment of social hierarchies, and the ability of some to exert control over others. This process of memory making and identity construction becomes the foundation for multiple memory communities that may be in competition or disagreement with one another or with the effort to produce a more encompassing, larger-scale totality through public acts of commemoration. The actions of these multiple memory communities allow one to approach how a historical consciousness is expressed through relations with the social, material, and physical world manifested in material culture, practice, and landscape. That such a historical consciousness does not necessarily conform to current academic or folk definitions does not, I would argue, reflect the workings of a premodern type of mind incapable of freeing itself from the undifferentiated repetitiveness of time's cycle. Instead, the differences discernable between what members of these ancient societies emphasized in the construction of their local histories and that which contemporary people would consider historical help demonstrate the value of an anthropological approach that treats history as another culturally constructed aspect of society (Parmentier 1987; Rosaldo 1980). I have deliberately rejected the argument that these people were "modern" because to make such a claim would be to imply that they were "as good" or "as smart" or "as advanced" as us (leaving aside the question of who "us" is). Rather than patronize the people living in the Copan and Cuyumapa valleys or at Cerro Palenque by assigning them the status of modern, I have worked to analyze the ways in which they produced local or more encompassing histories.

The use of hieroglyphic inscriptions at Copan to name individuals and fix their actions within a particular temporal framework reinforces and augments the way in which monumental images emphasize certain living or dead people. Text and image work in tandem to assert control over the space of the Main Group and to present the preferred history of one particular community of memory. It is easy to be seduced by these texts and images into assuming that Copan's royal dynasty was more historically minded than other societies in Honduras, such as the residents of the lower Ulua and Cuyumapa valleys. Privileging these products of royal authority suggests that memory crystallizes into something one recognizes as history only under a narrow range of circumstances having to do more with certain technologies of remembering than with anything else. This puts one at risk of assuming that only some things are worthy or capable of being remembered, while everything else must fall by the wayside into the undifferentiated morass of experience and the endlessly repeated lived moment. Figurines and pottery prove that residents of the lower Ulua and Cuyumapa valleys were capable of creating visual representations of people (or, more precisely, of human-looking entities). In fact, their abundance and the multiple sites of production suggest that people here reveled in the production of personlike figures. Thus the lack of personalized representation of the kind found at Copan must be seen as the result of a set of decisions or ideas about what political relations are and how they should be commemorated in material, durable form. I have found it productive to think about such differences as forming part of a political economy of remembering and forgetting (Melion and Küchler 1991). The choices people make about how to connect people and places and the present and past have political consequences that only sometimes resulted in the creation of a kingdom. The consolidation of authority and control in the hands of a relatively few members of society seems successful if one looks at what its promulgators chose to commemorate. Sociological houses do not, however, abandon their efforts to commemorate their own histories. Social, political, and historical circumstances result in some things being remembered differently or through different means.

Copan, Cerro Palenque, and Cuyumapa represent three societies that differ in size, political centralization, and social differentiation. They were complicated societies (Piot 1999). As the analysis presented here suggests, however, their differences are more of degree than of kind. That is to say, the construction of local histories out of the meaningful practices of daily life and special events is a thread running through all three societies. Local histories both bind people together and push them apart by emphasizing different bodies of memory. One might say the Copan ruling dynasty was the most successful at elevating its local history to the level of the history of the polity as a whole. While this is to some degree the case, this more "national" history never completely erases the practices through which other communities of memory persist in remembering their own significant events and markers of their local identity in their own ways. The expansion of ballcourts in Cuyumapa may not be an entirely voluntary or cooperative phenomenon. Several features, however, argue for the existence of overlapping and cross-cutting networks of power rather than bounded, congruent hierarchies. The dispersal throughout the region of these monumental constructions and the way in which they index the collective labor and participation of most or all members of society are two such features, while the third is the fact that they are not contained in a carapace of monumental architecture, as at Cerro Palenque and Copan.

THE ARCHAEOLOGICAL STUDY OF MEMORY AND IDENTITY

The persistence of multiple communities of memory in these societies ensures a multiplicity of opportunities for the social construction of memory to go forward. That these memory communities were most concerned with enshrining their own local histories that were integral to the continuation of their identity as social groups makes it highly probable that these histories varied in content. Although the information archaeologists work with is always incomplete and rarely includes directly the voices of the members of ancient societies, it does nevertheless reveal much about how, why, and where people engaged in the work of memory making. Remembering and forgetting are active processes, embedded in social practices that have material as well as verbal and mental components. My approach emphasizes how and why local histories are cherished by coresident communities of practice and the sociological houses to which they belong. My book does not desire to resolve any of the problems inherent in trying to write a seamless narrative account of political leadership or social evolution. Its purpose has been to address the interrelationship of memory and identity as intersubjective social practices that extend across space and through time and are susceptible to analysis through material remains. While this analysis has been immersed in the historical and cultural details of three societies living at a particular time in specific places, its emphasis on the interplay between archaeologically derived data and the theoretical and conceptual frameworks I have used hold out a promise for the archaeological study of social memory and identity in the context of everyday life and domestic spaces more generally.

NOTES

INTRODUCTION

1. This is the number found through excavation, but it is possible that more burials existed since the entire area was not exposed.

2. One of the most famous examples comes from the Olmec site of La Venta in the state of Tabasco, Mexico, where excavators found a carefully arranged deposit of human figurines and celts made from jade and other types of stone. Their excavations also revealed that the deposit was deliberately buried and covered by a floor. Much later, a hole was dug through the overlying deposits and through the floor and the fill below it to expose just the top of the cache. Then the hole was filled in again (Drucker, Heizer, and Squier 1959:152–61).

3. Elizabeth Boone (1994b:18–19) describes the writing systems of the Aztec and Mixtec as semasiographic, in which "meaning is carried by pictorial and conventionalized images, by their relative placement, and by the contexts in which they participate. . . . The Aztec and Mixtec writing

systems are intelligible to those who share a general cultural base even though they might speak different languages." Glass and Robertson (1975) provide a description of types of documents and an inventory of those known to have survived.

4. Here is one example that uses the day names as they occur in the Yucatec Maya language and starts with the day Manik and the number 1. The sequence is 1 Manik, 2 Lamat, 3 Muluc, 4 Oc, 5 Chuen, 6 Eb, 7 Ben, 8 Ix, 9 Men, 10 Cib, 11 Caban, 12 Eznab, 13 Cauac, 1 Ahau, 2 Imix, 3 **Manik,** and so on. Note that the numbers cycle back to their beginning point sooner than the names because there are fewer numbers than days and that it takes 260 days (20 x 13) to return to 1 Manik (B. Tedlock 1992b:89–96).

1. COMMUNITIES OF PRACTICE IN HONDURAS

1. The lack of comparable samples from Cerro Palenque or Cuyumapa makes it impossible to know if the same patterns existed among those populations. Rhoads (2002:206–11) did compare the Copan sample to ones from other sites or regions, including the site of Puerto Escondido in the lower Ulua valley. Cluster analysis shows Copan and Puerto Escondido as genetically distant populations. These results suggest, as a working hypothesis, that lower Ulua valley populations in general were not closely related to those living in the Copan valley.

2. This social formation has been referred to in the literature as the *social* house and the *sociological* house. I have opted for *sociological*, first, as a way to distinguish between physical houses, which figure prominently in my discussion; second, the term *social* appears frequently because of my interest in the interpenetration of the individual and the group. Thus I discuss social relations, identities, groups, and forms of memory.

2. THE ENCHANTMENT AND HUMILITY OF OBJECTS

1. The date of the Copan ruler's decapitation is transcribed as 9.15.6.14.6 6 Cimi 4 Tzec. The first part (9.15 . . .) is the Long Count. "6 Cimi" is the associated point in the 260-day cycle. "4 Tzec" indicates which day and month in the solar year. Riese (1984) and Sharer (1990) convert this to 737 CE, but all other authors cited agree on 738 CE. The names of the Copan and Quirigua rulers have been translated in various ways by those scholars who study the inscriptions from these sites, examples of which may be found in the sources cited. Over time, different readings have been proposed for the names. For the sake of simplicity, I refer to the rulers by the position they claimed in the dynastic line of succession—hence Ruler 13 for the thirteenth of the Copan royal line. The assertion of a continuous sequence of rulers does not mean all were related by blood or even were members of the same royal (sociological) house.

2. Also spelled *malangan*.

3. Sharer (1990:36) reports the height of Stela E, which he calls Monument 5, as 8 meters, or 26.5 feet.

4. Storey also divided the sample up by social status. Since she found no statistically significant variation in the height of people of the same sex placed in different status groups, I have collapsed these groups back together. Vera Tiesler Blos (2001:Tables 4 and 5) reports somewhat different results. In her analysis, the average female height is noticeably less at 147 centimeters (4 feet, 11 inches) but that of men closer at 159 centimeters (5 feet, 4 inches). I don't know the reason for the discrepancy between the two analyses but suspect it results from the somewhat different compositions of their samples and perhaps different formulas for estimating height. Tiesler Blos included human remains from a wider time range than Storey, who restricted herself to the Late Classic.

5. Boone (1994b:17–18) characterizes the Maya hieroglyphic writing system as "glottographic [which] employs a combination of logograms representing whole words, phonetic signs, and semantic qualifiers, which together reproduce a verbal text." It is pictorial without being "picture writing" in any literal sense of the term. "Maya hieroglyphs present the reader with a richness and visual elaboration unrivalled by any of the world's ancient scripts" (Martin and Grube 2000:11).

6. Claude Baudez disagrees with the mountain interpretation, arguing that the reptilian creature is a personification of the earth (the "earth monster") and that Temple 22 "as a whole represents the earth" (Baudez 1994:205, see also 257–58). He is thus presenting an alternative reading of the conventionalized signs embodied in sculpture; the disagreement represents one about how best to translate the iconographic "text."

3. EVERYDAY LIFE AND DOMESTIC SPACE

1. So much so that the park management has had to prohibit access to rooms in the Main Group and Sepulturas area.

4. EMBODIED FORMS OF KNOWING

1. My translation of "Juntos describen nuestro universo en el cual yo, mujer fecunda, estoy al centro."

2. Although Fung did not report any spindle whorls from his PACO 2 excavations, my field notes indicate that I found at least one while excavating in the Late to Terminal Classic residential area of PACO 15 in 1992.

BIBLIOGRAPHY

Abrams, Elliot M. 1987. "Economic Specialization and Construction Personnel in Classic Period Copan." *American Antiquity* 52:485–99.

———. 1994. *How the Maya Built Their World: Energetics and Ancient Architecture.* Austin: University of Texas Press.

Alcock, Susan E. 2001. "The Reconfiguration of Memory in the Eastern Roman Empire" in *Empires: Perspectives from Archaeology and History.* Edited by Susan E. Alcock, Terence N. D'Altroy, Kathleen D. Morrison, and Carla M. Sinopoli, 323–50. Cambridge: Cambridge University Press.

Anawalt, Patricia R. 1981. *Indian Clothing Before Cortés.* Norman: University of Oklahoma Press.

Andrews, E. Wyllys, and Cassandra R. Bill. 2005. "A Late Classic Royal Residence at Copan" in *Copan: The History of an Ancient Maya Kingdom.* Edited by E. Wyllys Andrews and William L. Fash, 239–314. Santa Fe: School of American Research Press.

Andrews, E. Wyllys, and Barbara W. Fash. 1992. "Continuity and Change in a Royal Maya Residential Complex at Copan." *Ancient Mesoamerica* 3:63–88.

Andrews, E. Wyllys, and William L. Fash. 2005. "Issues in Copan Archaeology" in *Copan: The History of an Ancient Maya Kingdom*. Edited by E. Wyllys Andrews and William L. Fash, 395–425. Santa Fe: School of American Research Press.

Aoyama, Kazuo. 1995. "Microwear Analysis in the Southeast Maya Lowlands: Two Case Studies at Copan, Honduras." *Latin American Antiquity* 6:129–44.

——. 1999. *Ancient Maya State, Urbanism, Exchange, and Craft Specialization: Chipped Stone Evidence from the Copan Valley and the La Entrada Region, Honduras / Estado, urbanismo, intercambio, y especialización artesanal entre los Mayas antiguos: Evidencia de lítica menor del valle de Copan y la región de La Entrada, Honduras*. Memoirs in Latin American Archaeology 12. Pittsburgh: Department of Anthropology, University of Pittsburgh.

——. 2001. "Classic Maya State, Urbanism, and Exchange: Chipped Stone Evidence of the Copan Valley and Its Hinterland." *American Anthropologist* 103:346–60.

Archibald, Robert R. 2002. "A Personal History of Memory" in *Social Memory and History: Anthropological Perspectives*. Edited by Jacob J. Climo and Maria G. Cattell, 65–80. Walnut Creek, Calif.: AltaMira Press.

Ardón Mejía, Mario. 1986. "Los indígenas jicaques de Honduras." *Tradiciones de Guatemala* 25:71–85.

Ashmore, Wendy. 1981. "Some Issues of Method and Theory in Lowland Maya Settlement Archaeology" in *Lowland Maya Settlement Patterns*. Edited by Wendy Ashmore, 37–69. Albuquerque: University of New Mexico Press.

——. 1991. "Site-Planning Principles and Concepts of Directionality among the Ancient Maya." *Latin American Antiquity* 2:199–226.

——. 2004. "Classic Maya Landscapes and Settlement" in *Mesoamerican Archaeology: Theory and Practice*. Edited by Julia A. Hendon and Rosemary A. Joyce, 169–91. Malden, Mass.: Blackwell.

Assmann, Jan. 1995. "Collective Memory and Cultural Identity." Translated by John Czaplicka. *New German Critique* 65:125–33.

Asturias de Barrios, Linda. 1998. "Weaving and Daily Life" in *The Maya Textile Tradition*. Edited by Margo Blum Schevill, 65–87. New York: Harry Abrams.

Bachand, Holly, Rosemary A. Joyce, and Julia A. Hendon. 2003. "Bodies Moving in Space: Ancient Mesoamerican Human Sculpture and Embodiment." *Cambridge Archaeological Journal* 13:238–47.

Ballinger, Diane A. 1999. "Sexual Dimorphism in Cortical Bone Geometry in Two Maya Populations." Ph.D. diss., Department of Anthropology, Indiana University.

Barrera Rivera, José Álvaro, Ma. de Lourdes Gallardo Parrodi, and Aurora Montúfar López. 2001. "La ofrenda 102 del Templo Mayor." *Arqueología Mexicana* 8:48:70–77.

Bassie-Sweet, Karen. 1991. *From the Mouth of the Dark Cave: Commemorative Sculpture of the Late Classic Maya*. Norman: University of Oklahoma Press.

Baudez, Claude F. 1984. "Le roi, la balle et le maïs: Images du jeu de balle maya." *Journal de la Société des américanistes* 70:139–52.

———. 1989. "The House of the Bacabs: An Iconographic Analysis" in *The House of the Bacabs, Copan, Honduras*. Edited by David Webster, 73–81. Studies in Pre-Columbian Art and Archaeology No. 29. Washington: Dumbarton Oaks.

———. 1991. "The Cross Pattern at Copan: Forms, Rituals, and Meanings" in *Sixth Palenque Round Table, 1986*. Edited by Virginia M. Fields, 81–88. Norman: University of Oklahoma Press.

———. 1994. *Maya Sculpture of Copan: The Iconography*. Norman: University of Oklahoma Press.

Beaudry, Marilyn P. 1984. *Ceramic Production and Distribution in the Southeastern Maya Periphery: Late Classic Painted Serving Vessels*. BAR International Series 203. Oxford: British Archaeological Reports.

Beaudry-Corbett, Marilyn, Pauline Caputi, John S. Henderson, Rosemary A. Joyce, Eugenia J. Robinson, and Anthony Wonderly. 1993. "Lower Ulua Region" in *Pottery of Prehistoric Honduras: Regional Classification and Analysis*. Edited by John S. Henderson and Marilyn Beaudry-Corbett, 65–135. Los Angeles: Institute of Archaeology, University of California.

Becker, Marshall J. 1992. "Burials as Caches, Caches as Burials: A New Interpretation of the Meaning of Ritual Deposits Among the Classic Period Lowland Maya" in *New Theories on the Ancient Maya*. Edited by Elin C. Danien and Robert J. Sharer, 185–96. University Museum Monograph 77. Philadelphia: University Museum, University of Pennsylvania.

Becker, Marshall J., and Charles D. Cheek. 1983. "La Estructura 10L-18" in *Introducción a la arqueología de Copán, Honduras, Tomo II*. Edited by Claude F. Baudez, 381–500. Tegucigalpa: Proyecto Arqueológico Copán, Secretaría de Estado en el Despacho de Cultura y Turismo.

Begley, Christopher. 2004. "Intercambio interregional, conexiones externas, y estratégias de poder en el Oriente de Honduras durante los períodos V y VI" in *Memoria VII Seminario de Antropología de Honduras "Dr. George Hasemann."* Edited by Kevin Rubén Ávalos, 298–302. Tegucigalpa: Instituto Hondureño de Antropología e Historia.

Bell, Catherine. 1992. *Ritual Theory, Ritual Practice*. New York: Oxford University Press.

Bell, Ellen E., Robert J. Sharer, Loa P. Traxler, David W. Sedat, Christine W. Carrelli, and Lynn A. Grant. 2004. "Tombs and Burials in the Early Classic Acropolis at Copan" in *Understanding Early Classic Copan*. Edited by Ellen E. Bell, Marcello A. Canuto, and Robert J. Sharer, 131–57. Philadelphia: University of Pennsylvania Museum of Archaeology and Anthropology.

Bell, Lilian A. 1983. *Papyrus, Tapa, Amate and Rice Paper: Papermaking in Africa, the Pacific, Latin America and Southeast Asia*. McMinnville, Ore.: Liliaceae Press.

Bender, Barbara. 1998. *Stonehenge: Making Space*. Oxford: Berg.

Berdan, Frances F., and Patricia R. Anawalt, eds. 1992. *The Codex Mendoza*. Berkeley: University of California Press.

Best, Steven, and Douglas Kellner. 1991. *Postmodern Theory: Critical Interrogations*. New York: Guilford Press.

Bill, Cassandra R. 1997a. "Patterns of Variation and Change in Dynastic Period Ceramics and Ceramic Production at Copan, Honduras." Ph.D. diss., Department of Anthropology, Tulane University. Ann Arbor: University Microfilms.

———. 1997b. "The Roles and Relationships of God M and Other Black Gods in the Codices, with Specific Reference to Pages 50–56 of the Madrid Codex" in *Papers on the Madrid Codex*. Edited by Victoria R. Bricker and Gabrielle Vail, 111–45. Middle American Research Institute Publication 64. New Orleans: Tulane University.

Birdwell-Pheasant, Donna, and Denise Lawrence-Zúñiga. 1999. "Introduction: Houses and Families in Europe" in *House Life: Space, Place and Family in Europe*. Edited by Donna Birdwell-Pheasant and Denise Lawrence-Zúñiga, 1–35. Oxford: Berg.

Bishop, Ronald L., Marilyn P. Beaudry, Richard M. Leventhal, and Robert J. Sharer. 1986. "Compositional Analysis of Copador and Related Pottery in the Southeastern Maya Area" in *The Southeast Maya Periphery*. Edited by Patricia A. Urban and Edward M. Schortman, 143–67. Austin: University of Texas Press.

Blier, Suzanne Preston. 1987. *The Anatomy of Architecture: Ontology and Metaphor in Batammaliba Architectural Expression*. Chicago: University of Chicago Press.

Bloch, Maurice. 1977. "The Past and the Present in the Present." *Man* n.s. 12:278–92.

Bodnar, John E. 1992. *Remaking America: Public Memory, Commemoration, and Patriotism in the Twentieth Century*. Princeton: Princeton University Press.

Boone, Elizabeth H. 1983. *The Codex Magliabechiano and the Lost Prototype of the Magliabechiano Group*. Berkeley: University of California Press.

———. 1994a. "Aztec Pictorial Histories: Records Without Words" in *Writing Without Words: Alternative Literacies in Mesoamerica and the Andes*. Edited by Elizabeth H. Boone and Walter D. Mignolo, 50–76. Durham: Duke University Press.

———. 1994b. "Introduction: Writing and Recording Knowledge" in *Writing Without Words: Alternative Literacies in Mesoamerica and the Andes*. Edited by Elizabeth H. Boone and Walter D. Mignolo, 3–26. Durham: Duke University Press.

Bourdieu, Pierre. 1977. *Outline of a Theory of Practice*. Translated by Richard Nice. Cambridge: Cambridge University Press.

———. 1990. *The Logic of Practice*. Translated by Richard Nice. Stanford: Stanford University Press.

———. 1993. "Conclusions: For a Sociogenetic Understanding." Translated by Nicole Kaplan, Craig Calhoun, and Leah Florence. In *Bourdieu: Critical Perspectives*. Edited by Craig Calhoun, Edward LiPuma, and Moishe Postone, 263–75. Chicago: University of Chicago Press.

———. 1998. "Social Space and Symbolic Space." Translated by Gisele Sapiro. In *Practical Reason: On the Theory of Action*, 1–13. Stanford: Stanford University Press.

Bradley, Douglas E. 2001. "Gender, Power, and Fertility in the Olmec Ritual Ballgame" in *The Sport of Life and Death: The Mesoamerican Ballgame*. Edited by E. Michael Whittington, 33–39. London: Thames and Hudson.

Bradley, Richard. 2003a. "A Life Less Ordinary: The Ritualization of the Domestic Sphere in Later Prehistoric Europe." *Cambridge Archaeological Journal* 13:1:5–23.

——. 2003b. "The Translation of Time" in *Archaeologies of Memory*. Edited by Ruth M. Van Dyke and Susan E. Alcock, 221–27. Malden, Mass.: Blackwell.

Bricker, Victoria R. 1991. "Faunal Offerings in the Dresden Codex" in *Sixth Palenque Round Table, 1986*. Edited by Virginia M. Fields, 285–92. Norman: University of Oklahoma Press.

Bricker, Victoria R., and Harvey M. Bricker. 1988. "The Seasonal Table in the Dresden Codex and Related Almanacs." *Archaeoastronomy* 12:S1-S62. Supplement to Volume 19 of the *Journal for the History of Astronomy*.

Brotherston, Gordon. 1992. *Book of the Fourth World: Reading the Native Americas Through Their Literature*. Cambridge: Cambridge University Press.

Brown, Linda A. 2000. "From Discard to Divination: Demarcating the Sacred through the Collection and Curation of Discarded Objects." *Latin American Antiquity* 11:319–33.

Brown, Linda A., and Andrea I. Gerstle. 2002. "Structure 10: Feasting and Village Festivals" in *Before the Volcano Erupted: The Ancient Ceren Village in Central America*. Edited by Payson Sheets, 97–103. Austin: University of Texas Press.

Brown, Linda A., Scott E. Simmons, and Payson Sheets. 2002. "Household Production of Extra-Household Ritual at the Ceren Site, El Salvador" in *Domestic Ritual in Ancient Mesoamerica*. Edited by Patricia S. Plunkett, 83–92. Cotsen Institute of Archaeology Monograph 46. Los Angeles: University of California.

Bulbeck, Chilla. 1998. *Re-Orienting Western Feminisms: Women's Diversity in a Postcolonial World*. Cambridge: Cambridge University Press.

Burke, Peter. 1989. "History as Social Memory" in *Memory: History, Culture and the Mind*. Edited by Thomas Butler, 97–113. Oxford: Basil Blackwell.

——. 2002. "Western Historical Thinking in a Global Perspective—10 Theses" in *Western Historical Thinking: An Intercultural Debate*. Edited by Jörn Rüsen, 15–30. New York: Berghahn Books.

Burkhart, Louise M. 1989. *The Slippery Earth: Nahua-Christian Moral Dialogue in Sixteenth-Century Mexico*. Tucson: University of Arizona Press.

Butler, Mary. 1935. "A Study of Maya Mouldmade Figurines." *American Anthropologist* n.s. 37:636–72.

Campbell, Lyle, Terrence Kaufman, and Thomas C. Smith-Stark. 1986. "Meso-America as a Linguistic Area." *Language* 62:530–70.

Canuto, Marcello A. 2002. "A Tale of Two Communities: Social and Political Transformation in the Hinterlands of the Maya Polity of Copan." Ph.D. diss., Department of Anthropology, University of Pennsylvania. Ann Arbor: University Microfilms.

——. 2004. "The Rural Settlement of Copan: Changes through the Early Classic" in *Understanding Early Classic Copan*. Edited by Ellen E. Bell, Marcello A. Canuto, and Robert J. Sharer, 29–50. Philadelphia: University of Pennsylvania Museum of Archaeology and Anthropology.

Canuto, Marcello A., and Jason Yaeger, eds. 2000. *The Archaeology of Communities: A New World Perspective*. London: Routledge.

Carlsen, Robert S. 1986. "Analysis of the Early Classic Period Textile Remains: Tomb 19, Rio Azul, Guatemala" in *Rio Azul Reports, No. 2: The 1984 Season.* Edited by R. E. W. Adams, 122–55. San Antonio: Center for Archaeological Research, University of Texas.

——. 1987. "Analysis of the Early Classic Period Textile Remains from Tomb 23, Rio Azul, Guatemala" in *Rio Azul Reports, No. 3: The 1985 Season.* Edited by R. E. W. Adams, 152–60. San Antonio: Center for Archaeological Research, University of Texas.

Carman, Taylor. 2005. "Sensation, Judgment, and the Phenomenal Field" in *The Cambridge Companion to Merleau-Ponty.* Edited by Taylor Carman and Mark B. N. Hansen, 50–73. Cambridge: Cambridge University Press.

Carrelli, Christine W. 2004. "Measures of Power: The Energetics of Royal Construction at Early Classic Copan" in *Understanding Early Classic Copan.* Edited by Ellen E. Bell, Marcello A. Canuto, and Robert J. Sharer, 113–27. Philadelphia: University of Pennsylvania Museum of Archaeology and Anthropology.

Carsten, Janet, and Stephen Hugh-Jones. 1995. "Introduction: About the House— Lévi-Strauss and Beyond" in *About the House: Lévi-Strauss and Beyond.* Edited by Janet Carsten and Stephen Hugh-Jones, 1–46. Cambridge: Cambridge University Press.

Cattell, Maria G., and Jacob J. Climo. 2002. "Introduction: Meaning in Social Memory and History: Anthropological Perspectives" in *Social Memory and History: Anthropological Perspectives.* Edited by Jacob J. Climo and Maria G. Cattell, 1–36. Walnut Creek, Calif.: AltaMira Press.

Chamoux, Marie-Noëlle. 1986. "Apprendre autrement: Aspects des pedagogies dites informelles chez les Indiens du Mexique" in *Demain l'artisanat?.* By Pierre Rossel et al., 211–35. Cahiers de l'Institut Universitaire d'Études de Développement No. 16. Paris: Presses Universitaires de France.

——. 1993. "La difusión de tecnologías entre los indígenas de México: Una interpretación" in *Semillas de industria: Transformaciones de la tecnología indígena en las Américas.* Edited by Mario Humberto Ruz, 123–44. Mexico City and Washington: Centro de Investigaciones y Estudios Superiores en Antropología Social and Smithsonian Institution Center for Folklife Programs and Cultural Studies.

Chance, John K. 2000. "The Noble House in Colonial Puebla, Mexico: Descent, Inheritance, and the Nahua Tradition." *American Anthropologist* 102:485–502.

Chapman, Anne. 1978. *Les enfants de la mort: Univers mythique des indiens tolupan (jicaque).* Etudes Mésoaméricaines 4. Mexico City: Mission Archéologique et Ethnologique Française au Mexique.

——. 1985. *Los Hijos del copal y la candela tomo I: Ritos agrarios y tradición oral de los lencas de Honduras.* Mexico City: Universidad Nacional Autónoma de México.

——. 1986. *Los Hijos del copal y la candela tomo II: Tradición católica de los lencas de Honduras.* Mexico City: Universidad Nacional Autónoma de México.

Chase, Diane Z., and Arlen F. Chase. 1998. "The Architectural Context of Caches, Burials, and Other Ritual Activities for the Classic Period Maya (as Reflected at Caracol, Belize)" in *Function and Meaning in Classic Maya Architecture.* Edited by Stephen D. Houston, 299–332. Washington: Dumbarton Oaks.

——. 2004. "Hermeneutics, Transitions, and Transformations in Classic to Postclassic Maya Society" in *The Terminal Classic in the Maya Lowlands: Collapse, Transition, and Transformation*. Edited by Arthur A. Demarest, Prudence M. Rice, and Don S. Rice, 12–27. Boulder: University Press of Colorado.

Cheek, Charles D. 1983. "Excavaciones en la Plaza Principal" in *Introducción a la arqueología de Copán, Honduras, Tomo II*. Edited by Claude F. Baudez, 191–289. Tegucigalpa: Proyecto Arqueológico Copán, Secretaría de Estado en el Despacho de Cultura y Turismo.

Christensen, Bodil, and Samuel Martí. 1979. *Witchcraft and Pre-Columbian Paper/Brujerías y papel precolombino*. 3d ed. Biblioteca Interamericana Bilingüe 1. Mexico City: Ediciones Euroamericanas.

Cobb, Charles R. 2005. "Archaeology and the 'Savage Slot': Displacement and Emplacement in the Premodern World." *American Anthropologist* 107:563–74.

Coe, Michael D. 1982. *Old Gods and Young Heroes: The Pearlman Collection of Maya Ceramics*. Jerusalem: Israel Museum.

——. 1999. *Breaking the Maya Code*. Rev. ed. London: Thames and Hudson.

Cohodas, Marvin. 1991. "Ballgame Imagery of the Maya Lowlands: History and Iconography" in *The Mesoamerican Ballgame*. Edited by Vernon L. Scarborough and David R. Wilcox, 251–88. Tucson: University of Arizona Press.

Cole, Jennifer. 2001. *Forget Colonialism? Sacrifice and the Art of Memory in Madagascar*. Berkeley: University of California Press.

Comaroff, John, and Jean Comaroff. 1992. *Ethnography and the Historical Imagination*. Boulder: Westview.

Connerton, Paul. 1989. *How Societies Remember*. Cambridge: Cambridge University Press.

Coser, Lewis A. 1992. "Introduction: Maurice Halbwachs, 1877–1945" in *On Collective Memory*. Edited and translated by Lewis A. Coser, 1–40. Chicago: University of Chicago Press.

Crane, Susan A. 1997. "Writing the Individual Back into Collective Memory." *American Historical Review* 102:1372–85.

Cressy, David. 1994. "National Memory in Early Modern England" in *Commemorations: The Politics of National Identity*. Edited by John R. Gillis, 61–73. Princeton: Princeton University Press.

Cutler, Hugh C., and Martin Cardenas. 1947. "Chicha, a Native South American Beer." *Botanical Museum Leaflets* 13:3:33–60. Cambridge: Harvard University.

Davis-Salazar, Karla L. 2007. "Ritual Consumption and the Origins of Social Inequality in Early Formative Copan, Honduras" in *Mesoamerican Ritual Economy: Archaeological and Ethnological Perspectives*. Edited by Christian Wells and Karla L. Davis-Salazar, 197–220. Boulder: University of Colorado Press.

Day, Jane Stevenson. 2001. "Performing on the Court" in *The Sport of Life and Death: The Mesoamerican Ballgame*. Edited by E. Michael Whittington, 65–77. London: Thames and Hudson.

de Certeau, Michel. 1984. *The Practice of Everyday Life*. Translated by Steven Rendall. Berkeley: University of California Press.

Demarest, Arthur A., Prudence M. Rice, and Don S. Rice. 2004. "The Terminal Classic in the Maya Lowlands: Assessing Collapses, Terminations, and Transformations" in *The Terminal Classic in the Maya Lowlands: Collapse, Transition, and Transformation*. Edited by Arthur A. Demarest, Prudence M. Rice, and Don S. Rice, 545–72. Boulder: University Press of Colorado.

Diamanti, Melissa. 2000. "Excavaciones en el conjunto de los Patios E, F, y M, Grupo 9N-8 (Operación XV)" in *Proyecto Arqueológico Copán Segunda Fase: Excavaciones en el área urbana de Copán, Tomo IV*. Edited by William T. Sanders, 21–341. Tegucigalpa: Secretaría de Cultura, Artes y Deportes, Instituto Hondureño de Antropología e Historia.

Dietler, Michael. 2003. "Clearing the Table: Some Concluding Reflections on Commensal Politics and Imperial States" in *The Archaeology and Politics of Food and Feasting in Early States and Empires*. Edited by Tamara L. Bray, 271–82. New York: Kluwer Academic/Plenum Publishers.

Dobres, Marcia-Anne. 2000. *Technology and Social Agency: Outlining a Practice Framework for Archaeology*. Oxford: Blackwell.

Doonan, William. 1996. "The Artifacts of Group 10L-2, Copan, Honduras: Variation in Material Culture and Behavior in a Royal Residential Compound." Ph.D. diss., Department of Anthropology, Tulane University. Ann Arbor: University Microfilms.

Douglas, Mary. 1993. "The Idea of a Home: A Kind of Space" in *Home: A Place in the World*. Edited by Arien Mack, 261–81. New York: New York University Press.

Dow, James. 1982. "Las figuras de papel y el concepto del alma entre los Otomies de la Sierra." *América Indígena* 42:629–50.

Drucker, Philip, Robert F. Heizer, and Robert J. Squier. 1959. *Excavations at La Venta, Tabasco, 1955*. Bureau of American Ethnology Bulletin 170. Washington: Government Printing Office.

Dupiech-Cavaleri, Danielle. 1999. "L'image des ancêtres: Quelques réflexions sur les motifs des tissages mayas" in *Textiles mayas: La trame d'un peuple*. Edited by Danielle Dupiech-Cavaleri, Mario H. Ruz, Marta Turok, and Linda Asturias de Barrios, 96–155. Paris: Editions U N E S C O.

Durán, Diego. 1971. *Book of the Gods and Rites and The Ancient Calendar*. Edited and translated by Fernando Horcasitas and Doris Heyden. Norman: University of Oklahoma Press.

Elsner, Jaś. 2003. "Iconoclasm and the Preservation of Memory" in *Monuments and Memory, Made and Unmade*. Edited by Robert S. Nelson and Margaret Olin, 209–31. Chicago: University of Chicago Press.

Farnell, Brenda. 1999. "Moving Bodies, Acting Selves." *Annual Review of Anthropology* 28:341–73.

——. 2000. "Getting out of the *Habitus*: An Alternative Model of Dynamically Embodied Social Action." *Journal of the Royal Anthropological Institute* n.s. 6:397–418.

Fash, Barbara W. 1992. "Late Classic Architectural Sculpture Themes in Copan." *Ancient Mesoamerica* 3:89–104.

——. 2005. "Iconographic Evidence for Water Management and Social Organization at Copan" in *Copan: The History of an Ancient Maya Kingdom*. Edited by E. Wyllys Andrews and William L. Fash, 103–38. Santa Fe: School of American Research Press.

Fash, Barbara W., and William L. Fash. 2007. "The Roles of Ballgames in Meso-american Ritual Economy" in *Mesoamerican Ritual Economy: Archaeological and Ethno-logical Perspectives*. Edited by E. Christian Wells and Karla L. Davis-Salazar, 267–84. Boulder: University Press of Colorado.

Fash, Barbara W., William L. Fash, Sheree Lane, Rudy Larios, Linda Schele, Jeff Stomper, and David Stuart. 1992. "Investigations of a Classic Maya Council House at Copan, Honduras." *Journal of Field Archaeology* 19:419–42.

Fash, William L. 1983a. "Maya State Formation: A Case Study and its Implications." Ph.D. diss., Department of Anthropology, Harvard University.

——. 1983b. "Reconocimiento y excavaciones en el valle" in *Introducción a la arqueología de Copán, Honduras, Tomo I*. Edited by Claude F. Baudez, 229–469. Tegucigalpa: Proyecto Arqueológico Copán, Secretaría de Estado en el Despacho de Cultura y Turismo.

——. 1989. "The Sculptural Façade of Structure 9N-82: Content, Form, and Signifi-cance" in *The House of the Bacabs, Copan, Honduras*. Edited by David Webster, 41–72. Studies in Pre-Columbian Art and Archaeology 29. Washington: Dumbarton Oaks.

——. 1998. "Dynastic Architectural Programs: Intention and Design in Classic Maya Buildings at Copan and Other Sites" in *Function and Meaning in Classic Maya Archi-tecture*. Edited by Stephen D. Houston, 223–70. Washington: Dumbarton Oaks.

——. 2001. *Scribes, Warriors and Kings: The City of Copan and the Ancient Maya*, 2d ed. London: Thames and Hudson.

——. 2005. "Toward a Social History of the Copan Valley" in *Copan: The History of an Ancient Maya Kingdom*. Edited by E. Wyllys Andrews and William L. Fash, 73–101. Santa Fe: School of American Research Press.

Fash, William L., E. Wyllys Andrews, and T. Kam Manahan. 2004. "Political Decen-tralization, Dynastic Collapse, and the Early Postclassic in the Urban Center of Copan, Honduras" in *The Terminal Classic in the Maya Lowlands: Collapse, Transition, and Transformation*. Edited by Arthur A. Demarest, Prudence M. Rice, and Don S. Rice, 260–87. Boulder: University Press of Colorado.

Fash, William, L., Barbara Fash, and Karla Davis-Salazar. 2004. "Setting the Stage: Origins of the Hieroglyphic Stairway Plaza on the Great Period Ending" in *Under-standing Early Classic Copan*. Edited by Ellen E. Bell, Marcello A. Canuto, and Robert J. Sharer, 65–83. Philadelphia: University of Pennsylvania Museum of Archaeol-ogy and Anthropology.

Fash, William L., and Sheree Lane. 1983. "El juego de pelota B" in *Introducción a la arqueología de Copán, Honduras, Tomo II*. Edited by Claude F. Baudez, 501–62. Tegucigalpa: Proyecto Arqueológico Copán, Secretaría de Estado en el Despacho de Cultura y Turismo.

Fash, William L., and Kurt Z. Long. 1983. "Mapa arqueológico del valle de Copán" in *Introducción a la arqueología de Copán, Honduras, Tomo III*. Edited by Claude F. Baudez. Tegucigalpa: Secretaría de Estado en el Despacho de Cultura y Turismo.

Fash, William L., and Robert J. Sharer. 1991. "Sociopolitical Developments and Methodological Issues at Copan, Honduras: A Conjunctive Perspective." *Latin American Antiquity* 2:166–87.

Fash, William L., and David S. Stuart. 1991. "Dynastic History and Cultural Evolution at Copan, Honduras" in In *Classic Maya Political History: Hieroglyphic and Archaeological Evidence*. Edited by T. Patrick Culbert, 147–79. Cambridge: Cambridge University Press.

Fash, William L., Richard V. Williamson, Carlos Rudy Larios, and Joel Palka. 1992. "The Hieroglyphic Stairway and Its Ancestors: Investigations of Copan Structure 10L-26." *Ancient Mesoamerica* 3:105–15.

Featherstone, Mike. 1995. *Undoing Culture: Globalization, Postmodernism and Identity*. London: Sage.

Felski, Rita. 2000. *Doing Time: Feminist Theory and Postmodern Culture*. New York: New York University Press.

Fentress, James, and Chris Wickham. 1992. *Social Memory*. Oxford: Blackwell.

Fisette, Denis. 2003. "Descriptive Phenomenology and the Problem of Consciousness" in *The Problem of Consciousness: New Essays in Phenomenological Philosophy of Mind*. Edited by Evan Thompson, 33–66. Canadian Journal of Philosophy Supplementary Volume 29. Calgary: University of Calgary Press.

Forty, Adrian. 1999. "Introduction" in *The Art of Forgetting*. Edited by Adrian Forty and Susanne Küchler, 1–18. Oxford: Berg.

Fox, James J. 1993. "Comparative Perspectives on Austronesian Houses: An Introductory Essay" in *Inside Austronesian Houses: Perspectives on Domestic Designs for Living*. Edited by James J. Fox, 1–28. Canberra: Department of Anthropology, Australian National University.

Fox, John G. 1994. "Putting the Heart Back in the Court: Ballcourts and Ritual Action in Mesoamerica." Ph.D. diss., Department of Anthropology, Harvard University. Ann Arbor: University Microfilms.

——. 1996. "Playing with Power: Ballcourts and Political Ritual in Southern Mesoamerica." *Current Anthropology* 37:483–509.

Frémont, Armand. 1997. "The Land." Translated by Arthur Goldhammer. In *Realms of Memory: Rethinking the French Past. Volume 2: Traditions*. Edited by Pierre Nora and Lawrence D. Kritzman, 3–35. New York: Columbia University Press.

Freter, AnnCorinne. 1988. "The Classic Maya Collapse at Copan, Honduras: A Regional Settlement Perspective." Ph.D. diss., Department of Anthropology, Pennsylvania State University. Ann Arbor: University Microfilms.

Fung, Christopher D. 1995. "Domestic Labor, Gender and Social Power: Household Archaeology in Terminal Classic Yoro, Honduras." Ph.D. diss., Department of Anthropology, Harvard University. Ann Arbor: University Microfilms.

——. 1996. "Domestic Labor, Gender and Power on the Mesoamerican Frontier" in *Debating Complexity: Proceedings of the 26th Annual Chac Mool Conference*. Edited by

Daniel A. Meyer, Peter C. Dawson, and Donald T. Hanna, 65–75. Calgary: Archaeology Association of the University of Calgary.

Furst, Peter T. 1986. "Human Biology and the Origin of the 260-Day Sacred Alma-
nac: The Contributions of Leonhard Schultze Jena (1872–1955)" in *Symbol and
Meaning Beyond the Closed Community: Essays in Mesoamerican Ideas*. Edited by Gary H.
Gossen, 69–76. Albany: Institute for Mesoamerican Studies, State University of
New York.

Gallagher, Shaun, and Francisco J. Varela. 2003. "Redrawing the Map and Resetting
the Time: Phenomenology and the Cognitive Sciences" in *The Problem of Consciousness: New Essays in Phenomenological Philosophy of Mind*. Edited by Evan Thompson,
93–132. Canadian Journal of Philosophy Supplementary Volume 29. Calgary: University of Calgary Press.

Gardiner, Michael E. 2000. *Critiques of Everyday Life*. London: Routledge.

Gell, Alfred. 1977. "Magic, Perfume, Dream . . ." in *Symbols and Sentiments: Cross-
cultural Studies in Symbolism*. Edited by Ioan Lewis, 25–38. London: Academic
Press.

——. 1992. "The Technology of Enchantment and the Enchantment of Technology"
in *Anthropology, Art and Aesthetics*. Edited by Jeremy Coote and Anthony Shelton,
40–63. Oxford: Clarendon Press.

——. 1998. *Art and Agency: An Anthropological Theory*. Oxford: Clarendon Press.

——. 1999a. "Strathernograms, or the Semiotics of Mixed Metaphors" in *The Art of
Anthropology: Essays and Diagrams*. Edited by Eric Hirsch, 29–75. London School of
Economics Monographs in Social Anthropology Volume 67. London: Athlone
Press.

——. 1999b. "Vogel's Net: Traps as Artworks and Artworks as Traps" in *The Art of
Anthropology: Essays and Diagrams*. Edited by Eric Hirsch, 187–214. London School
of Economics Monographs in Social Anthropology Volume 67. London: Athlone
Press.

Geller, Pamela L. 2004. "Transforming Bodies, Transforming Identities: A Consid-
eration of Pre-Columbian Maya Corporeal Beliefs and Practices." Ph.D. diss.,
Department of Anthropology, University of Pennsylvania. Ann Arbor: University
Microfilms.

Gerry, John P., and Meredith S. Chesson. 2000. "Classic Maya Diet and Gender Relationships" in *Gender and Material Culture in Archaeological Perspective*. Edited by Moira
Donald and Linda Hurcombe, 250–64. New York: St. Martin's Press.

Gerry, John P., and Harold W. Krueger. 1997. "Regional Diversity in Classic Maya
Diets" in *Bones of the Maya: Studies of Ancient Skeletons*. Edited by Stephen L. Whit-
tington and David M. Reed, 196–207. Washington: Smithsonian Institution
Press.

Gerstle, Andrea I. 1987. "Ethnic Diversity and Interaction at Copan, Honduras."
*Interaction on the Southeast Mesoamerican Frontier: Prehistoric and Historic Honduras and El
Salvador*. Edited by Eugenia J. Robinson, 328–56. BAR International Series 327.
Oxford: British Archaeological Reports.

——. 1988. "Maya-Lenca Ethnic Relations in Late Classic Period Copan, Honduras."

Ph.D. diss., Department of Anthropology, University of California, Santa Barbara. Ann Arbor: University Microfilms.

Gerstle, Andrea I., and David L. Webster. 1990. "Excavaciones en 9N-8, conjunto del patio D" in *Proyecto Arqueológico Copán Segunda Fase: Excavaciones en el área urbana de Copán, Tomo III*. Edited by William T. Sanders, 25–368. Tegucigalpa: Secretaría de Estado en el Despacho de Cultura y Turismo, Instituto Hondureño de Antropología e Historia.

Giard, Luce. 1998. "Doing-Cooking" in *The Practice of Everyday Life*. Volume 2: *Living and Cooking*. Edited by Luce Giard and translated by Timothy J. Tomasik, 149–247. Rev. ed. Minneapolis: University of Minnesota Press.

Giddens, Anthony. 1981. *A Contemporary Critique of Historical Materialism*. Volume 1: *Power, Property and the State*. Berkeley: University of California Press.

——. 1990. *The Consequences of Modernity*. Stanford: Stanford University Press.

Giedion, Sigfried, Fernand Léger, and José Luis Sert. 1984. "Nine Points on Monumentality." *The Harvard Architectural Review IV: Monumentality and the City*. 62–63. Cambridge: MIT Press.

Gillespie, Susan D. 1989. *The Aztec Kings: The Construction of Rulership in Mexica History*. Tucson: University of Arizona Press.

——. 1991. "Ballcourts and Boundaries" in *The Mesoamerican Ballgame*. Edited by Vernon L. Scarborough and David R. Wilcox, 317–45. Tucson: University of Arizona Press.

——. 1999. "Olmec Thrones as Ancestral Altars: The Two Sides of Power" in *Material Symbols: Culture and Economy in Prehistory*. Edited by John E. Robb, 224–53. Center for Archaeological Investigations Occasional Paper No. 26. Carbondale: Southern Illinois University.

——. 2000a. "Lévi-Strauss: *Maison* and *Société à maisons*" in *Beyond Kinship: Social and Material Reproduction in House Societies*. Edited by Rosemary A. Joyce and Susan D. Gillespie, 22–52. Philadelphia: University of Pennsylvania Press.

——. 2000b. "Maya 'Nested Houses': The Ritual Construction of Place" in *Beyond Kinship: Social and Material Reproduction in House Societies*. Edited by Rosemary A. Joyce and Susan D. Gillespie, 135–60. Philadelphia: University of Pennsylvania Press.

——. 2000c. "Rethinking Ancient Maya Social Organization: Replacing 'Lineage' with 'House.'" *American Anthropologist* 102:467–84.

——. 2001. "Personhood, Agency, and Mortuary Ritual: A Case Study from the Ancient Maya." *Journal of Anthropological Archaeology* 20:73–112.

Gillespie, Susan D., and Rosemary A. Joyce. 1997. "Gendered Goods: The Symbolism of Maya Hierarchical Exchange Relations" in *Women in Prehistory: North American and Mesoamerica*. Edited by Cheryl Claassen and Rosemary A. Joyce, 189–207. Philadelphia: University of Pennsylvania Press.

Gillis, John R. 1994. "Memory and Identity: The History of a Relationship" in *Commemorations: The Politics of National Identity*. Edited by John R. Gillis, 3–24. Princeton: Princeton University Press.

Glass, John B., with Donald Robertson. 1975. "A Census of Native Middle American

Pictorial Manuscripts" in *Guide to Ethnohistorical Sources Part Three*. Edited by Howard F. Cline, 81–252. Handbook of Middle American Indians Volume 14. Austin: University of Texas Press.

Goethe, Johann Wolfgang von. 1891. *The Autobiography of Goethe. Truth and Poetry: From My Own Life*. Translated by John Oxenford. Rev. ed. London: George Bell and Sons.

Gonlin, Nancy. 1985. "The Architectural Variation of Two Small Sites in the Copan Valley, Honduras: A Rural/Urban Dichotomy?" M.A. thesis, Department of Anthropology, Pennsylvania State University. Ann Arbor: University Microfilms.

——. 1993. "Rural Household Archaeology at Copan, Honduras." Ph.D. diss., Department of Anthropology, Pennsylvania State University. Ann Arbor: University Microfilms.

——. 1994. "Rural Household Diversity in Late Classic Copan, Honduras" in *Archaeological Views from the Countryside: Village Communities in Early Complex Societies*. Edited by Glenn M. Schwartz and Steven E. Falconer, 177–97. Washington: Smithsonian Institution Press.

——. 2000. "Lo que las mujeres y los hombres hacen: Investigaciones recientes en hogares antiguos en Copan, Honduras." *Yaxkin* 13:23–39.

Goody, Jack. 1986. *The Logic of Writing and the Organization of Society*. Cambridge: Cambridge University Press.

Gordon, George B. 1970. *Prehistoric Ruins of Copan, Honduras: A Preliminary Report of the Explorations by the Museum, 1891–1895*. Memoirs of the Peabody Museum of American Archaeology and Ethnology Volume 1, Number 1. New York: Kraus Reprint.

Gossen, Gary H. 1996. "Animal Souls, Co-essences, and Human Destiny in Mesoamerica" in *Monsters, Tricksters, and Sacred Cows: Animal Tales and American Identities*. Edited by A. James Arnold, 80–107. Charlottesville: University Press of Virginia.

Gould, Stephen Jay. 1987. *Time's Arrow, Time's Cycle: Myth and Metaphor in the Discovery of Geological Time*. Cambridge: Harvard University Press.

Graeber, David. 2001. *Toward an Anthropological Theory of Value: The False Coin of Our Own Dreams*. New York: Palgrave.

Greenfield, Patricia Marks. 1984. "A Theory of the Teacher in the Learning Activities of Everyday Life" in *Everyday Cognition: Its Development in Social Context*. Edited by Barbara Rogoff and Jean Lave, 117–38. Cambridge: Harvard University Press.

——. 2004. *Weaving Generations Together: Evolving Creativity in the Maya of Chiapas*. Santa Fe: School of American Research Press.

Grube, Nikolai. 1992. "Classic Maya Dance: Evidence from Hieroglyphs and Iconography." *Ancient Mesoamerica* 3:201–18.

——. 2006. "Ancient Maya Royal Biographies in a Comparative Perspective" in *Janaab' Pakal of Palenque: Reconstructing the Life and Death of a Maya Ruler*. Edited by Vera Tiesler and Andrea Cucina, 146–66. Tucson: University of Arizona Press.

Halbwachs, Maurice. 1992. "The Social Frameworks of Memory" in *On Collective Memory*. Edited and translated by Lewis A. Coser, 41–189. Chicago: University of Chicago Press.

——. 1994. *Les cadres sociaux de la mémoire*. Paris: Albin Michel.

——. 1997. *La mémoire collective*. Edited by Gérard Namer. Rev. ed. Paris: Albin Michel.

Hall, Jay, and René Viel. 2004. "The Early Classic Copan Landscape: A View from the Preclassic" in *Understanding Early Classic Copan*. Edited by Ellen E. Bell, Marcello A. Canuto, and Robert J. Sharer, 17–28. Philadelphia: University of Pennsylvania Museum of Archaeology and Anthropology.

Halliwell, Stephen. 2002. *The Aesthetics of Mimesis: Ancient Texts and Modern Problems*. Princeton: Princeton University Press.

Halverson, John. 1992. "Goody and the Implosion of the Literacy Thesis." *Man* n.s. 27:301–17.

Hamann, Byron. 2002. "The Social Life of Pre-Sunrise Things." *Current Anthropology* 43:351–82.

Handler, Richard. 1994. "Is 'Identity' a Useful Cross-Cultural Concept?" *Commemorations: The Politics of National Identity*. Edited by John R. Gillis, 27–40. Princeton: Princeton University Press.

Hanks, William F. 1990. *Referential Practice: Language and Lived Space Among the Maya*. Chicago: University of Chicago Press.

——. 1996. *Language and Communicative Practices*. Boulder: Westview.

Hart, Gillian. 1992. "Imagined Unities: Constructions of 'the Household' in Economic Theory" in *Understanding Economic Processes*. Edited by Sutti Ortiz and Susan Lees, 111–29. Monographs in Economic Anthropology No. 10. Lanham, Md.: University Press of America.

Harvey, David. 1990. *The Condition of Postmodernity*. Cambridge, Mass.: Blackwell.

Hassig, Ross. 2001. *Time, History, and Belief in Aztec and Colonial Mexico*. Austin: University of Texas Press.

Hayden, Brian. 1996. "Feasting in Prehistoric and Traditional Societies" in *Food and the Status Quest: An Interdisciplinary Perspective*. Edited by Polly Wiessner and Wulf Schiefenhövel, 127–47. Providence: Berghahn Books.

Heath, Christian, and Paul Luff. 2000. *Technology in Action*. Cambridge: Cambridge University Press.

Hegel, Georg Wilhelm Friedrich. 1975. *Lectures on the Philosophy of World History. Introduction: Reason in History*. Edited by Johannes Hoffmeister and translated by H. B. Nisbet. Cambridge: Cambridge University Press.

Henderson, John S., and Rosemary A. Joyce. 2005. "Social Networks and Cultural Identity: Changing Perspectives on the Prehistory of Southeastern Mesoamerica." Presented at the 70th Annual Meeting of the Society for American Archaeology, Salt Lake City, Utah.

——. 2006. "Brewing Distinction: The Development of Cacao Beverages in Formative Mesoamerica" in *Chocolate in Mesoamerica: A Cultural History of Cacao*. Edited by Cameron L. McNeil, 140–53. Gainesville: University of Florida Press.

Henderson, John S., Rosemary A. Joyce, Gretchen R. Hall, W. Jeffrey Hurst, and Patrick E. McGovern. 2007. "Chemical and Archaeological Evidence for the Earliest Cacao Beverages" in *PNAS* 104:18937–940.

Hendon, Julia A. 1987. "The Uses of Maya Structures: A Study of Architecture and

Artifact Distribution at Sepulturas, Copan, Honduras." Ph.D. diss., Department of Anthropology, Harvard University. Ann Arbor: University Microfilms.

———. 1988. "Discusión preliminar del estudio de áreas de actividad en Las Sepulturas, Copán: Forma, función y distribución de las vasijas de barro." Yaxkin 11:1:47–82.

———. 1989. "Elite Household Organization at Copan, Honduras: Analysis of Activity Distribution in the Sepulturas Zone" in Household and Communities. Edited by Sean MacEachern et al., 371–80. Proceedings of the 21st Annual Chacmool Conference. Calgary: Archaeological Association of the University of Calgary.

———. 1991. "Status and Power in Classic Maya Society: An Archeological Study." American Anthropologist 93: 894–918.

———. 1992. "Architectural Symbols of the Maya Social Order: Residential Construction and Decoration in the Copan Valley, Honduras" in Ancient Images, Ancient Thought: The Archaeology of Ideology. Edited by A. Sean Goldsmith, Sandra Garvie, David Selin, and Jeannette Smith, 481–95. Proceedings of the 23rd Annual Chacmool Conference. Calgary: Archaeological Association of the University of Calgary.

———. 1996. "Archaeological Approaches to the Organization of Domestic Labor: Household Practice and Domestic Relations." Annual Review of Anthropology 25:45–61.

———. 1997. "Women's Work, Women's Space and Women's Status among the Classic Period Maya Elite of the Copan Valley, Honduras" in Women in Prehistory: North America and Mesoamerica. Edited by Cheryl Claassen and Rosemary A. Joyce, 33–46. Philadelphia: University of Pennsylvania Press.

———. 1998. "Informe preliminar: Excavaciones en CR 157 (Cerro Palenque), 1998." Report on file with the Instituto Hondureño de Antropología e Historia, Tegucigalpa.

———. 1999a. "Multiple Sources of Prestige and the Social Evaluation of Women in Prehispanic Mesoamerica" in Material Symbols: Culture and Economy in Prehistory. Edited by John E. Robb, 257–76. Center for Archaeological Investigations Occasional Paper No. 26. Carbondale: Southern Illinois University.

———. 1999b. "The Pre-Classic Maya Compound as the Focus of Social Identity" in Social Patterns in Pre-Classic Mesoamerica. Edited by David C. Grove and Rosemary A. Joyce, 97–125. Washington: Dumbarton Oaks.

———. 1999c. "Spinning and Weaving in Pre-Hispanic Mesoamerica: The Technology and Social Relations of Textile Production" in Mayan Clothing and Weaving through the Ages. Edited by B. Knoke de Arathoon, N. L. González, and J. M. Willemsen Devlin, 7–16. Guatemala City: Museo Ixchel del Traje Indígena.

———. 2000a. "Excavaciones en el sitio CR-157 (Cerro Palenque), temporada 2000: Informe preliminar del Proyecto Arqueológico Cerro Palenque." Report on file with the Instituto Hondureño de Antropología e Historia, Tegucigalpa.

———. 2000b. "Having and Holding: Storage, Memory, Knowledge, and Social Relations." American Anthropologist 102:42–53.

———. 2002a. "Excavaciones en Cerro Palenque (CR-157), temporada 2002: Informe preliminar del Proyecto Arqueológico Cerro Palenque." Report on file with the Instituto Hondureño de Antropología e Historia, Tegucigalpa.

——. 2002b. "Household and State in Prehispanic Maya Society: Gender, Identity, and Practice" in *Ancient Maya Gender Identity and Relations*. Edited by Lowell Gustafson and Amelia Trevelyan, 75–92. Westport, Conn.: Greenwood.

——. 2002c. "Social Relations and Collective Identities: Household and Community in Ancient Mesoamerica" in *The Dynamics of Power*. Edited by Maria O'Donovan, 273–300. Center for Archaeological Investigations Occasional Paper No. 30. Carbondale: Southern Illinois University.

——. 2003a. "El papel de los enterramientos en la construcción y negociación de la identidad social en los mayas prehispánicos" in *Antropología de la eternidad: La muerte en la cultura maya*. Edited by Andrés Ciudad Ruiz, Mario Humberto Ruz Sosa, and María Josefa Iglesia Ponce de León, 161–74. Madrid: Sociedad Española de Estudios Mayas, Centro de Estudios Mayas, Instituto de Investigaciones Filológicas, Universidad Nacional Autónoma de México.

——. 2003b. "Feasting at Home: Community and House Solidarity among the Maya of Southeastern Mesoamerica" in *The Archaeology and Politics of Food and Feasting in Early States and Empires*. Edited by Tamara L. Bray, 203–33. New York: Kluwer Academic/Plenum Publishers.

——. 2003c. "Honor, Shame and Reciprocity: Feasting in Southeastern Mesoamerican Complex Societies during the Late to Terminal Classic Period." Presented at the 102d Annual Meeting of the American Anthropological Association, Chicago.

——. 2003d. "In the House: Maya Nobility and Their Figurine Whistles." *Expedition* 45(3):28–33.

——. 2004a. "Importación de obsidiana a Cerro Palenque, Depto. de Cortés: resultados de una análisis por FRX." Presented at the 8th Seminario de Antropología Hondureña, Tegucigalpa.

——. 2004b. "Living and Working at Home: The Social Archaeology of Household Production and Social Relations" in *A Companion to Social Archaeology*. Edited by Lynn Meskell and Robert W. Preucel, 272–86. Malden, Mass.: Blackwell.

——. 2004c. "Postclassic and Colonial Period Sources on Maya Society and History" in *Mesoamerican Archaeology: Theory and Practice*. Edited by Julia A. Hendon and Rosemary A. Joyce, 296–322. Malden, Mass.: Blackwell.

——. 2005. "Social Identity and Practice in the Terminal Classic Community of Cerro Palenque, Honduras." Presented at the 70th Annual Meeting of the Society for American Archaeology, Salt Lake City, Utah.

——. 2006a. "The Engendered Household" in *Handbook of Gender in Archaeology*. Edited by Sarah Milledge Nelson, 171–98. Lanham, Md.: AltaMira Press.

——. 2006b. "Social Identity and Daily Life in the Terminal Classic: Local Histories and Global Connections in the Ulua Valley, Honduras." Presented at the 52nd International Congress of Americanists, Seville, Spain.

——. 2006c. "Textile Production as Craft in Mesoamerica: Time, Labor, and Knowledge." *Journal of Social Archaeology* 6:354–78.

——. 2007. "Memory, Materiality, and Practice: House Societies in Southeastern

Mesoamerica" in *The Durable House: House Society Models in Archaeology*. Edited by Robin A. Beck, 292–316. Center for Archaeological Investigations Occasional Paper No. 35. Carbondale: Southern Illinois University.

Hendon, Julia A., Ricardo Agurcia F., William L. Fash, and Eloísa Aguilar P. 1990. "Excavaciones en 9N-8, Conjunto del Patio C" in *Proyecto Arqueológico Copán Segunda Fase: Excavaciones en el área urbana de Copán, Tomo II*. Edited by William T. Sanders, 11–109. Tegucigalpa: Secretaría de Estado en el Despacho de Cultura y Turismo, Instituto Hondureño de Antropología e Historia.

Hendon, Julia A., William L. Fash, and Eloísa Aguilar P. 1990. "Excavaciones en 9N-8, Conjunto del Patio B" in *Proyecto Arqueológico Copán Segunda Fase: Excavaciones en el área urbana de Copán Tomo II*. Edited by William T. Sanders, 110–293. Tegucigalpa: Secretaría de Estado en el Despacho de Cultura y Turismo, Instituto Hondureño de Antropología e Historia.

Hendon, Julia A., and Rosemary Joyce. 1993. "Questioning 'Complexity' and 'Periphery': Archaeology in Yoro, Honduras." Presented at the 58th Annual Meeting of the Society for American Archaeology, St. Louis.

Hendon, Julia A., and Jeanne Lopiparo. 2004. "Investigaciones recientes en Cerro Palenque, Cortés, Honduras" in *Memoria VII Seminario de Antropología de Honduras "Dr. George Hasemann."* Edited by Kevin Rubén Ávalos, 187–95. Tegucigalpa: Instituto Hondureño de Antropología e Historia.

Herzfeld, Michael. 1991. *A Place in History: Social and Monumental Time in a Cretan Town*. Princeton: Princeton University Press.

Heyden, Doris. 1983. "Las diosas del agua y la vegetación." *Anales de Antropología* 20:2:129–45.

——. 1986. "Metaphors, *Nahualtocaitl*, and Other 'Disguised' Terms among the Aztecs" in *Symbol and Meaning Beyond the Closed Community: Essays in Mesoamerican Ideas*. Edited by Gary H. Gossen, 35–43. Albany: Institute for Mesoamerican Studies, University at Albany, State University of New York.

Highmore, Ben. 2002. *Everyday Life and Cultural Theory: An Introduction*. London: Routledge.

Hill, Walter, and John Clark. 2001. "Sports, Gambling, and Government: America's First Social Contract?" *American Anthropologist* 103:1–15.

Hirst, William, and David Manier. 1995. "Opening Vistas for Cognitive Psychology" in *Sociocultural Psychology: Theory and Practice of Doing and Knowing*. Edited by Laura M. W. Martin, Katherine Nelson, and Ethel Tobach, 89–124. Cambridge: Cambridge University Press.

Hohmann, Hasso, and Annegrete Vogrin. 1982. *Die Architektur von Copan (Honduras)*. Graz: Akademische Druck und Verlagsanstalt.

Holtorf, Cornelius. 1997. "Megaliths, Monumentality and Memory." *Archaeological Review from Cambridge* 14:2:45–66.

Houston, Stephen. 1994. "Literacy among the Pre-Colombian Maya: A Comparative Perspective" in *Writing Without Words: Alternative Literacies in Mesoamerica and the Andes*. Edited by Elizabeth H. Boone and Walter D. Mignolo, 27–49. Durham: Duke University Press.

——. 2000. "In the Minds of Ancients: Advances in Maya Glyph Studies." *Journal of World Prehistory* 14:121–201.

Houston, Stephen, and Karl Taube. 2000. "An Archaeology of the Senses: Perception and Cultural Expression in Ancient Mesoamerica." *Cambridge Archaeological Journal* 10:261–94.

Howes, David. 1991. "Sensorial Anthropology" in *The Varieties of Sensory Experience: A Sourcebook in the Anthropology of the Senses*. Edited by David Howes, 167–91. Toronto: University of Toronto Press.

Hunt, Eva. 1977. *The Transformation of the Hummingbird: Cultural Roots of a Zinacantecan Mythical Poem*. Ithaca: Cornell University Press.

Hutton, Patrick H. 1993. *History as an Art of Memory*. Hanover, N.H.: University Press of New England.

Jackson, Michael. 1998. *Minima Ethnographica: Intersubjectivity and the Anthropological Project*. Chicago: University of Chicago Press.

Joyce, Rosemary A. 1982. "La zona arqueológica de Cerro Palenque." *Yaxkin* 5:2:95–101.

——. 1985. "Cerro Palenque, Valle de Ulua, Honduras: Terminal Classic Interaction on the Southern Mesoamerican Periphery." Ph.D. diss., Department of Anthropology, University of Illinois at Urbana-Champaign. Ann Arbor: University Microfilms.

——. 1986. "Terminal Classic Interaction on the Southeastern Maya Periphery." *American Antiquity* 51:313–29.

——. 1987a. "Intraregional Ceramic Variation and Social Class: Developmental Trajectories of Classic Period Ceramic Complexes from the Ulua Valley" in *Interaction on the Southeast Mesoamerican Frontier: Prehistoric and Historic Honduras and El Salvador*. Edited by Eugenia J. Robinson, 280–303. BAR International Series 327. Oxford: British Archaeological Reports.

——. 1987b. "The Terminal Classic Ceramics of Cerro Palenque: An Eastern Outlier of the Boca Ceramic Sphere" in *Maya Ceramics: Papers from the Maya Ceramic Conference, 1985*. Edited by Prudence Rice and Robert Sharer, 397–430. BAR International Series 345. Oxford: British Archaeological Reports.

——. 1988. "Ceramic Traditions and Language Groups in Prehispanic Honduras." *Journal of the Steward Anthropological Society* 15:158–86.

——. 1991. *Cerro Palenque: Power and Identity on the Maya Periphery*. Austin: University of Texas Press.

——. 1993a. "The Construction of the Mesoamerican Frontier and the Mayoid Image of Honduran Polychromes" in *Reinterpreting Prehistory of Central America*. Edited by Mark Miller Graham, 51–101. Niwot: University Press of Colorado.

——. 1993b. "Women's Work: Images of Production and Reproduction in Pre-Hispanic Southern Central America." *Current Anthropology* 34:255–73.

——. 1996. "Construction of Gender in Classic Maya Monuments" in *Gender and Archaeology*. Edited by Rita P. Wright, 167–95. Philadelphia: University of Pennsylvania Press.

——. 1998. "Performing the Body in Prehispanic Central America." *Res* 33:147–65.

——. 2000a. *Gender and Power in Prehispanic Mesoamerica.* Austin: University of Texas Press.

——. 2000b. "Girling the Girl and Boying the Boy: The Production of Adulthood in Ancient Mesoamerica." *World Archaeology* 31:473–83.

——. 2000c. "Heirlooms and Houses: Materiality and Social Memory" in *Beyond Kinship: Social and Material Reproduction in House Societies.* Edited by Rosemary A. Joyce and Susan D. Gillespie, 189–212. Philadelphia: University of Pennsylvania Press.

——. 2000d. "A Precolumbian Gaze: Male Sexuality among the Ancient Maya" in *Archaeologies of Sexuality.* Edited by Barbara Voss and Rob Schmidt, 263–83. London: Routledge.

——. 2001. "Burying the Dead at Tlatilco: Social Memory and Social Identities" in *Social Memory, Identity, and Death: Anthropological Perspectives on Mortuary Analysis.* Edited by Meredith Chesson, 12–26. Archeological Paper No. 10. Naperville, Ill.: American Anthropological Association.

——. 2002. "Desiring Women: Classic Maya Sexualities" in *Ancient Maya Gender Identity and Relations.* Edited by Lowell Gustafson and Amelia Trevelyan, 329–44. Westport, Conn.: Greenwood.

——. 2003. "Concrete Memories: Fragments of the Past in the Classic Maya Present (500–1000 AD)" in *Archaeologies of Memory.* Edited by Ruth M. Van Dyke and Susan E. Alcock, 104–25. Malden, Mass.: Blackwell.

——. 2004. "Mesoamerica: A Working Model for Archaeology" in *Mesoamerican Archaeology: Theory and Practice.* Edited by Julia A. Hendon and Rosemary A. Joyce, 1–42. Malden, Mass.: Blackwell.

——. 2005. "Archaeology of the Body." *Annual Review of Anthropology* 34:139–58.

——. 2007. "Figurines, Meaning, and Meaning-Making in Early Mesoamerica" in *Image and Imagination: A Global Prehistory of Figurative Representation.* Edited by Colin Renfrew and Iain Morley, 107–16. Cambridge: McDonald Institute for Archaeological Research.

Joyce, Rosemary A., and Susan D. Gillespie, eds. 2000. *Beyond Kinship: Social and Material Reproduction in House Societies.* Philadelphia: University of Pennsylvania Press.

Joyce, Rosemary A., and John S. Henderson. 2001. "Beginnings of Village Life in Eastern Mesoamerica." *Latin American Antiquity* 12:5–24.

Joyce, Rosemary A., and Julia A. Hendon. 2000. "Heterarchy, History, and Material Reality: 'Communities' in Late Classic Honduras" in *The Archaeology of Communities: A New World Perspective.* Edited by Marcello-Andrea Canuto and Jason Yaeger, 143–59. London: Routledge.

Joyce, Rosemary A., Julia A. Hendon, Christopher D. Fung, and John G. Fox. 2001. "Expanding the Terminal Classic in Honduras: Implications from Research in the Cuyumapa River Drainage, Department of Yoro." Manuscript on file in the Department of Anthropology, Gettysburg College, Gettysburg, Penn.

Joyce, Rosemary A., Julia A. Hendon, and Jeanne Lopiparo. 2009. "Being in Place:

Intersections of Identity and Experience on the Honduran Landscape" in *The Archaeology of Meaningful Places*. Edited by Brenda J. Bowser and M. Nieves Zedeño, 53–72. Salt Lake City: University of Utah Press.

Joyce, Rosemary A., Russell N. Sheptak, Julia A. Hendon, Christopher D. Fung, and John Gerry. 1989. "Settlement Patterns in Yoro, Honduras." Presented at the 88th Annual Meeting of the American Anthropological Association, Washington, D.C.

Kahn, Anna Lee. 1990. "A Thematic Study of the Female Figures in Late Classic Maya Vessel Paintings." Ph.D. diss., Department of Anthropology, University of Texas, Dallas. Ann Arbor: University Microfilms.

Kan, Sergei. 1989. *Symbolic Immortality: The Tlingit Potlatch of the Nineteenth Century*. Washington: Smithsonian University Press.

Karttunen, Frances. 1994. *Between Worlds: Interpreters, Guides, and Survivors*. New Brunswick: Rutgers University Press.

Keane, Webb. 1995. "The Spoken House: Text, Act, and Object in Eastern Indonesia." *American Ethnologist* 22:102–24.

——. 1997. *Signs of Recognition: Powers and Hazards of Representation in an Indonesian Society*. Berkeley: University of California Press.

——. 2001. "Money Is No Object: Materiality, Desire, and Modernity in an Indonesian Society" in *The Empire of Things: Regimes of Value and Material Culture*. Edited by Fred R. Myers, 65–90. Santa Fe: School of American Research Press.

——. 2005. "Signs Are Not the Garb of Meaning: On the Social Analysis of Material Things" in *Materiality*. Edited by Daniel Miller, 182–205. Durham: Duke University Press.

Keller, Charles M., and Janet Dixon Keller. 1996. *Cognition and Tool Use: The Blacksmith at Work*. Cambridge: Cambridge University Press.

Kelly, Sean Dorrance. 2005. "Seeing Things in Merleau-Ponty" in *The Cambridge Companion to Merleau-Ponty*. Edited by Taylor Carman and Mark B. N. Hansen, 74–110. Cambridge: Cambridge University Press.

Kerr, Justin. 1989. *The Maya Vase Book*. Volume 1. New York: Kerr Associates.

Ketelaar, Eric. 2002. "Archival Temples, Archival Prisons: Modes of Power and Protection." *Archival Science* 2:221–38.

Kirshner, David, and James A. Whitson. 1997. "Editors' Introduction to *Situated Cognition: Social, Semiotic, and Psychological Perspectives*" in *Situated Cognition: Social, Semiotic, and Psychological Perspectives*. Edited by David Kirshner and James A. Whitson, 1–16. Mahwah, N.J.: Lawrence Erlbaum Associates.

Klein, Cecilia F. 2001. "Conclusions: Envisioning Pre-Columbian Gender Studies" in *Gender in Pre-Hispanic Mesoamerica*. Edited by Cecilia F. Klein, 363–85. Washington: Dumbarton Oaks.

Klor de Alva, J. Jorge. 1989. "European Spirit and Mesoamerican Matter: Sahagún and the 'Crisis of Representation' in Sixteenth-Century Ethnography" in *The Imagination of Matter: Religion and Ecology in Mesoamerican Traditions*. Edited by Davíd Carrasco, 17–29. BAR International Series 515. Oxford: British Archaeological Reports.

——. 1993. "Aztec Spirituality and Nahuatized Christianity" in *South and Meso-*

American Native Spirituality: From the Cult of the Feathered Serpent to the Theology of Liberation. Edited by Gary H. Gossen, 173–97. New York: Crossroad.

Knapp, A. Bernard, and Wendy Ashmore. 1999. "Archaeological Landscapes: Constructed, Conceptualized, Ideational" in *Archaeologies of Landscape: Contemporary Perspectives.* Edited by Wendy Ashmore and A. Bernard Knapp, 1–30. Oxford: Blackwell.

Knappett, Carl. 2005. *Thinking Through Material Culture: An Interdisciplinary Perspective.* Philadelphia: University of Pennsylvania Press.

Koshar, Rudy. 2000. *From Monuments to Traces: Artifacts of German Modernity, 1870–1990.* Berkeley: University of California Press.

Kowalski, Jeff K., and William L. Fash. 1991. "Symbolism of the Maya Ball Game at Copan: Synthesis and New Aspects" in *Sixth Palenque Round Table, 1986.* Edited by Virginia M. Fields, 59–67. Norman: University of Oklahoma Press.

Küchler, Susanne. 1987. "Malangan: Art and Memory in a Melanesian Society." *Man* 22:238–55.

——. 1988. "Malangan: Objects, Sacrifice and the Production of Memory." *American Ethnologist* 15:625–37.

——. 1992. "Making Skins: *Malangan* and the Idiom of Kinship in Northern New Ireland" in *Anthropology, Art and Aesthetics.* Edited by Jeremy Coote and Anthony Shelton, 94–112. Oxford: Clarendon Press.

——. 1999. "The Place of Memory" in *The Art of Forgetting.* Edited by Adrian Forty and Susanne Küchler, 53–72. Oxford: Berg.

——. 2002. *Malanggan: Art, Memory, and Sacrifice.* Oxford: Berg.

——. 2005. "Materiality and Cognition: The Changing Face of Things" in *Materiality.* Edited by Daniel Miller, 206–30. Durham: Duke University Press.

Laughlin, Robert M., trans., and Carol Karasik, ed. 1988. *The People of the Bat: Mayan Tales and Dreams from Zinacantan.* Washington: Smithsonian Institution Press.

Lave, Jean. 1988. *Cognition in Practice: Mind, Mathematics and Culture in Everyday Life.* Cambridge: Cambridge University Press.

——. 1993. "The Practice of Learning" in *Understanding Practice: Perspectives on Activity and Context.* Edited by Seth Chaiklin and Jean Lave, 3–32. Cambridge: Cambridge University Press.

Lave, Jean, and Etienne Wenger. 1991. *Situated Learning: Legitimate Peripheral Participation.* Cambridge: Cambridge University Press.

Lee, Carla S. 1995. "A Bioarchaeological Study of Differential Food Access and Activity Type at an Elite Classic Maya Site, Copan, Honduras." M.A. thesis, Department of Anthropology, University of Houston. Ann Arbor: University Microfilms.

Lefebvre, Henri. 1987. "The Everyday and Everydayness." Translated by Christine Levich. *Yale French Studies* 73:7–11.

——. 1991a. *Critique of Everyday Life.* Volume 1: *Introduction.* Translated by John Moore. London: Verso.

——. 1991b. *The Production of Space*. Translated by Donald Nicholson-Smith. Oxford: Blackwell.

——. 2004. *Rhythmanalysis: Space, Time and Everyday Life*. Translated by Stuart Elden and Gerald Moore. London: Continuum.

Le Goff, Jacques. 1992. *History and Memory*. Translated by Steven Rendall and Elizabeth Claman. New York: Columbia University Press.

Leibsohn, Dana. 1994. "Primers for Memory: Cartographic Histories and Nahua Identity" in *Writing Without Words: Alternative Literacies in Mesoamerica and the Andes*. Edited by Elizabeth H. Boone and Walter D. Mignolo, 161–87. Durham: Duke University Press.

Lele, Veerendra P. 2006. "Material Habits, Identity, Semeiotic." *Journal of Social Archaeology* 6:48–70.

Lenz, Hans. 1961. *Mexican Indian Paper: Its History and Survival*. Translated by H. Murray Campbell. Mexico City: Editorial Libros de México.

Leonard, Anne, and John Terrell. 1980. *Patterns of Paradise: The Styles and Significance of Bark Cloth Around the World*. Chicago: Field Museum of Natural History.

León-Portilla, Miguel. 1969. *Pre-Columbian Literatures of Mexico*. Norman: University of Oklahoma Press.

Leventhal, Richard M. 1979. "Settlement Patterns at Copan, Honduras." Ph.D. diss., Department of Anthropology, Harvard University.

Levinson, Sanford. 1998. *Written in Stone: Public Monuments in Changing Societies*. Durham: Duke University Press.

Lévi-Strauss, Claude. 1982. *The Way of the Masks*. Translated by Sylvia Modelski. Seattle: University of Washington Press.

——. 1987. *Anthropology and Myth: Lectures, 1951–1982*. Translated by Roy Willis. Oxford: Basil Blackwell.

Leyenaar, Ted J. J., and Lee A. Parsons. 1988. *Ulama: The Ballgame of the Mayas and the Aztecs 2000 BC–AD 2000*. Leiden: Spruyt, Van Mantgem and De Does.

LiPuma, Edward. 1998. "Modernity and Forms of Personhood in Melanesia" in *Bodies and Persons: Comparative Perspectives from Africa and Melanesia*. Edited by Michael Lambek and Andrew Strathern, 53–79. Cambridge: Cambridge University Press.

Longyear, John M. 1952. *Copan Ceramics: A Study of Southeastern Maya Pottery*. Publication 597. Washington: Carnegie Institution of Washington.

Looper, Matthew G. 1998. "A Note on the Carved Bone from Copan Temple 11." *Glyph Dwellers Report* 4. Electronic document at http://nas.ucdavis.edu/NALC /R4.pdf. Accessed 1/4/06.

——. 1999. "New Perspectives on the Late Classic Political History of Quirigua, Guatemala." *Ancient Mesoamerica* 10:263–80.

——. 2002. "Women-Men (and Men-Women): Classic Maya Rulers and the Third Gender" in *Ancient Maya Women*. Edited by Traci Ardren, 171–202. Walnut Creek, Calif.: AltaMira Press.

——. 2003. *Lightning Warrior: Maya Art and Kingship at Quirigua*. Austin: University of Texas Press.

——. 2009. *To Be Like Gods: Dance in Ancient Maya Civilization.* Austin: University of Texas Press.

Lopiparo, Jeanne L. 2003. "Household Ceramic Production and the Crafting of Society in the Terminal Classic Ulua Valley, Honduras." Ph.D. diss., Department of Anthropology, University of California, Berkeley. Ann Arbor: University Microfilms.

——. 2006. "Crafting Children: Materiality, Social Memory, and the Reproduction of Terminal Classic House Societies in the Ulua Valley, Honduras" in *The Social Experience of Childhood in Ancient Mesoamerica.* Edited by Traci Ardren and Scott R. Hutson, 133–68. Boulder: University of Colorado Press.

——. 2007. "House Societies and Heterarchy in the Terminal Classic Ulua Valley, Honduras" in *The Durable House: House Society Models in Archaeology.* Edited by Robin A. Beck, 73–96. Center for Archaeological Investigations Occasional Paper No. 35. Carbondale: Southern Illinois University.

Lopiparo, Jeanne L., and Julia A. Hendon. 2006. "Honduran Figurines and Whistles in Context: Production, Use, and Meaning in the Ulua Valley" in *Mesoamerican Figurines: Small-Scale Indices of Large-Scale Social Phenomenon.* Edited by Christina T. Halperin, Katherine A. Faust, Rhonda Taube, and Aurore Giguet, 51–74. Gainesville: University of Florida Press.

Lopiparo, Jeanne L., Rosemary A. Joyce, and Julia A. Hendon. 2005. "Terminal Classic Pottery Production in the Ulua Valley, Honduras" in *Geographies of Power: Understanding the Nature of Terminal Classic Pottery in the Maya Lowlands.* Edited by Sandra L. López Varela and Antonia E. Foias, 107–19. BAR International Series 1447. Oxford: Archaeopress.

Lounsbury, Floyd G. 1983. "The Base of the Venus Table in the Dresden Codex, and Its Significance for the Calendar-Correlation Problem" in *Calendars in Mesoamerica and Peru: Native American Computations of Time.* Edited by Anthony F. Aveni and Gordon Brotherston, 1–26. BAR International Series 174. Oxford: British Archaeological Reports.

Love, Bruce. 1989. "Yucatec Sacred Breads through Time" in *Word and Image in Maya Culture: Explorations in Language, Writing, and Representation.* Edited by William F. Hanks and Don S. Rice, 336–50. Salt Lake City: University of Utah Press.

Lovell, Terry. 2000. "Thinking Feminism With and Against Bourdieu" in *Reading Bourdieu on Society and Culture.* Edited by Bridget Fowler, 27–48. Oxford: Blackwell/Sociological Review.

Lovibond, Sabina. 1993. "Feminism and Postmodernism" in *Postmodernism: A Reader.* Edited by Thomas Docherty, 390–414. New York: Columbia University Press.

Low, Setha M., and Denise Lawrence-Zúñiga. 2003. "Locating Culture" in *The Anthropology of Space and Place: Locating Culture.* Edited by Setha M. Low and Denise Lawrence-Zúñiga, 1–47. Malden, Mass.: Blackwell.

Lüdtke, Alf. 1995. "Introduction: What Is the History of Everyday Life and Who Are Its Practitioners?" in *The History of Everyday Life: Reconstructing Historical Experiences and Ways of Life.* Edited by Alf Lüdtke and translated by William Templer, 3–40. Princeton: Princeton University Press.

Luke, Christina. 2004. "Los vasos de mármol: Los períodos Clásico Tardío y Clásico Terminal en el valle del Río Ulúa, Honduras" in *Memoria VII Seminario de Antropología de Honduras "Dr. George Hasemann."* Edited by Kevin Rubén Ávalos, 161–85. Tegucigalpa: Instituto Hondureño de Antropología e Historia.

Luke, Christina, and Robert H. Tykot. 2002. "Marble Sources and Artifacts from the Ulua Valley, Honduras" in *ASMOSIA 5: Interdisciplinary Studies on Ancient Stone.* Edited by John J. Herrmann, Norman Herz, and Richard Newman, 394–400. London: Archetype.

MacGregor, Gavin. 1999. "Making Sense of the Past in the Present: A Sensory Analysis of Carved Stone Balls." *World Archaeology* 31:258–71.

Mahler, Joy. 1965. "Garments and Textiles of the Maya Lowlands" in *Archaeology of Southern Mesoamerica Part Two.* Edited by Gordon R. Willey, 581–93. Handbook of Middle American Indians Volume 3. Austin: University of Texas Press.

Maleuvre, Didier. 1999. *Museum Memories: History, Technology, Art.* Stanford: Stanford University Press.

Mallory, John K. 1981. "Excavaciones en el complejo residencial de las Sepulturas, Copan." *Yaxkin* 4:2:145–58.

——. 1984. "Late Classic Maya Economic Specialization: Evidence from the Copan Obsidian Assemblage." Ph.D. diss., Department of Anthropology, Pennsylvania State University. Ann Arbor: University Microfilms.

Manahan, T. Kam. 2004. "The Way Things Fall Apart: Social Organization and the Classic Maya Collapse of Copan." *Ancient Mesoamerica* 15:107–25.

Marcus, Joyce. 1978. "Archaeology and Religion: A Comparison of the Zapotec and Maya." *World Archaeology* 10:172–91.

——. 1992a. *Mesoamerican Writing Systems: Propaganda, Myth, and History in Four Ancient Civilizations.* Princeton: Princeton University Press.

——. 1992b. "Royal Families, Royal Texts: Examples from the Zapotec and Maya" in *Mesoamerican Elites: An Archaeological Assessment.* Edited by Diane Z. Chase and Arlen F. Chase, 221–41. Norman: University of Oklahoma Press.

——. 2002. "Maya Hieroglyphs: History or Propaganda?" *Archaeology: Original Readings in Method and Theory.* Edited by Peter Peregrine, Melvin Ember, and Carol R. Ember, 192–209. Englewood Cliffs, N.J.: Prentice-Hall.

Márquez, Lourdes, Patricia Hernández, and Carlos Serrano. 2006. "Pakal's Age in the Demographic Context of Late Classic Palenque Society" in *Janaab' Pakal of Palenque: Reconstructing the Life and Death of a Maya Ruler.* Edited by Vera Tiesler and Andrea Cucina, 68–83. Tucson: University of Arizona Press.

Martin, Simon, and Nikolai Grube. 2000. *Chronicle of the Maya Kings and Queens: Deciphering the Dynasties of the Ancient Maya.* London: Thames and Hudson.

Matos Moctezuma, Eduardo. 2001. "The Ballcourt in Tenochtitlan" in *The Sport of Life and Death: The Mesoamerican Ballgame.* Edited by E. Michael Whittington, 88–95. London: Thames and Hudson.

Maudslay, Alfred P. 1974. *Biologia Centrali-Americana: Archaeology.* Edited by F. Ducane Godman and Osbert Salvin. 6 volumes. New York: Milpatron Publishing.

Mauss, Marcel. 1990. *The Gift: The Form and Reason for Exchange in Archaic Societies*. Translated by W. D. Halls. New York: W. W. Norton.

——. 2006. "Techniques of the Body." Translated by Ben Brewster. In *Techniques, Technology and Civilisation*. Edited by Nathan Schlanger, 77–95. New York: Durkheim Press/Berghahn Books.

Maxwell, Judith M. 1997. "Discourse Strategies, Then and Now" in *The Language of Maya Hieroglyphs*. Edited by Martha J. Macri and Anabel Ford, 97–110. San Francisco: Pre-Columbian Art Research Institute.

McAnany, Patricia. 1995. *Living with the Ancestors*. Austin: University of Texas Press.

——. 1998. "Ancestors and the Classic Maya Built Environment" in *Function and Meaning in Classic Maya Architecture*. Edited by Stephen D. Houston, 271–98. Washington: Dumbarton Oaks.

McKie, Linda, Sophia Bowlby, and Susan Gregory. 1999. "Connecting Gender, Power, and the Household" in *Gender, Power and the Household*. Edited by Linda McKie, Sophia Bowlby, and Susan Gregory, 3–21. New York: St. Martin's Press.

McKinnon, Susan. 1991. *From a Shattered Sun: Hierarchy, Gender, and Alliance in the Tanimbar Islands*. Madison: University of Wisconsin Press.

McNeil, Cameron L., W. Jeffrey Hurst, and Robert J. Sharer. 2006. "The Use and Representation of Cacao During the Classic Period at Copan, Honduras" in *Chocolate in Mesoamerica: A Cultural History of Cacao*. Edited by Cameron L. McNeil, 224–52. Gainesville: University of Florida Press.

Melion, Walter, and Susanne Küchler. 1991. "Introduction: Memory, Cognition, and Image Production" in *Images of Memory: On Remembering and Representation*. Edited by Susanne Küchler and Walter Melion, 1–46. Washington: Smithsonian Institution Press.

Mendieta, Gerónimo de. 1945. *Historia Eclesiástica Indiana*. Mexico City: Salvador Chávez Hayhoe.

Merleau-Ponty, Maurice. 1958. *Phenomenology of Perception*. Translated by Colin Smith. London: Routledge.

Meskell, Lynn M. 2000. "Writing the Body in Archaeology" in *Reading the Body: Representations and Remains in the Archaeological Record*. Edited by Alison E. Rautman, 13–21. Philadelphia: University of Pennsylvania Press.

——. 2002. *Private Life in New Kingdom Egypt*. Princeton: Princeton University Press.

——. 2004. *Object Worlds in Ancient Egypt: Material Biographies Past and Present*. Oxford: Berg.

Meskell, Lynn M., and Rosemary A. Joyce. 2003. *Embodied Lives: Figuring Ancient Maya and Egyptian Experience*. London: Routledge.

Miller, Daniel. 1987. *Material Culture and Mass Consumption*. Oxford: Basil Blackwell.

——. 1998a. *A Theory of Shopping*. Ithaca: Cornell University Press.

——. 1998b. "Why Some Things Matter" in *Material Cultures: Why Some Things Matter*. Edited by Daniel Miller, 3–21. Chicago: University of Chicago Press.

——. 2001. "Behind Closed Doors" in *Home Possessions: Material Culture Behind Closed Doors*. Edited by Daniel Miller, 1–19. Oxford: Berg.

———. 2005. "Materiality: An Introduction" in *Materiality*. Edited by Daniel Miller, 1–50. Durham: Duke University Press.

Miller, Mary. 1986. "Copan, Honduras: Conference with a Perished City" in *City-States of the Maya: Art and Architecture*. Edited by Elizabeth P. Benson, 72–108. Denver: Rocky Mountain Institute for Pre-Columbian Studies.

———. 1999. *Maya Art and Architecture*. London: Thames and Hudson.

———. 2001. "The Maya Ballgame: Rebirth in the Court of Life and Death" in *The Sport of Life and Death: The Mesoamerican Ballgame*. Edited by E. Michael Whittington, 78–87. London: Thames and Hudson.

Miller, Mary, and Stephen D. Houston. 1987. "The Classic Maya Ballgame and Its Architectural Setting." *Res* 14:46–65.

Miller, Mary, and Karl Taube. 1993. *An Illustrated Dictionary of the Gods and Symbols of Ancient Mexico and the Maya*. New York: Thames and Hudson.

Mills, Barbara J., and William H. Walker. 2008. "Introduction: Memory, Materiality, and Depositional Practice" in *Memory Work: Archaeologies of Material Practices*. Edited by Barbara J. Mills and William H. Walker, 3–23. Santa Fe: School for Advanced Research Press.

Mitchell, Jon P. 2006. "Performance" in *Handbook of Material Culture*. Edited by Christopher Tilley, Webb Keane, Susanne Küchler, Michael Rowlands, and Patricia Spyer, 384–401. London: Sage Publications.

Monaghan, John. 1994. "The Text in the Body, the Body in the Text: The Embodied Sign in Mixtec Writing" in *Writing Without Words: Alternative Literacies in Mesoamerica and the Andes*. Edited by Elizabeth H. Boone and Walter D. Mignolo, 87–101. Durham: Duke University Press.

———. 1995. *The Covenants with Earth and Rain: Exchange, Sacrifice, and Revelation in Mixtec Sociality*. Norman: University of Oklahoma Press.

———. 1998a. "Dedication: Ritual or Production?" *The Sowing and the Dawning: Termination, Dedication, and Transformation in the Archaeological and Ethnographic Record of Mesoamerica*. Edited by Shirley B. Mock, 47–52. Albuquerque: University of New Mexico Press.

———. 1998b. "The Person, Destiny, and the Construction of Difference in Mesoamerica." *Res* 33:137–46.

Moore, Henrietta. 1992. "Households and Gender Relations: The Modelling of the Economy" in *Understanding Economic Process*. Edited by S. Ortiz and S. Lees, 131–48. Monographs in Economic Anthropology No. 10. Lanham, Md.: University Press of America.

———. 1994. *A Passion for Difference: Essays in Anthropology and Gender*. Bloomington: Indiana University Press.

Morley, Sylvanus G. 1920. *The Inscriptions at Copan*. Publication 219. Washington: Carnegie Institution of Washington.

Morris, Walter F. 1985. "Warped Glyphs: A Reading of Maya Textiles" in *Fourth Palenque Round Table, 1980*. Edited by Elizabeth P. Benson, 317–23. San Francisco: Pre-Columbian Art Research Institute.

Morris, Walter F., and Jeffrey J. Foxx. 1987. *Living Maya*. New York: Harry N. Abrams.

Moshenska, Gabriel. 2007. "Oral History in Historical Archaeology: Excavating Sites of Memory." *Oral History* 35:91–97.

Munn, Nancy D. 1992. "The Cultural Anthropology of Time: A Critical Essay." *Annual Review of Anthropology* 21:93–123.

Muriuki, Godfrey. 2002. "Western Uniqueness? Some Counterarguments from an African Perspective" in *Western Historical Thinking: An Intercultural Debate*. Edited by Jörn Rüsen, 142–47. New York: Berghahn Books.

Myers, Fred R. 2001. "Introduction: The Empire of Things" in *The Empire of Things: Regimes of Value and Material Culture*. Edited by Fred R. Myers, 3–61. Santa Fe: School of American Research Press.

Nabokov, Vladimir. 1966. *Speak, Memory: An Autobiography Revisited*. Rev. ed. New York: G. P. Putnam's Sons.

Nakamura, Seiichi, Kazuo Aoyama, and Eiji Uratsuji, eds. 1991. *Investigaciones arqueológicas en la región de la Entrada, Primera Fase*. San Pedro Sula: Servicio de Volunatrios Japoneses para la Cooperación con el Extranjero and the Instituto Hondureño de Antropología e Historia.

Nelson Sutherland, Cyril Hardy. 1986. *Plantas comunes de Honduras*. 2 volumes. Tegucigalpa: Editorial Universitaria.

Nicholson, H. B. 1988. "Introduction: Research Concerning the Mesoamerican Ritual Ballgame." In *Ulama: The Ballgame of the Mayas and the Aztecs 2000 BC–AD 2000*, 11–21. Leiden: Spruyt, Van Mantgem and De Does.

Nora, Pierre. 1989. "Between Memory and History: Les Lieux de Mémoire." *Representations* 26:7–24.

——. 1996. "General Introduction: Between Memory and History." Translated by Arthur Goldhammer. In *Realms of Memory: Rethinking the French Past*. Volume 1: *Conflicts and Divisions*. Edited by Pierre Nora and Lawrence D. Kritzman, 1–20. New York: Columbia University Press.

Nora, Pierre, ed. 1996. *Realms of Memory: Rethinking the French Past*. Volume 1: *Conflicts and Divisions*. Edited by Pierre Nora and Lawrence D. Kritzman and translated by Arthur Goldhammer. New York: Columbia University Press.

——. 1997. *Realms of Memory: Rethinking the French Past*. Volume 2: *Traditions*. Edited by Pierre Nora and Lawrence D. Kritzman and translated by Arthur Goldhammer. New York: Columbia University Press.

——. 2001. *Rethinking France: Les Lieux de mémoire*. Volume 1: *The State*. Translated by Mary Trouille. Chicago: University of Chicago Press.

Norkunas, Martha K. 2002. *Monuments and Memory: History and Representation in Lowell, Massachusetts*. Washington: Smithsonian Institution Press.

Noyes, Ernest, trans. 1932. "Fray Alonso Ponce in Yucatan, 1588" in *Middle American Papers: Studies Relating to Research in Mexico, the Central American Republics, and the West Indies*. Edited by Maurice Ries, 297–372. Middle American Research Series Publication No. 4. New Orleans: Tulane University.

Olick, Jeffrey K., and Joyce Robbins. 1998. "Social Memory Studies: From 'Collective Memory' to the Historical Sociology of Mnemonic Practices." *Annual Review of Sociology* 24:105–40.

Oliver, Paul. 1990. *Dwellings: The House Across the World*. Austin: University of Texas Press.

O'Neale, Lila M. 1945. *Textiles of Highland Guatemala*. Publication 567. Washington: Carnegie Institution of Washington.

Padgett, Paige M. 1996. "The Effects of Social Status and Residency Patterns on Infection among the Late Classic Maya at Copan, Honduras." M.A. thesis, Department of Anthropology, University of Houston. Ann Arbor: University Microfilms.

Pahl, Gary W. 1977. "The Inscriptions of Rio Amarillo and Los Higos: Secondary Centers of the Southeastern Maya Frontier." *Journal of Latin American Lore* 3:133–54.

Parmentier, Richard J. 1987. *The Sacred Remains: Myth, History and Polity in Belau*. Chicago: University of Chicago Press.

Pennebaker, James W. and Becky L. Banasik. 1997. "On the Creation and Maintenance of Collective Memories: History as Social Psychology" in *Collective Memory of Political Events: Social Psychological Perspectives*. Edited by James W. Pennebaker, Dario Paez, and Bernard Rimé, 3–19. Mahwah, N.J.: Lawrence Erlbaum Associates.

Petrov, Krinka Vidaković. 1989. "Memory and Oral Tradition" in *Memory: History, Culture and the Mind*. Edited by Thomas Butler, 77–96. Oxford: Basil Blackwell.

Pfaffenberger, B. 1992. "Social Anthropology of Technology." *Annual Review of Anthropology* 21:491–516.

Phelan, John L. 1970. *The Millennial Kingdom of the Franciscans in the New World*. Berkeley: University of California Press.

Piot, Charles. 1999. *Remotely Global: Village Modernity in West Africa*. Chicago: University of Chicago Press.

Pohl, Mary. 1981. "Ritual Continuity and Transformation in Mesoamerica: Reconstructing the Ancient Maya Cuch Ceremony." *American Antiquity* 46:513–29.

Pohl, Mary, and Larry H. Feldman. 1982. "The Traditional Role of Women and Animals in Lowland Maya Economy" in *Maya Subsistence*. Edited by Kent V. Flannery, 295–311. New York: Academic Press.

Pohl, Mary E. D., and John M. D. Pohl. 1994. "Cycles of Conflict and Political Factionalism in the Maya Lowlands" in *Factional Competition and Political Development in the New World*. Edited by Elizabeth M. Brumfiel and John W. Fox, 138–57. Cambridge: Cambridge University Press.

Poster, Mark. 1997. *Cultural History and Postmodernity: Disciplinary Readings and Challenges*. New York: Columbia University Press.

Prechtel, Martin, and Robert S. Carlsen. 1988. "Weaving and Cosmos among the Tzutujil Maya of Guatemala." *Res* 15:123–32.

Pred, Allan. 1990. *Making Histories and Constructing Human Geographies: The Local Transformation of Practice, Power Relations, and Consciousness*. Boulder: Westview.

Press, Gerald A. 1982. *The Development of the Idea of History in Antiquity*. Kingston: McGill-Queen's University Press.

Preucel, Robert W. 2006. *Archaeological Semiotics*. Malden, Mass.: Blackwell.

Preucel, Robert W., and Alexander A. Bauer. 2001. "Archaeological Pragmatics." *Norwegian Archaeological Review* 34:85–96.

Proskouriakoff, Tatiana. 1978. "Olmec Gods and Maya God-Glyphs." *Codex Wauchope: A Tribute Roll*. Edited by M. Giardino, B. Edmonson, and W. Creamer. *Human Mosaic* 12:113–17.

Prost, Antoine. 1997. "Monuments to the Dead." Translated by Arthur Goldhammer. In *Realms of Memory: Rethinking the French Past*. Volume 2: *Traditions*. Edited by Pierre Nora and Lawrence D. Kritzman, 307–30. New York: Columbia University Press.

Pyburn, K. Anne. 1989. "Maya Cuisine: Hearths and the Lowland Economy." *Research in Economic Anthropology Supplement* 4:325–44. Greenwich, Conn.: JAI Press.

———. 1998. "Consuming the Maya." *Dialectical Anthropology* 23:111–29.

Quiñones Keber, Eloise. 1995. *Codex Telleriano-Remensis: Ritual, Divination, and History of a Pictorial Aztec Manuscript*. Austin: University of Texas Press.

Rabinow, Paul. 1994. "Modern and Counter-Modern: Ethos and Epoch in Heidegger and Foucault" in *The Cambridge Companion to Foucault*. Edited by Gary Gutting, 197–214. Cambridge: Cambridge University Press.

Rands, Robert L. and Barbara C. Rands. 1965. "Pottery Figurines of the Maya Lowlands" in *Archaeology of Southern Mesoamerica, Part 1*. Edited by Gordon R. Willey, 535–60. Handbook of Middle American Indians Volume 2. Austin: University of Texas Press.

Rappaport, Joanne. 1990. *The Politics of Memory: Native Historical Interpretations in the Colombian Andes*. Cambridge: Cambridge University Press.

Reed, David M. 1998. "Ancient Maya Diet at Copan, Honduras." Ph.D. diss., Department of Anthropology, Pennsylvania State University. Ann Arbor: University Microfilms.

———. 1999. "Cuisine from Hun-Nal-Ye" in In *Reconstructing Ancient Maya Diet*. Edited by Christine D. White, 183–96. Salt Lake City: University of Utah Press.

Reents-Budet, Dorie. 1994. *Painting the Maya Universe: Royal Ceramics of the Classic Period*. Durham: Duke University Press.

———. 2006. "The Social Context of *Kakaw* Drinking Among the Ancient Maya" in *Chocolate in Mesoamerica: A Cultural History of Cacao*. Edited by Cameron L. McNeil, 202–23. Gainesville: University of Florida Press.

Rhoads, Megan L. 2002. "Population Dynamics at the Southern Periphery of the Ancient Maya World: Kinship at Copan." Ph.D. diss., Department of Anthropology, University of New Mexico.

Rice, Prudence M., Arthur A. Demarest, and Don S. Rice. 2004. "The Terminal Classic and the 'Classic Maya Collapse' in Perspective" in *The Terminal Classic in the Maya Lowlands: Collapse, Transition, and Transformation*. Edited by Arthur A. Demarest, Prudence M. Rice, and Don S. Rice, 1–11. Boulder: University Press of Colorado.

Rice, Prudence M., and Donald W. Forsyth. 2004. "Terminal Classic-Period Lowland Ceramics" in *The Terminal Classic in the Maya Lowlands: Collapse, Transition, and Trans-*

formation. Edited by Arthur A. Demarest, Prudence M. Rice, and Don S. Rice, 28–59. Boulder: University Press of Colorado.

Riese, Berthold. 1984. "Relaciones clásico tardías entre Copán y Quiriguá: Algunas evidencias epigráficas." *Yaxkin* 7:1:23–30.

Robin, Cynthia. 2002. "Outside of Houses: The Practices of Everyday Life at Chan Noohol, Belize." *Journal of Social Archaeology* 2:245–68.

Rodman, Margaret C. 2003. "Empowering Place: Multilocality and Multivocality" in *The Anthropology of Space and Place: Locating Culture.* Edited by Setha M. Low and Denise Lawrence-Zúñiga, 204–23. Malden, Mass.: Blackwell.

Rogoff, Barbara, Barbara Radziszewska, and Tracy Masiello. 1995. "Analysis of Developmental Processes in Sociocultural Activity" in *Sociocultural Psychology: Theory and Practice of Doing and Knowing.* Edited by Laura M. W. Martin, Katherine Nelson, and Ethel Tobach, 125–49. Cambridge: Cambridge University Press.

Rosaldo, Renato. 1980. "Doing Oral History." *Social Analysis* 4:89–99.

Rowlands, Michael. 2005. "A Materialist Approach to Materiality" in *Materiality.* Edited by Daniel Miller, 72–87. Durham: Duke University Press.

Roys, Ralph, trans. and ed. 1965. *The Ritual of the Bacabs.* Norman: University of Oklahoma Press.

———. 1967. *The Book of Chilam Balam of Chumayel.* Norman: University of Oklahoma Press.

Rüsen, Jörn. 2002. "Introduction: Historical Thinking as Intercultural Discourse" in *Western Historical Thinking: An Intercultural Debate.* Edited by Jörn Rüsen, 1–11. New York: Berghahn Books.

Sahagún, Bernardino de. 1953–82. *Florentine Codex: General History of the Things of New Spain.* Translated by Arthur J. O. Anderson and Charles E. Dibble. Monographs of the School of American Research and the Museum of New Mexico, No. 14, Parts 1–13. Santa Fe and Salt Lake City: School of American Research and the University of Utah.

Sanders, William T. 1989. "Household, Lineage, and State at Eighth-Century Copan, Honduras" in *House of the Bacabs, Copan, Honduras.* Edited by David Webster, 89–105. Studies in Pre-Columbian Art and Archaeology No. 29. Washington: Dumbarton Oaks.

Sandstrom, Alan R. 1978. *The Image of Disease: Medical Practices of Nahua Indians of the Huasteca.* Monographs in Anthropology 3. Columbia: Department of Anthropology, University of Missouri-Columbia.

———. 2000. "Toponymic Groups and House Organization: The Nahuas of Northern Veracruz, Mexico" in *Beyond Kinship: Social and Material Reproduction in House Societies.* Edited by Rosemary A. Joyce and Susan D. Gillespie, 53–72. Philadelphia: University of Pennsylvania Press.

———. 2001. "Papermaking" in *The Oxford Encyclopedia of Mesoamerican Cultures: The Civilizations of Mexico and Central America.* Edited by Davíd Carrasco, 2:442–43. Oxford: Oxford University Press.

———. 2003. "Sacred Mountains and Miniature Worlds: Altar Design among the

Nahua of Northern Veracruz, Mexico" in *Mesas and Cosmologies in Mesoamerica*. Edited by Douglas Sharon, 51–70. San Diego: San Diego Museum of Man.

Sandstrom, Alan R., and Pamela E. Sandstrom. 1986. *Traditional Papermaking and Paper Cult Figures of Mexico*. Norman: University of Oklahoma Press.

Saturno, William A. 2000. "In the Shadow of the Acropolis: Rio Amarillo and Its Role in the Copan Polity." Ph.D. diss., Department of Anthropology, Harvard University. Ann Arbor: University Microfilms.

Sawicki, Jana. 1994. "Foucault, Feminism and Questions of Identity" in *The Cambridge Companion to Foucault*. Edited by Gary Gutting, 286–313. Cambridge: Cambridge University Press.

Scarborough, Vernon L. 1991. "Courting the Southern Maya Lowlands: A Study in Pre-Hispanic Ballgame Architecture" in *The Mesoamerican Ballgame*. Edited by Vernon L. Scarborough and David R. Wilcox, 129–44. Tucson: University of Arizona Press.

Scarborough, Vernon L., and David R. Wilcox, eds. 1991. *The Mesoamerican Ballgame*. Tucson: University of Arizona Press.

Schama, Simon. 1995. *Landscape and Memory*. New York: Knopf.

Schele, Linda. 1987. "The Figures on the Central Marker of Ballcourt AIIb at Copan." *Copan Note 13*. Copan Mosaics Project. Electronic version: Mesoamerica Center, University of Texas at Austin. At www.utmesoamerica.org/CopanNotes.php. Accessed 7/29/07.

——. 1997. *Hidden Faces of the Maya*. Singapore: ALTI Publishing.

Schele, Linda, and David A. Freidel. 1991. "The Courts of Creation: Ballcourts, Ballgames, and Portals to the Maya Underworld" in *The Mesoamerican Ballgame*. Edited by Vernon L. Scarborough and David R. Wilcox, 289–316. Tucson: University of Arizona Press.

Schele, Linda, and Peter Mathews. 1998. *The Code of Kings: The Language of Seven Sacred Maya Temples and Tombs*. New York: Scribner.

Schele, Linda, and Mary Ellen Miller. 1986. *The Blood of Kings: Dynasty and Ritual in Maya Art*. Fort Worth: Kimball Art Museum.

Schevill, Margot Blum. 1993. *Maya Textiles of Guatemala: The Gustavus A. Eisen Collection, 1902, the Hearst Museum of Anthropology, the University of California at Berkeley*. Austin: University of Texas Press.

Schlosser, Ann L. 1978. "Ceramic Lowland Maya Figurine Development with Special Reference to Piedras Negras, Guatemala." Ph.D. diss., Department of Anthropology, Southern Illinois University at Carbondale. Ann Arbor: University Microfilms.

Schor, Naomi. 1992. "*Cartes Postales*: Representing Paris 1900." *Critical Inquiry* 18:188–244.

Schortman, Edward M., and Patricia A. Urban. 2004. "Marching Out of Step: Early Classic Copan and Its Honduran Neighbors" in *Understanding Early Classic Copan*. Edited by Ellen E. Bell, Marcello A. Canuto, and Robert J. Sharer, 319–35. Philadelphia: University of Pennsylvania Museum of Archaeology and Anthropology.

Schöttler, Peter. 1995. "Mentalities, Ideologies, Discourses: On the 'Third Level' as a Theme in Social-Historical Research" in *The History of Everyday Life: Reconstructing Historical Experiences and Ways of Life*. Edited by Alf Lüdtke and translated by William Templer, 72–115. Princeton: Princeton University Press.

Scott, John F. 2001. "Dressed to Kill: Stone Regalia of the Mesoamerican Ballgame" in *The Sport of Life and Death: The Mesoamerican Ballgame*. Edited by E. Michael Whittington, 51–63. London: Thames and Hudson.

Sedat, David, and Fernando López. 2004. "Initial Stages in the Formation of the Copan Acropolis" in *Understanding Early Classic Copan*. Edited by Ellen E. Bell, Marcello A. Canuto, and Robert J. Sharer, 85–99. Philadelphia: University of Pennsylvania Museum of Archaeology and Anthropology.

Seler, Eduard. 1991. *Collected Works in Mesoamerican Linguistics and Archaeology*. Volume 2. Edited by Frank E. Comparato. Culver City, Calif.: Labyrinthos.

Serageldin, Ismail, Ephim Shluger, and Joan Martin-Brown, eds. 2001. *Historic Cities and Sacred Sites: Cultural Roots for Urban Futures*. Washington: World Bank.

Sharer, Robert J. 1990. *Quirigua: A Classic Maya Center and Its Sculptures*. Durham: Carolina Academic Press.

——. 1994. *The Ancient Maya*. 5th ed. Stanford: Stanford University Press.

Sharer, Robert J., David W. Sedat, Loa P. Traxler, Julia C. Miller, and Ellen E. Bell. 2005. "Early Classic Royal Power in Copan: The Origins and Development of the Acropolis (ca. A.D. 250–600)" in *Copan: The History of an Ancient Maya Kingdom*. Edited by E. Wyllys Andrews and William L. Fash, 201–36. Santa Fe: School of American Research Press.

Sheehy, James J. 1991. "Structure and Change in a Late Classic Maya Domestic Group at Copan, Honduras." *Ancient Mesoamerica* 2:1–19.

Sheets, Payson. 1992. *The Ceren Site: A Prehistoric Village Buried by Volcanic Ash in Central America*. Orlando: Holt, Rinehart, and Winston.

Sheptak, Russell N. 1987. "Interaction between Belize and the Ulua Valley" in *Interaction on the Southeast Mesoamerican Frontier: Prehistoric and Historic Honduras and El Salvador*. Edited by Eugenia J. Robinson, 247–66. BAR International Series 327. Oxford: British Archaeological Reports.

——. 2005. "The Continuity of Social Practices in the Colonial Period Ulua Valley, Northern Honduras." Presented at the 70th Annual Meeting of the Society for American Archaeology, Salt Lake City, Utah.

Sigal, Pete. 2000. *From Moon Goddesses to Virgins: The Colonization of Yucatecan Maya Sexual Desire*. Austin: University of Texas Press.

Simmel, Georg. 1997. "Sociology of the Meal." Translated by Mark Ritter and David Frisby. In *Simmel on Culture: Selected Writings*. Edited by David Frisby and Mike Featherstone, 130–35. London: Sage.

Smolka, Ana Luiza B., Maria Cecília R. de Goes, and Angel Pino. 1995. "The Constitution of the Subject: A Persistent Question" in *Sociocultural Studies of Mind*. Edited by James V. Wertsch, Pablo del Río, and Amelia Alvarez, 165–84. Cambridge: Cambridge University Press.

Soja, Edward W. 1985. "The Spatiality of Social Life: Towards a Transformative Retheorisation" in *Social Relations and Spatial Structures*. Edited by Derek Gregory and John Urry, 90–127. New York: St. Martin's Press.

Sperber, Dan. 1975. *Rethinking Symbolism*. Translated by Alice L. Morton. Cambridge: Cambridge University Press.

Sperlich, Norbert, and Elizabeth Katz Sperlich. 1980. *Guatemalan Backstrap Weaving*. Norman: University of Oklahoma Press.

Spink, Mary L. 1983. "Metates as Socioeconomic Indicators during the Classic Period of Copan, Honduras." Ph.D. diss., Department of Anthropology, Pennsylvania State University. Ann Arbor: University Microfilms.

Spores, Ronald. 1984. *The Mixtecs in Ancient and Colonial Times*. Norman: University of Oklahoma Press.

Stephen, Lynn. 1993. "Weaving in the Fast Lane: Class, Ethnicity, and Gender in Zapotec Craft Commercialization" in *Crafts in the World Market: The Impact of Global Exchange on Middle American Artisans*. Edited by June Nash, 25–57. Albany: State University of New York Press.

Stilgoe, John R. 2005. *Landscape and Images*. Charlottesville: University of Virginia Press.

Stone, Andrea J. 1995. *Images from the Underworld: Naj Tunich and the Tradition of Maya Cave Painting*. Austin: University of Texas Press.

Stone, Doris. 1941. *Archaeology of the North Coast of Honduras*. Memoirs of the Peabody Museum of Archaeology and Ethnology, Harvard University, Volume 9, No. 1. Cambridge: Peabody Museum of Archaeology and Ethnology.

———. 1957. *The Archaeology of Central and Southern Honduras*. Papers of the Peabody Museum of Archaeology and Ethnology, Harvard University, Volume 49, No. 3. Cambridge: Peabody Museum of Archaeology and Ethnology.

Storey, Rebecca. 1992. "The Children of Copan: Issues in Paleopathology and Paleodemography." *Ancient Mesoamerica* 3:161–67.

———. 1997. "Individual Frailty, Children of Privilege, and Stress in Late Classic Copan" in *Bones of the Maya: Studies of Ancient Skeletons*. Edited by Stephen L. Whittington and David M. Reed, 116–26. Washington: Smithsonian Institution Press.

———. 1998. "The Mothers and Daughters of a Patrilineal Civilization: The Health Status of Females among the Late Classic Maya of Copan, Honduras" in *Sex and Gender in Paleopathological Perspective*. Edited by Anne L. Grauer and Patricia Stuart-Macadam, 133–48. Cambridge: Cambridge University Press.

———. 1999. "Late Classic Nutrition and Skeletal Indicators at Copan, Honduras" in *Reconstructing Ancient Maya Diet*. Edited by Christine D. White, 169–79. Salt Lake City: University of Utah Press.

———. 2005. "Health and Lifestyle (Before and After Death) among the Copan Elite" in *Copan: The History of an Ancient Maya Kingdom*. Edited by E. Wyllys Andrews and William L. Fash, 315–43. Santa Fe: School of American Research Press.

Strathern, Marilyn. 1988. *The Gender of the Gift: Problems with Women and Problems with Society in Melanesia*. Berkeley: University of California Press.

Strömsvik, Gustav. 1941. *Substela Caches and Stela Foundations at Copan and Quirigua*. Publication 528. Washington: Carnegie Institution of Washington.

——. 1952. *The Ball Courts at Copan with Notes on the Courts at La Union, Quirigua, San Pedro Pinula, and Asunción Mitla*. Publication 596. Washington: Carnegie Institution of Washington.

Stuart, David. 1997. "The Hills Are Alive: Sacred Mountains in the Maya Cosmos." *Symbols* (spring):13–17.

——. 1998. " 'The Fire Enters His House': Architecture and Ritual in Classic Maya Texts" in *Function and Meaning in Classic Maya Architecture*. Edited by Stephen D. Houston, 373–425. Washington: Dumbarton Oaks.

——. 2002. "Copan's Last *Saklaktuun*." Electronic document on *Mesoweb*, at www.mesoweb.com/stuart/notes/Saklaktuun.pdf. Accessed 4 January 2006.

——. 2005. "A Foreign Past: The Writing and Representation of History on a Royal Ancestral Shrine at Copan" in *Copan: The History of an Ancient Maya Kingdom*. Edited by E. Wyllys Andrews and William L. Fash, 373–94. Santa Fe: School of American Research Press.

Sweetman, Paul. 2003. "Twenty-first Century Dis-ease? Habitual Reflexivity or the Reflexive Habitus." *Sociological Review* 2003:528–49.

Tacchi, Jo. 1998. "Radio Texture: Between Self and Others" in *Material Cultures: Why Some Things Matter*. Edited by Daniel Miller, 25–45. Chicago: University of Chicago Press.

Tai, Hue-Tam Ho. 2001. "Introduction: Situating Memory" in *The Country of Memory: Remaking the Past in Late Socialist Vietnam*. Edited by Hue-Tam Ho Tai, 1–17. Berkeley: University of California Press.

Taladoire, Eric. 1981. *Les terrains de jeu de balle (Mésoamérique et Sud-ouest des Etats-Unis)*. Etudes mésoaméricaines series II vol. 4. Mexico City: Mission Archéologique et Ethnologiques Française au Mexique.

Taladoire, Eric, and Benoit Colsenet. 1991. " 'Bois ton sang, Beaumanoir:' The Political and Conflictual Aspects of the Ballgame in the Northern Chiapas Area" in *The Mesoamerican Ballgame*. Edited by Vernon L. Scarborough and David R. Wilcox, 161–74. Tucson: University of Arizona Press.

Taube, Karl A. 1989. "The Maize Tamale in Classic Maya Diet, Epigraphy, and Art." *American Antiquity* 54:31–51.

Taylor, Charles. 1993. "To Follow a Rule . . " in *Bourdieu: Critical Perspectives*. Edited by Craig Calhoun, Edward LiPuma, and Moishe Postone, 45–60. Chicago: University of Chicago Press.

——. 2005. "Merleau-Ponty and the Epistemological Picture" in *The Cambridge Companion to Merleau-Ponty*. Edited by Taylor Carman and Mark B. N. Hansen, 26–49. Cambridge: Cambridge University Press.

Taylor, Dicey. 1992. "Painted Ladies: Costumes for Women on Tepeu Ceramics" in *The Maya Vase Book*. Edited by Justin Kerr, 3:513–25. New York: Kerr Associates.

Tedlock, Barbara. 1986. "On a Mountain in the Dark: Encounters with the Quiché Maya Culture Hero" in *Symbol and Meaning beyond the Closed Community: Essays in Mesoamerican Ideas*. Edited by Gary H. Gossen, 125–38. Albany: Institute for Mesoamerican Studies, University of Albany.

——. 1992a. "Mayan Calendars, Cosmology, and Astronomical Commensuration" in *New Theories on the Ancient Maya*. Edited by Elin C. Danien and Robert J. Sharer, 217–27. University Museum Monograph 77. Philadelphia: University Museum, University of Pennsylvania.

——. 1992b. *Time and the Highland Maya*. Rev. ed. Albuquerque: University of New Mexico Press.

Tedlock, Dennis. 1983. *The Spoken Word and the Work of Interpretation*. Philadelphia: University of Pennsylvania Press.

——. 1992. "The Popol Vuh as a Hieroglyphic Book" in In *New Theories on the Ancient Maya*. Edited by Elin C. Danien and Robert J. Sharer, 229–40. University Museum Monograph 77. Philadelphia: University Museum, University of Pennsylvania.

——. 1993. *Breath on the Mirror: Mythic Voices and Visions of the Living Maya*. New York: HarperCollins.

Tedlock, Dennis, trans. 1996. *Popol Vuh: The Mayan Book of the Dawn of Life*. Rev. ed. New York: Simon and Schuster.

Tercero, Geraldina. 1996. "Figurines from the Ulua Valley, Honduras: A Preliminary Study of Their Distribution and Uses." M.A. thesis, Department of Anthropology, Arizona State University.

Thapar, Romila. 2002. "Some Reflections on Early Indian Historical Thinking" in *Western Historical Thinking: An Intercultural Debate*. Edited by Jörn Rüsen, 178–86. New York: Berghahn Books.

Thompson, J. Eric S. 1970. *Maya History and Religion*. Norman: University of Oklahoma Press.

Tiesler Blos, Vera. 1999. "Rasgos bioculturales entre los antiguos mayas: aspectos arqueológicos y sociales." Ph.D. diss., Doctoral Program in Anthropology, Universidad Nacional Autónoma de México. Mexico City: Universidad Nacional Autónoma de México.

——. 2001. "La estatura entre los mayas prehispánicos: Consideraciones bioculturales." *Estudios de Antropología Biológica* 10:257–73.

Tilley, Christopher. 2006. "Objectification" in *Handbook of Material Culture*. Edited by Christopher Tilley, Webb Keane, Susanne Küchler, Michael Rowlands, and Patricia Spyer, 60–73. London: Sage Publications.

Todes, Samuel. 2001. *Body and World*. Cambridge: MIT Press.

Tozzer, Alfred M., trans. 1978. *Landa's Relación de las cosas de Yucatan*. Papers of the Peabody Museum of American Archaeology and Ethnology Volume 18. Millwood, N.Y.: Kraus Reprint.

Traxler, Loa. 2001. "The Royal Court of Early Classic Copan" in *Royal Courts of the Ancient Maya*. Volume 2: *Data and Case Studies*. Edited by Takeshi Inomata and Stephen D. Houston, 46–73. Boulder: Westview.

——. 2004. "Redesigning Copan: Early Architecture of the Polity Center" in *Understanding Early Classic Copan*. Edited by Ellen E. Bell, Marcello A. Canuto, and Robert J. Sharer, 53–64. Philadelphia: University of Pennsylvania Museum of Archaeology and Anthropology.

Trigger, Bruce G. 1990. "Monumental Architecture: A Thermodynamic Explanation of Symbolic Behaviour." *World Archaeology* 22:119–32.

Trik, Aubrey S. 1939. *Temple XXII at Copan*. Publication 509. Washington: Carnegie Institution of Washington.

Trouillot, Michel-Rolph. 1991. "Anthropology and the Savage Slot: The Poetics and Politics of Otherness" in *Recapturing Anthropology: Working in the Present*. Edited by Richard G. Fox, 17–44. Santa Fe: School of American Research Press.

Tuan, Yi-Fu. 1977. *Space and Place: The Perspective of Experience*. Minneapolis: University of Minnesota Press.

Turok, Marta. 1988. *Cómo acercarse a la artesanía*. Mexico City: Plaza y Valdés and Consejo Nacional para la Cultura y las Artes.

——. 1996. "Xiuhquilitl, nocheztl y tixinda: Tintes del México antiguo." *Arqueología Mexicana* 3:17:26–33.

Turok, Marta, and Walter F. Morris. 1994. "La urdimbre del tiempo maya" in *Semillas de industria: Transformaciones de la tecnología indígena en las Américas*. Edited by Mario Humberto Ruz, 147–65. Mexico City and Washington: Centro de Investigaciones y Estudios Superiores en Antropología Social and Smithsonian Institution Center for Folklife Programs and Cultural Studies.

Uriarte, María Teresa. 2006. "The Teotihuacan Ballgame and the Beginning of Time." *Ancient Mesoamerica* 17:17–38.

Van de Mieroop, Marc. 1999. *Cuneiform Texts and the Writing of History*. London: Routledge.

Van Dyke, Ruth M., and Susan E. Alcock, eds. 2003. *Archaeologies of Memory*. Malden, Mass.: Blackwell.

Viel, René. 1993a. "Copán Valley" in *Pottery of Prehistoric Honduras: Regional Classification and Analysis*. Edited by John S. Henderson and Marilyn Beaudry-Corbett, 13–29. Los Angeles: Institute of Archaeology, University of California.

——. 1993b. *Evolución de la cerámica de Copán, Honduras*. Tegucigalpa: Instituto Hondureño de Antropología e Historia.

——. 1998. "La interacción entre Copan y Kaminaljuyu" in *XI Simposio de investigaciones arqueológicas en Guatemala 1997*. Edited by Juan Pedro Laporte and Héctor L. Escobedo, 427–30. Guatemala City: Ministerio de Cultura y Deportes, Instituto de Antropología e Historia, Asociación Tikal.

——. 1999. "The Pectorals of Altar Q and Structure 11: An Interpretation of the Political Organization at Copan, Honduras." *Latin American Antiquity* 10:377–99.

Viel, René, and Charles D. Cheek. 1983. "Sepulturas" in *Introducción a la arqueología de Copán, Honduras, Tomo I*. Edited by Claude F. Baudez, 551–609. Tegucigalpa: Proyecto Arqueológico Copán, Secretaría de Estado en el Despacho de Cultura y Turismo.

Viesca Treviño, Carlos. 2001. "*Curanderismo* in Mexico and Guatemala: Its Historical Evolution from the Sixteenth to the Nineteenth Century" in *Mesoamerican Healers*. Edited by Brad R. Huber and Alan R. Sandstrom, 47–65. Austin: University of Texas Press.

Vogt, Evon Z. 1969. *Zinacantan: A Maya Community in the Highlands of Chiapas*. Cambridge: Belknap Press, Harvard University Press.

——. 1998. "Zinacanteco Dedication and Termination Rituals" in *The Sowing and the*

Dawning: Termination, Dedication, and Transformation in the Archaeological and Ethnographic Record of Mesoamerica. Edited by Shirley B. Mock, 21–30. Albuquerque: University of New Mexico Press.

von Hagen, Victor Wolfgang. 1943. *The Jicaque (Torrupan) Indians of Honduras.* Indian Notes and Monographs 53. New York: AMS Press.

———. 1977. *The Aztec and Maya Papermakers.* New York: Hacker Art Books.

Warnier, Jean-Pierre. 2001. "A Praxeological Approach to Subjectivation in a Material World." *Journal of Material Culture* 6:5–24.

———. 2006. "Inside and Outside: Surfaces and Containers" in *Handbook of Material Culture.* Edited by Christopher Tilley, Webb Keane, Susanne Küchler, Michael Rowlands, and Patricia Spyer, 186–95. London: Sage Publications.

Watanabe, John M. 1992. *Maya Saints and Souls in a Changing World.* Austin: University of Texas Press.

Waterson, Roxana. 1995. "Houses and Hierarchies in Island Southeast Asia" in *About the House: Lévi-Strauss and Beyond.* Edited by Janet Carsten and Stephen Hugh-Jones, 47–68. Cambridge: Cambridge University Press.

———. 1997. *The Living House: An Anthropology of Architecture in South-East Asia.* New York: Watson-Guptill.

Webster, David. 1999. "The Archaeology of Copan, Honduras." *Journal of Archaeological Research* 7:1–53.

Webster, David, ed. 1989. *The House of the Bacabs, Copan, Honduras.* Studies in Pre-Columbian Art and Archaeology 29. Washington: Dumbarton Oaks.

Webster, David, Barbara Fash, Randolph Widmer, and Scott Zeleznik. 1998. "The Skyband Group: Investigation of a Classic Maya Residential Complex at Copan, Honduras." *Journal of Field Archaeology* 25:319–43.

Webster, David, William L. Fash, and Elliot Abrams. 1986. "Excavaciones en el conjunto 9N-8, Patio A (Operación VII)" in *Proyecto Arqueológico Copán Segunda Fase: Excavaciones en el área urbana de Copán, Tomo I.* Edited by William T. Sanders, 155–317. Tegucigalpa: Secretaría de Estado en el Despacho de Cultura y Turismo.

Webster, David, AnnCorinne Freter, and Rebecca Storey. 2004. "Dating Copan Culture-History: Implications for the Terminal Classic and the Collapse" in *The Terminal Classic in the Maya Lowlands: Collapse, Transition, and Transformation.* Edited by Arthur A. Demarest, Prudence M. Rice, and Don S. Rice, 231–59. Boulder: University Press of Colorado.

Webster, David, and Nancy Gonlin. 1988. "Household Remains of the Humblest Maya." *Journal of Field Archaeology* 15:169–90.

Weedon, Chris. 1997. *Feminist Practice and Poststructuralist Theory.* 2d ed. Oxford: Blackwell.

———. 1999. *Feminism, Theory and the Politics of Difference.* Oxford: Blackwell.

Weiner, Annette B. 1992. *Inalienable Possessions: The Paradox of Keeping-While-Giving.* Berkeley: University of California Press.

Weiss-Krejci, Estella. 2004. "Mortuary Representations of the Noble House: A Cross-Cultural Comparison between Collective Tombs of the Ancient Maya and Dynastic Europe." *Journal of Social Anthropology* 4:368–404.

Wenger, Etienne. 1998. *Communities of Practice: Learning, Meaning, and Identity.* Cambridge: Cambridge University Press.

Whittington, Stephen L. 1999. "Caries and Antemortem Tooth Loss at Copan: Implications from Commoner Diet" in *Reconstructing Ancient Maya Diet.* Edited by Christine D. White, 151–67. Salt Lake City: University of Utah Press.

Whittington, Stephen L., and David M. Reed. 1997. "Commoner Diet at Copan: Insights from Stable Isotopes and Porotic Hyperostosis" in *Bones of the Maya: Studies of Ancient Skeletons.* Edited by Stephen L. Whittington and David M. Reed, 157–70. Washington: Smithsonian Institution Press.

Whittington, Stephen L., and Scott Zeleznik. 1991. "History and Functions of a Pair of Neighboring Rural Elite Residential Compounds in the Ostuman Pocket, Copan, Honduras." Presented at the 56th Annual Meeting of the Society for American Archaeology, New Orleans.

Wichmann, Søren. 2006. "Mayan Historical Linguistics and Epigraphy: A New Synthesis." *Annual Review of Anthropology* 35:279–94.

Widmer, Randolph J. 1997. "Especialización económica en Copán." *Yaxkin* 15:141–60.

Wilk, Richard R., and William L. Rathje. 1982. "Household Archaeology." *American Behavioral Scientist* 25:617–39.

Willey, Gordon R. 1972. *The Artifacts of Altar de Sacrificios.* Papers of the Peabody Museum of Archaeology and Ethnology, Volume 64, No. 1. Cambridge: Harvard University.

——. 1978. *Excavations at Seibal, Department of Petén, Guatemala: Artifacts.* Memoirs of the Peabody Museum of Archaeology and Ethnology, Volume 14, No. 1. Cambridge: Harvard University.

Willey, Gordon R., and William R. Bullard. 1965. "Prehistoric Settlement Patterns in the Maya Lowlands" in *Archaeology of Southern Mesoamerica Part One.* Edited by Gordon R. Willey, 360–77. Handbook of Middle American Indians Volume 2. Austin: University of Texas Press.

Willey, Gordon R., and Richard M. Leventhal. 1979. "Settlement at Copan" in *Maya Archaeology and Ethnohistory.* Edited by Norman Hammond and Gordon R. Willey, 75–102. Austin: University of Texas Press.

Willey, Gordon R., Richard M. Leventhal, Arthur A. Demarest, and William L. Fash. 1994. *Ceramics and Artifacts from Excavations in the Copan Residential Zone.* Papers of the Peabody Museum of Archaeology and Ethnology Volume 80. Cambridge: Harvard University.

Willey, Gordon R., Richard M. Leventhal, and William L. Fash. 1978. "Maya Settlement in the Copan Valley." *Archaeology* 31:4:32–43.

Williams, Harold. 2001. "Historic Cities: The Sense of Place, Sacred and Secular" in *Historic Cities and Sacred Sites: Cultural Roots for Urban Futures.* Edited by Ismail Serageldin, Ephim Shluger, and Joan Martin-Brown, 401–5. Washington: World Bank.

Williams, Howard, ed. 2003. *Archaeologies of Remembrance: Death and Memory in Past Societies.* New York: Kluwer Academic/Plenum.

Williamson, Richard. 2003. "Excavations, Interpretations, and Implications of the Earliest Structures Beneath Structure 10L-26 at Copan, Honduras." Electronic document on P.A.R.I. Online Publications, at www.mesoweb.com/pari /publications/RT10/17_Excavations.html. Accessed 7/26/07.

Woda, Christine, and Lilian Zeller. 2005. "Tuno, una técnica tradicional de procesar tela entra en el mercado moderno." *Yaxkin* 24:2:127–47.

Wu Hung. 2003. "Monumentality of Time: Giant Clocks, the Drum Tower, the Clock Tower" in *Monuments and Memory, Made and Unmade*. Edited by Robert S. Nelson and Margaret Olin, 107–32. Chicago: University of Chicago Press.

Yarnell, Amy. 2005. "Cost Surface Analysis of Travel Between Cerro Palenque and Mesoamerican Obsidian Sources." Paper on file in the Department of Anthropology, Gettysburg College, Gettysburg, Pennsylvania.

Yates, Frances A. 1966. *The Art of Memory*. Chicago: University of Chicago Press.

Young, Iris Marion. 1997. *Intersecting Voices: Dilemmas of Gender, Political Philosophy, and Policy*. Princeton: Princeton University Press.

Zahavi, Dan. 2003. "Intentionality and Phenomenality: A Phenomenological Take on the Hard Problem" in *The Problem of Consciousness: New Essays in Phenomenological Philosophy of Mind*. Edited by Evan Thompson, 63–92. Canadian Journal of Philosophy Supplementary Volume 29. Calgary: University of Calgary Press.

Zambrano, Isabel, and Patricia Greenfield. 2004. "Ethnoepistemologies at Home and at School" in *Culture and Competence: Contexts of Life Success*. Edited by Robert J. Sternberg and Elena L. Grigorenko, 251–72. Washington: American Psychological Association.

INDEX

Page numbers in italics refer to illustrations. A "t" following a page number denotes a table.

JULIA A. HENDON is associate professor of anthropology at Gettysburg College. She is the co-editor of *Mesoamerican Archaeology: Theory and Practice* (2004).

Library of Congress Cataloging-in-Publication Data

Hendon, Julia A. (Julia Ann)
Houses in a landscape : memory and everyday life in Mesoamerica / Julia A. Hendon.
p. cm. — (Material worlds)
Includes bibliographical references and index.
ISBN 978-0-8223-4693-7 (cloth : alk. paper)
ISBN 978-0-8223-4704-0 (pbk. : alk. paper)
1. Mayas—Honduras—Antiquities. 2. Copán Site (Honduras) 3. Maya architecture—Honduras.
4. Honduras—Antiquities. I. Title.
II. Series: Material worlds.
F1435.1.C7H46 2010
792.83'01—dc22   2009044002